Beyond Employment

In the series Labor and Social Change, edited by Paula Rayman and Carmen Sirianni.

Beyond Employment

Time, Work and the Informal Economy

Claus Offe and Rolf G. Heinze

*with assistance from Ulrike Götting,
Karl Hinrichs and Ruud Vlek*

translated by Alan Braley

Temple University Press
Philadelphia

Temple University Press, Philadelphia 19122

Copyright © Claus Offe and Rolf G. Heinze 1992;
copyright © this translation Polity Press 1992

ISBN 0–87722–951–1

CIP data available from the Library of Congress

Printed in Great Britain

This book is printed on acid-free paper.

Contents

Part IV   The Cooperation Circle System

Foreword

This book explores economic and social phenomena in the 'grey area' between commercial market provision and domestic self-supply. We were chiefly concerned to discover whether the 'useful activities' that take place in this sphere are only performed individually, spontaneously and perhaps according to the traditional rules of certain social groupings, or whether they can also be organized and distributed according to formal rules. If it can be shown that labour can also be organized differently from the way the market does it without loss of efficiency and other features of rationality, and that the results of useful human activity can be allocated otherwise than through the medium of money, without the need to solve the problems of production and distribution via the state and bureaucratic hierarchies, this would be a discovery not only of theoretical interest but also of practical importance.

What are the possible solutions to the problems of production and distribution which conform neither to the pattern of the market nor that of the state, and yet are 'organized', that is, not dependent upon the arrangements that individuals and small communities happen to make?

The first part of this study contains an overview of data on the resources and needs of individuals and private households, culled from conditions and developments in the Federal Republic of Germany. Its main emphasis is on the provision of the resources 'money' and 'time' to households. It is important to build up a detailed picture of the quantitative relationship between 'time-rich' and 'time-poor', 'money-rich' and 'money-poor' types of households and circumstances, if we are to assess the structural preconditions necessary to induce people to devote their 'active time' outside their own households to purposes other than the one usually considered normal in our societies, namely to exchange time for money by taking paid employment, or to 'consume' it by simultaneously spending money.

In the second, descriptive part of our study we have given 'on the spot' descriptions – drawn from the Federal German Republic, the Netherlands, the USA and Canada – of exchange networks and similar economic arrangements based on interviews, observation, documents and the collation of sociological research findings; and have cited historical precedents for such organized networks. Here we have concentrated on a small number of examples, and we make no claim to have provided a representative sample.

In the third, theoretical part of the study the structural difficulties, especially those inhering in the 'transaction costs problems' of multi-household exchange networks, are presented.

The fourth and final section is mainly concerned with the problems involved in organizing non-monetary exchange systems on a scale larger than that of occasional exchange between friends, neighbours, relatives or members of a club. We believe it is not unrealistic to suppose that such developments toward a non-monetary but exchange-led parallel economy can make a very positive contribution to the solution of many social and economic problems characteristic of societies suffering from high unemployment, from much personal isolation and from a poorly functioning welfare state.

This volume is an abbreviated version of the book published in 1989 by Campus (Frankfurt). The research was undertaken for the Ministry for Urban Development, Housing and Transport of Land North Rhine-Westphalia in 1988. The authors wish to thank those who took part in the research project and the many people who made themselves available for interviews and discussions, as well as all those colleagues in the social sciences who helped us with comments, both encouraging and sceptical.

Clause Offe and Rolf G. Heinze
Bremen/Bochum

1
Introduction

Work is measured in time and paid for in money. That is how we as citizens of industrial societies normally perceive the nature of human work and the causes of social wealth. This perception appears to be confirmed by an objective trend in social development. The number of persons whose work (or, more generally, whose useful activity) is not measured in units of time and paid for in units of money is decreasing. The desire to have a job and to meet all the costs of living from the income received for this work has become the accepted pattern for most people when making their plans and projecting their hopes for the future. The steadily rising number of women entering employment has been a prime cause of the fact that in 1989 the number of gainfully employed people in the Federal Republic of Germany reached a historical high of 27 million. Schools and universities justify their activities by claiming that their task is to train schoolchildren and students to become effective *employees*. Researchers and technologists boast that their labours will result in the creation of new jobs. Numbers of people emigrate to another country or even another continent, motivated by the hope of finding regular, well-paid *employment* in the country of their choice. We all know that the effectiveness of social security systems depends on the performance of a sufficient amount of work in the formal, employment economy; only in this way can adequate social wages for the temporarily 'inactive' part of the population (children and mothers, pensioners and the unemployed) be financed. All these justifications, trends and attitudes appear to confirm that in our societies 'being employed' is increasingly held to be the normal psychological, social and economic situation.

And yet the experiences of the 1970s and 1980s with their persistent crisis of employment have shown us that 'being employed' is not really the normal state of affairs; people only think it is. Throughout the 1980s the unemployed have outnumbered the farmers – despite an agricultural policy under which vast sums were paid out to ensure that farmers could remain farmers and not turn up in the unemployed statistics. The gap between the *imagined* normality of employment and a steady job and the *experienced* reality of unemployment, underemployment and precarious or irregular employment is widening, resulting in a growing contingent of marginalized, discouraged and powerless sections of the population, who are often called the 'new underclass'. But because it is supposedly 'normal' that entitlement to 'income' can only be based on the performance of paid work (or that of family members, or at least on the preparedness to do paid work), the income situation suffers the same vicissitudes as the employment situation, save for a social minimum of public assistance. Because of the shaky employment prospects to which they are directly and indirectly exposed, many people are very unsure whether in the long run their income will be sufficient, and sufficiently dependable, to enable them to live what they would call a 'normal' life. Even when the current level of their income gives no cause for unease and fear of poverty, they still harbour understandable doubts as to whether this income flow will in the future be steady and reliable enough to secure them against unpleasant surprises and poverty. This is particularly true of that most unprotected section of the workforce who, because of age, have retired from the work process and now draw pensions that have to be earned by those who are still at work. It is perhaps paradoxical that precisely in the rich societies of the West, where work has been institutionalized as a cardinal value, concerns about the safety of their jobs and the regularity of their incomes are looming ever larger in many people's thoughts.

There is a second universal trend, and it is this: ever since the beginning of the present century the work week per employee in all countries in Western Europe has been getting shorter. On average we work fewer hours in the day, fewer days in the week, fewer weeks in the year and fewer years in our life than our grandparents did. We could conclude from this that there is an increasing 'bonanza of time' in society, provided we also recognize that this 'wealth' is by no means an unmixed blessing. Yes, we do enjoy more time for leisure and recreation; but we also need more time, not only to cover the long journey to and from work and to purchase the goods and services we crave, but also to update our job qualifications and maintain our health. Then there is the downright disastrous 'time bonus' for people whose working time is brusquely reduced to zero as a result of unemployment they did not want. Nevertheless it is universally assumed that the members of society – at least in certain phases and situations of life – typically enjoy a more generous allotment of time than their forebears two or three generations ago. This at least is the theory: practice often belies it, because of the lack of institutions in which time could be passed in a useful, satisfying and socially recognized way *without* the possession of additional disposable income. The consequence is that available time is often experienced not as enrichment but as boredom and social isolation.

For goods and services are bought with money, not time. Or, to speak more accurately, not only can nothing be bought with time (if it could, that would *save* money) but, in order to experience free time as life enhancing, money has also to be *spent* (for example on air fares or a sailing boat). Many critics of the culture and living conditions of industrial society seem to agree that money has gained a worldwide victory over time. This is true at least in the sense that a satisfactory quality of life is increasingly coming to depend on individuals having money not only to enable them to buy material goods but also as a necessary precondition for obtaining all other kinds of pleasant experiences and satisfactions. To say this is not to deny that a sufficiently high and secure money income, such as the middle class enjoys, seems to be a prerequisite for people seeking to emancipate themselves from regarding money as essential to happiness, whether in their ideological thinking or beyond that in the practical decisions of life. This is the outlook of the new social movements (most of which originate in the middle classes).

The decisive influence of money income on living standards, quality of life and the subjective experiences of happiness and contentment is accompanied by a fourth trend, which could be characterized as a concurrent decrease in the 'welfare productivity' of time. Time spent in other than business activities (and not directly related to them) is often stigmatized by 'others' as 'wasted' and, what is more, felt subjectively to be burdensome and unsatisfying. This is partly connected with the fact that the use value of time – unlike that of money – is fully realized only when the use of time is interwoven into social contexts, in other words, when it is shared with others. Compared with individual consumption, which clearly requires both money *and* time to be available, 'pure' time can be enjoyed only in the company of others – who must also be free at the same time. It is an observed fact that people who have intensive and satisfying relationships with their family, with friends, politically likeminded people or members of societies 'have' much more time for these activities (or are prepared to sacrifice activities for them) than those who do not have such 'communal' social relationships of 'shared time'. In so far as such observations can be generalized, the converse may also be surmised, namely that when the social environment tends to become individualized and anonymous, time ceases to be an 'attractive' resource. If this assumption is correct it would suggest a cyclical dynamic: when the ideal of normality of industrial society – that (nearly) every adult person is gainfully employed (almost) full-time – wins the day, this does away with the social forms and contexts of the productive and satisfying use of time; instead the most economically efficient use of time is to use it in gainful employment and transform it into money. But in so far as the idealized conception of normality of gainful employment becomes in fact unrealistic, society suffers from a condition which we have described as 'the modernization trap' (Offe and Heinze 1986:473ff.).

The notion of a 'modernization trap' refers to the following paradox: on the one hand, a growing number of persons find themselves in a situation in which not all of their active time – or even none of it if they are unemployed – is absorbed by the labour market and gainful activities; but, at the same time, more traditional, socially respected and institutionalized ways of spending time outside work together with others (who have time to spend at the same time) are less easily found and practised – due to the very same process of modernization the economic dimension of which has generated more 'free' time.

To summarize, we have so far formulated four trend hypotheses. These refer to:

- overall, an increasing amount of available time (hypothesis 1);
- a tendency for institutional opportunities and social contexts for a productive and satisfying use of time outside gainful employment to disappear (hypothesis 2);
- increasing uncertainty with respect to the level and dependability of monetary income flows (hypothesis 3); and
- the growing importance of money for the distribution of welfare values and opportunities in life (hypothesis 4).

These are very broad, rough hypotheses; their validity and limits will be examined in more detail in chapter 2.

PART I

Household Needs and Systems for Meeting Them: Initial Assumptions and Trends

2

Time, Money and Types of Household: The Example of the Federal Republic of Germany

This chapter deals in more detail with the socioeconomic preconditions, supply situations and interests of households and members
of households in relation to institutional arrangements of use-value
production in the institutional no man's land between the market
and the state, on the one hand, and individual self-supply, on the
other. In particular it examines the empirical validity of the broad
assumptions as to the political and social context of the Federal
Republic of Germany that were sketched in the introduction, and
how these assumptions need to be hedged about and made more
nuanced.

Our investigations are concerned with *households* as functional
units of consumption and production, not with individuals. It is clear
even from a cursory glance at the four trend hypotheses that they
do not apply to all the 26 million-odd private households in the
Federal Republic to the same degree. Therefore it is useful to distinguish between different types of households, and to examine each
type separately. Although the variety of the households in the population makes it difficult to group *all* private households in categories,
nevertheless the following typology illustrated in figure 1 covers
about 92 per cent of the 26.4 million households in the Federal
Republic in 1985.

This typology does not take account of such groups as the very
heterogeneous households of single parents with children or those of
students and others in education or training. Household type I
(single-person households of the gainfully employed) is one of the
types of household that have shown the greatest increase during the
postwar period – 7.2 per cent of all private households in 1957, 12.9
per cent in 1985 (Federal Statistical Office 1985:191). This trend will

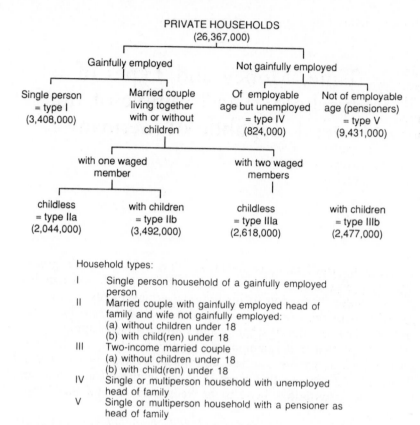

Household types:

I   Single person household of a gainfully employed person

II   Married couple with gainfully employed head of family and wife not gainfully employed:
(a) without children under 18
(b) with child(ren) under 18

III   Two-income married couple
(a) without children under 18
(b) with child(ren) under 18

IV   Single or multiperson household with unemployed head of family

V   Single or multiperson household with a pensioner as head of family

Figure 1. A typology of households based on the Federal Republic of Germany in 1985 (*Sources*: Federal Statistical Office (StBA), *Fachserie 1, Reihe 3: Haushalte und Familien 1985*, 1985, pp. 65, 84f., 117; K. Schüler, 'Demographischer Bezugsrahmen zur Einkommensverteilung nach Haushaltstypen in den Volkswirtschaftlichen Gesamtrechungen', *Wirtschaft und Statistik*, 1987, p. 369)

continue in the future because of the rise in the average age for marriage and the increase of divorced or separated couples. This growth seems set to continue for the households not gainfully employed as well, in particular for households of pensioners (type V), which in 1985 consisted of single-person and multiperson households in equal proportions. The increase in life expectancy, with growing numbers of people living to an advanced age, is the main reason for the increase of type V households. Within the category of households not gainfully employed it is pertinent to distinguish between these pensioners' households and those of the unemployed (type IV). Households where the head is unemployed do not form a homogeneous category, but in total they have shown a marked increase, from a figure of 102,000 in 1972. They also merit special attention because, unlike those in employment, they have a time potential that is at present unsaleable and because they regularly have less disposable money income.

The category of married people living together, with a male gainfully employed head of household (types II and III), do not in all cases make up the whole household (for instance, in the case of three-generation families); nevertheless, they do so in the vast majority of cases.[1] With regard to the availability of the resources 'money' and 'time' it appears necessary to distinguish according to both the number of earners (that is to say, whether the wife is gainfully employed or not) and also whether or not the household includes children under 18. The proportion of employed-person households in which only one member is gainfully employed is falling. In 1970 it amounted to 60.1 per cent, falling to 52.1 per cent by 1985. This reflects the fact that in a growing number of families of economically active age, both husband and wife are gainfully employed (cf. Federal Statistical Office 1970:53f.; 1985:117). In families with children and a gainfully employed husband aged between 25 and 45, in 1985 42.1 per cent of the wives were also in employment, while in childless families this proportion was as high as 80.3 per cent. We now turn to the question whether and to what extent the hypothesis 1 mentioned on page 4 ('increasing amount of time not institutionally preempted') can be confirmed as a description of the current situation and of the trend.

Increasing amounts of available time?

SHORTER WORKING HOURS AND INCREASE OF 'FREE' TIME RESOURCES

By far the greater part of the waking time of people of working age is spent working for remuneration. It is common knowledge that since about the 1870s the hours worked by *employees* have been considerably reduced. Between 1950 and 1985 the average working year of the employed workforce in the Federal Republic of Germany was reduced by at least a quarter as a result of collective bargaining agreements – from 2,344 to 1,730 hours (cf. Kohler and Reyher 1988:210). The transition from the 48-hour week to the 40-hour week (and since 1984 to less than 40 hours) accounted for some three-fifths of this decrease, the rest being made up by longer annual leave. Since 1960 independent workers and family members helping at home have also been spending less time in gainful employment, though they certainly work on average longer hours than employees. It seems probable, too, that collective agreements will continue to effect further reductions in working hours, in view of the persistent imbalance in the labour market, though the extent of such reductions is unpredictable. It may be confidently assumed that employees will not wish working hours to be further reduced unless earnings rise to an extent that would enable the increased leisure time to be spent in satisfying ways in terms of the prevailing cultural and institutional customs and standards (that is to say, primarily in consumption) – unless new institutional opportunities of using time in a less money intensive or even money substituting way were to arise. At all events it would be a mistake to conclude that less working time would mean more disposable free time for all working households without exception.

At this stage of the analysis we can ignore households of types IV and V, because there is, either temporarily or permanently, no contribution flowing from the waking hours of the unemployed and pensioners into the system of gainful employment. In the case of working households the reductions in standard working hours have increased the proportion of time not appropriated by paid employment in types I and II (for the employed head of household). However, over time type II households have lost some weight to type III – in other words, in an increasing number of employed families both marriage and partners are taking paid employment, thus *increasing* the amount of time spent in paid work per household. The net effect is an increase in the number of hours per household spent in paid employment, even though in about half of these households the women work fewer hours after marriage or after resuming their careers after the 'family break' (83.5 per cent of female part-time workers are married, cf. Heidenrich 1986:983). Thus in 1950 in what was then the 'typical' working family the husband spent an average of 2,434 hours a year in paid employment; in only 14 per cent of these families did the wife contribute to the family income through paid employment. Since then (by 1985) the annual working time of employees had fallen to 1,819 hours, but 44 per cent of the wives of employees were also in paid employment, raising the total time *per family* spent in paid employment to well above the norm for 1950 (for the numbers involved cf. Hinrichs 1988:180).

But the standard time spent in paid employment (even including any overtime worked) does not acount for all the time spent in economic activity. There is also travel time, unpaid work breaks, time spent on refresher courses, as well as the personal recreation and holidy periods. Kramer and Lakemann (1987:23) have calculated using data obtained from mini-surveys that in 1961 employees spent an average of 22 minutes each way travelling to and from work. In 1982 the average time so spent amounted to 17 minutes, and the projection of this calculation with data from the 1985 mini-census shows, at 18 minutes, little change from 1982. For those in ancillary industries the time spent getting to work was still over 20 minutes. Hence the following can be compiled for the time spent daily in connection with work (1985 data):

Standard working time:	8.0 hours
Overtime per day:	0.3 hours
Travel time (twice 20 min.):	0.7 hours
Unpaid work breaks:	0.75 hours
Total:	9.75 hours

If to this ten-odd hours of time devoted to earning a living on working days, which does not include retraining and holiday time, we add a further 9.3 hours for personal needs (sleeping, eating and personal hygiene) then on working days (from Monday to Friday) people in full-time work have only an average of about five hours' free time – which again must be subdivided into 'real' leisure time and that spent in household tasks.

During the last few decades other changes in the structure of working time have had an even more significant effect than the shortening of the working week. Already by 1960 the gradual introduction of the 40-hour week had brought half the workforce a gain of a 'block' of work-free time in the form of a two-day weekend. Even though in 1981 about one employee in five still had to do regular Saturday work, 90 per cent of employees enjoyed a five-day week. Furthermore, since 1960 standard annual leave as another kind of blocked 'leisure time' has just about doubled, since nearly all employees in the Federal German Republic became entitled to 30 working days, or six weeks, annual leave. In sum this means that whereas in 1950 employees had to go to work on 293 days in the year, by 1985 this obligation had fallen to 219 days. Moreover, the conversion of the shorter working week that had been agreed in 1984 in several areas of the collective labour agreement in the form of 'free days' – often called 'bridging days' linked to public holidays – provided some employees with a virtual prolongation of their leave entitlement; even before that, extra 'free shifts' or 'senior worker free periods' had been laid down in various parts of the agreement for older employees and those doing particularly arduous work. Thus the reduction in the number of working days in the year is the crucial gain of work-free time. These blocks of work-free time also represent a possible time resource for new patterns of economic activity.

At least as important as the shortening of the working *year* is the shortening of the working *life*. The prolongation of pre-vocational education at the 'lower end' of the working life, resulting in a higher average age of entry to the labour market, is relevant here only in the sense that although there are fewer children per family overall, they represent a financial burden for their families for a longer period of education. What is more important is the foreshortening of the 'top end' of the working life by earlier retirement. Between 1973 and 1986 the pensionable age for male insured persons fell from 62.2 to 58.8 years (cf. VDR 1975:45, 125; 1987:76). The take-up of the flexible age limit introduced in 1973, and the increased award of retirement pensions on health grounds (due in large part to the deterioration in the employment situation), together with earlier retirement under the pre-retirement law of 1984, brought about a noticeable lowering of the numbers employed in the higher age groups (55 and upwards), with a consequent increase in the number of households headed by a pensioner (type V). Since it can be assumed that only a small proportion of the increasingly 'youthful' new pensioners is unfit for work, this group represents a growing and largely untapped potential pool of productive labour that cannot be absorbed by the paid employment system. The fact that early (and not always entirely voluntary) retirement entails a correspondingly larger drop in income makes it all the more likely that this pool could be tapped by suitable self-employment arrangements.

Whereas for pensioners' households the exit from the active earning phase is permanent, households not in paid employment, headed by an unemployed person (type IV) mainly represent a category of varying composition but one which overall was growing up to the middle of the 1980s. In this type of household the (temporary) availability of portions of time not taken up by gainful employment and the need to operate in the informal economy in order to secure a level of welfare are comparable with the situation of pensioners' households.

THE TREND OF TIME NOT GAINFULLY EMPLOYED — RESULTS OF TIME BUDGET STUDIES

Regrettably, information about the extent of, and changes in, activities outside the field of paid employment is much more limited and less reliable than that relating to the field itself. The available data for the Federal German Republic do not allow firm conclusions to be drawn as to whether working time within households has decreased absolutely and relatively during recent decades in favour of 'leisure'. There are, it is true, some studies on the subjectively estimated extent of 'leisure' time, (routine) household work, the activities of home workers, etc., but no consistent picture emerges from data of this kind.

Disregarding basic problems of data collection, time budget studies can provide more valid data regarding various patterns of time use than such appraisals, because they call for a systematic listing by respondents over a given period of how they spent units of time in different activities, how long they spent on them and how often they did them. The activities might be freely chosen, or prescribed by the researcher. (See, among others, Gershuny et al. 1986:14ff.; Andorka 1987; Haugg and Schweitzer 1987:233ff.; Ehling and Schäfer 1988; Hinrichs 1988:320). However, up to the present no suitable theory has been advanced as to the determining causes of time use, so that the results of time budget investigations are almost exclusively descriptive (cf. Gershuny and Jones 1987:11f.; Haugg and Schweitzer 1987:233f.). With regard to the estimation of the amount of 'leisure' the problem remains that this is determined by how the *observer* defines this category and now how such activities are regarded by the respondents. Gardening is an interesting instance. This perception may differ from one person to another and even from one time to another by the same person, with the result that the assessment of the utility of the process (which is present either positively or negatively in *every* activity) is one of the determinants of the allocation of time.

But the recorded allocation of time does not indicate whether the observed uses of time actually indicate preferences. Hitherto in the Federal Republic time budget surveys of this kind have been carried out either with specially selected, unrepresentative survey populations, or only budgets of portions of time (for instance, work performed) have been recorded, or else more extensive surveys were not replicated, so that unambiguous demographic comparisons have not so far been possible. In contrast, more careful surveys providing an insight into changes in the pattern of time usage by the population have been carried out in Britain (cf. Gershuny et al. 1986; Gershuny and Jones 1987) and in the Netherlands (cf. Knulst 1977; Knulst and Schoonderwoerd 1983). Since it may be assumed that developments are taking place in these two countries comparable to those in the Federal Republic, the following conspectus of some survey results on the situation and changes in the field of home work and leisure also makes use of the data from Britain and the Netherlands.[2]

Particular attention is given in this summary to the way in which domestic work and leisure are divided between the members of the household. For participation in novel, informal systems of economic activity cannot disregard existing (unequal) demands on time and possible welfare gains or losses by individual members of households. The following findings seem to be established and relatively uncontested:

- For those in employment there is a distinct difference in the pattern of time use between weekends and working days. Saturday is 'housework day' for employed wives and husbands. Employed persons have least free time on working days; at weekends (especially on Sunday) all groups of persons have the greatest amount of leisure time and it is *approximately* evenly distributed.

- The amount of time spent on housework rises with the size of the household, but less than proportionately. In married couple households the presence of children, and their age, makes a marked difference, and this is reflected in the employment profile of the mother.

- Women who are married do *more* housework than those who are single; they lose leisure time if they take up paid employment, and still more if they have to look after children living at home. Consequently mothers in full-time employment have to devote the greatest amount of time to (paid and unpaid) work.

- The amount of unpaid work performed per two-person household is determined by whether and, if so, for how long the wife goes to work outside the home. Other things being equal – for example the age and number of the children – married women with jobs devote *many* fewer hours to domestic chores than their sisters without jobs.[3] Whether a wife goes out to work and, if so, for how many hours a week, has only a small effect on the absolute extent to which the (working) husband helps with the housework (unless the wife has a *full-time* job). But since employed housewives do less housework, the longer a wife's working hours are the greater is the proportion of housework contributed by her husband.

- There is in any event a *dual sex-specific division of labour*; women in the partnership regularly take the (distinctly) greater share of housework *and* more often than not the 'routine' tasks of cooking, laundry, etc., while in the main the men see to the 'technical' tasks and non-repetitive ones, such as repairs, redecoration and gardening, as well as dealing with the finances.

- For married women in employment who have children the 'natural' result of a shortened working day is more housework, and not necessarily more leisure.

- Unemployed males utilize the time that would otherwise be spent at work in doing more housework (including typically 'women's' jobs), but most of them only go in for *passive* leisure activities as provided by the mass media and out-of-home leisure activities – social contacts.
- As household income increases the proportion of unpaid working time to total working time decreases; in other words there is a greater use of paid help and of purchased goods and services.
- The *amount* of 'free time' and the *uses* to which it is put vary according to time of life, household situation, the arrangement of paid employment time, sex, region (town or country), education, occupation, income and so on, so that any attempt at typecasting or creating a Mr or Mrs Average would falsify the complex reality. Yet out-of-house leisure activities are clearly directed towards a widening of experience, and leisure activities have increased in number and variety.
- Until the mid-1970s the amount of time spent by women on household duties was showing a slight decrease. Actual free time increased for both sexes, but for men not in proportion to the increased leisure they gained through shortening of working hours, because they used some of this time on housework. Since then the amount of housework done by women has remained about constant, whereas with (married) men it has risen more sharply than the reduction in working and travel time, giving them a net loss of 'leisure'.
- In the younger families (with small children, also those living in large cities) and in couples with a high educational level the man takes an *appreciably* larger share in the housework. In older married couples too, the husband takes a larger share in the household chores, but this is probably due less to a gradual weakening of traditional role consciousness than to the amount of time no longer preempted by outside employment.
- Over the years the total working time of married men and women of economically active age has tended to approximate more closely. Housewives not gainfully employed have more leisure than their husbands and than other married women.
- The proportions of time taken by different household tasks have shifted in that relatively more time is spent on shopping, transport and care of the children.
- The technical equipment in households has no significant influence on the time taken by housework. The only clear correlation

is with income: the higher the household income, the more domestic appliances the household has.

- If we look at the freely disposable time resources (those not taken up by paid and unpaid work) by types of household, it emerges that employed persons living alone (type I) and 'two-income' married couples with children needing care (type IIIb) have the smallest amounts of 'leisure' time, while in contrast households not gainfully employed (type V) have by far the largest amount of disposable leisure time. In between come childless (married) couple households in which the wife is not gainfully employed (type IIa) as well as households of types IIb and IIIa, which in fact show a somewhat longer total working time. In fairly broad terms we could speak of a *polarization* of the availability of 'free' time resources: there is an increased relative weighting both for households with little time left for alternative uses (types I and IIIb) and also for households with a high proportion of uncommitted time (type V and – to some extent – IV).

- If we disregard the lengthening of annual leave and the increase in (associated) non-working days, it becomes clear that for every type of household 'real' leisure time has risen only slightly in recent years and that the time taken up by housework has remained almost unaltered. This being so, a change in the *aggregate* of leisure time or the number of hours of unpaid work done would result mainly from a change in the composition of the types of household.

It is noticeable, but after all not surprising, that the amount of housework has not declined. The belief that housework would be reduced because of improvements in technical household equipment or because of its partial mechanization has been sufficiently exposed as a myth (cf. for example Bose et al. 1984). In many production processes the introduction of so-called 'time savers' has indeed altered the factor input and brought about an increase in productivity, but has often failed to effect an immediate saving in time. The change in the work process induced by the availability of such equipment simply made the work easier and increased the 'comfort' by improving cleanliness (for example in the frequency of changes of linen, quality (for example by diversifying meals) and so on. From the standpoint of productivity enhancement there has so far been no observable 'increase in the efficiency of domestic applicances application'; therefore on purely operating cost criteria many purchasing decisions must ultimately be considered as misconceived (Schweitzer and Pross 1976:262f.).

Furthermore there are not only more goods to be procured, transported, operated and serviced;[4] the range of consumer goods and services has become much wider. Nowadays holiday travel, yoga courses, and psychological counselling for children with behavioural problems have to be provided[5] and all these activities duly administered through registrations and signing off, bookings and cancellations, invoices, complaints, credit applications, extracts of accounts and so on. 'Consumption management' is a growth industry that multiplies the functions of homework. Therefore the vast increases of the 'output' of household production seem to have outweighed the productivity increases on the 'input' side. This despite the average decrease in the size of households and the smaller number of children per (multiperson) household, since work is saved less than proportionately to the decrease in the size of household. Moreover in recent decades each member of a household has occupied more space, partly in consequence of a growing proportion of owner-occupiers; and when higher standards are set for children's upbringing, fewer children in a household does not signify less housework – rather the reverse. Indeed, more time is now spent on bringing up children (cf. Gershuny and Jones 1987; Rerrich 1983).

Finally, the acceptance of self-service and do-it-yourself activities, which owing to the 'cost sickness of the services sector' (cf. Baumol 1967) assures access to certain services and/or makes a given income go farther, has caused an increasing amount of work to be done at home. And yet the cost advantage is not the only reason why householders use their own tools and unpaid labour time instead of bought-in services; frequently they have no other option, because private and public suppliers curtail their services in order to shed costs (one thinks of longer intervals between local trains) or else offer them at prohibitively high prices, as in the delivery and assembly of furniture, or even cut them out altogether. These curtailments of services are often reactions to rationalization measures taken by individual households, and they may have selective distribution effects which disadvantage households with below average resources.

It is becoming less and less possible to acquire goods and services which satisfy contemporary expectations of an appropriate lifestyle and give individuals more freedom, by using time as a substitute for money. Nevertheless there is still no substitute for (home-work) time for people wanting access to ready-for-use goods which after all are important for well-being. For developments in marketing have introduced an inescapable trend to closer integration of households into the market, crosslinking them with services supplied by other social institutions and hence multiplying the external relations of households (cf. Thiele-Wittig 1987). The imputation of simple alternatives such as 'depletion' vs 'enrichment' or 'immigration vs emigration' yields only an inadequate picture of this process. Entertainment, transport, relaxation in new environments, security arrangements, etc., have to be purchased in the market for money and they require both time to earn the income and time outside earning time to learn about, operate and administer these goods or services. Linder (1971) described this development as the 'paradox of welfare'. The general increase in incomes reduces the scarcity of goods and replaces it by scarcity of time. This 'time scarcity' is further intensified by the growing involvement of households in market and public organizations, because the 'on' times of the organizations (for example the opening hours of nursery schools, clinics and shops and the office hours of public authorities) follow a collective rhythm in their daily, weekly and to a degree their annual cycles which is largely identical with the working hours of the majority of employed people, and hence is particularly apt to cause them 'frictional losses', rationing (difficulties of access) and conflicts, either because there are too many outside demands pressing on a given period of time, or because it leads to waiting time, hold-ups or 'unusable' remainders of time.

So if despite enhanced prosperity on the one hand and greater complexity of the daily round on the other, none of the household types defined above has been able to reduce the amount of time spent in unpaid work – necessary work often done in a hurry and under pressure of time – it is not surprising that the feeling of having '(far) too little time' (cf. Keller 1984:198f.; EMNID 1983:89) or that 'I'm being swamped by work' (cf. IfD 1985:25ff.) is widespread among the adult population. Nor is it surprising that the proportion of the population thinking that people now have '*more* free time' (than previously) showed a marked decline between 1972/3 and 1982 (from 47 to 32 per cent, cf. EMNID 1983:103).

Hence although in the postwar period there has been a considerable decrease in the yearly quota of time spent in paid employment, especially the working lifetime, the amount of time perceived as being 'freely disposable' has not significantly increased. The numbers both of households with a high proportion of uncommitted time (predominantly those of pensioners) and of households which clearly have little time left over for additional work calculated to enhance welfare and not market dependent (married couple households with two incomes) have increased and are still increasing.

While the mix of household types, now and for the foreseeable future, shows the *polarity* of 'time scarcity' and 'time abundance', it does not bring out the fact that in a lifetime everybody belongs to several types of household. For instance, a young male wage-earner may start off in category I, then form a type IIIa household, progress to a type IIb and then revert to category IIIa, finally passing the evening of his life as a pensioner in household type V. During these transformations there will be changing needs for household work, and similar fluctuations as regards his 'freely' available time resources, and the former are likely under the given circumstances not to be fully covered. In the career viewed as a whole there is a certain lack of 'time banks' and 'capacitors', in which the surpluses of the 'seven fat years' can be stored and drawn on to ease the 'seven lean years'; there is, alas!, no 'time credit' facility to be drawn on in the lean years and repaid in the fat ones. Nor is there a workable system of demand smoothing that could be applied across the social spectrum between 'time poor' and 'time rich' households, to their mutual advantage.

A proposal for an institutional reform that would be very apposite in this connection was worked out by Gösta Rehn (1977). This concept called for 'drawing rights' on paid sabbaticals from work and on temporary undershoots of 'normal paid working time' to be suitably financially compensated from a social insurance fund which would offset the varying needs for off-the-job activities arising across the social spectrum and along the career profile by building into paid working time the necessary flexibility. A pattern of this kind would not finance *shortening* of working time, only the *redistribution* of a fixed-length working life in accordance with proven needs.

Declining welfare productivity of time?

While at first glance it is plausible to assert that resources of 'free' time in households have increased (even though, as has been shown, on closer analysis this is seen to need some qualification), there would seem little immediate reason to think that the 'value' of the resource, Time, that is to say the institutional opportunities and social contexts for its productive use outside paid working time, should decrease (hypothesis 2). Thus in 1983 the value of capital goods in private households was only a quarter less than the value of capital equipment per working place in the private and state sector (disregarding in both cases the value of the buildings). In other words, private households as decentralized places of work and production formed a very important part of the total production of wealth in society. Depending on the method of calculation, the value of home production equals between 30 and 50 per cent of the national product (cf. the comparison of a number of estimates in Schäfer 1988:309). Even if the order of magnitude of such estimates must be treated with some reserve on methodological grounds, the calculations still show one thing quite clearly – that in the postwar period non-market-led production in private households related to the national product as a measurable variable in the national accounts has remained approximately constant. In other words, however household production is measured, it has grown *pari passu* with statistically recorded production.

We shall now state and examine a number of arguments that seem to confirm the initial assertion that time not spent in paid employment represents a loss in value. These arguments rely on the logical advantage of money over time, the growth of 'defensive' (household) production bound up with productivity losses through the 'privatistic propensity to consume' of households that are constantly shrinking in size, and on the limited opportunities for the expansion of home production and self-supply. At this point our consideration of factors militating against the assumption that time not gainfully employed reduces the production of wealth will be confined to 'do-it-yourself'. Another field of activity, the provision of social services in family and neighbourhood networks, will be considered in more detail later in the chapter.

WHY 'MONEY' IS WORTH MORE THAN 'TIME'

We should now like to substantiate the thought that was only mentioned in passing in the introduction, namely that the medium 'money' is in general superior to the medium 'time' on account of the specific characteristics of the two media: in any denomination, at any time and in all social contexts, *money* represents its nominal face value,[6] whereas *time* is not 'homogenous' in such a way that the chronological value resulting from the position of a 'piece' of time along the time axis or in a cycle containing a quantity of time is always the same. Both as a potential offer of work and as 'leisure' its 'value' changes because of the rhythms of natural or social time (for example, between three and five o'clock in the morning time is relatively 'valueless', except for sleeping). But its value depends not only on *which* activities are in principle possible or not, but also on the issue of with *whom* these activities can be structured in common. Moreover, time cannot be 'parcelled up' at will into meaningful units. There is always a residue of unusable remainders of time, which have to be 'spent' because they can neither be saved and added to units currently needed nor passed on to other people. Hence the value of time depends on present opportunities for making use of it, and choice is correspondingly restricted. Superfluous money, on the other hand, can actually be increased if placed on deposit, because interest received enlarges future opportunities of satisfaction.

There is moreover an asymmetrical convertibility relationship between 'money' and 'time' in the sense that although, by spending money, portions of time appropriate to requirements can be 'bought', in order to harmonize the chronologically differing potentials of time or shortages of time, it is on the other hand far more difficult to convert available resources of time into money or to make a tight monetary budget go further by spending time. Working time can be sold only if there is a demand for it in the market, and the chances of saving money by time-intensive home production depend both on what time resources are available and how they are distributed, and on the possession of suitable skills and premises. If time alone is available, and not money as well, its use value *falls*. For under the influence of the socioculturally determined standards and forms of the use of time, the availability of time means boredom, exclusion (from valued activities) unless appropriate money resources are also available – in fact, disutility. Because money in hand is in principle not liable to lose its value and at the same time makes possible an endless variety of uses in the future, an increase in a person's money resources is not accompanied by a decrease in marginal utility, and there is probably no absolute saturation point for money. By contrast, the marginal utility of time resources falls with their availability. For obviously a satisfying experience of time presupposes – especially in a 'work society' – a certain tension in relation to compulsory activities, whether by experiencing and/or demonstrating one's own 'usefulness' or because of the experienced contrast between 'the working day' and 'leisure time' or between 'the common round' and 'high days and holidays'.

Continuing this train of thought, one might say that the 'wealth value' of a given quantity of time not put into gainful employment is assessed in the case both of home work and of 'originative' leisure activities according to (a) how 'rhythmic' the social environment is, (b) whether the position and distribution of time spent in employment are the same as most other people's, and (c) how free the subject is to decide how leisure time shall be spent. We have already mentioned the limitations placed on the 'quality of time' for customers, clients and patients by the fact that organizations servicing them have the same opening and closing hours. Thus in Anglo-Saxon terminology shiftwork, night and weekend work is rightly termed 'unsocial hours', because people working such hours are unable to take part in many activities during 'socially valuable' times, structured by the 'work/-rest' rhythm of the majority. These barriers to access affect family leisure activities and participation in cultural events after working hours or during the 'free' weekend, as well as hampering productive activities in neighbourhood or extended family networks, which are also usually organized at such times.

Employers in West Germany have been pressing ahead with the introduction of flexitime, and this should have the effect of freeing unused reserves of productivity by lengthening machine utilization time, adapting employees' working hours to the demands of the market and increasing the spread of the regular length of working time. This should make the pattern of working hours more heterogeneous and increase the number of hours worked outside the existing 'normal framework' by means of weekend and shift working.

Lastly, the wealth value of time to the individual is determined by the extent to which one is a 'consumer of time'. Because the increasing complexity of society and the involvement of households with public and market service systems confer added importance on punctuality and timekeeping and attention to opening hours, the opportunity of *unfettered choice* of the hours spent in gainful employment acquires added importance. Instead of simply having 'a lot of time' it is more advantageous to be able to 'tailor' periods of time that are meaningful in terms of what one wishes to do. A person who is able actively to structure the time required for doing what he has to do, and when and in what order to do it, is 'master/mistress of his/her time' and can 'upgrade' the quality of the time by avoiding unusable odds and ends of time ('idling'), bottleneck (queues and tailbacks) and conflicting claims on time. What is more, money can be saved if scarcity mark-ups can be avoided. Therefore it is likely that a *longer* time spent in gainful employment, provided the hours can be largely self-chosen, will yield *more* profitably usable 'leisure' with *more* alternative ways of spending it, and consequently a *higher* use quality than shorter working hours inflexibly prescribed.

Empirically there is a distinct covariance between high socioeconomic status and longer hours spent gainfully employed, together with greater control of the timing and distribution of the hours. On the other hand, employees who have a comparatively large amount of leisure time usually have this time *allocated* to them, often at times or in 'parcels' that do leave less choice of palatable alternative uses. As a rule they have more limited opportunities of self-determination and self-development at work and a smaller income, which still further reduces the alternative ways of spending their leisure time open to them. As a function of the differing wealth productivity those who have to content themselves with a smaller amount of free time husband it more carefully and display a more active, less routine-bound attitude to leisure in a larger social environment and are less subject to feelings of boredom.[7] Thus the variety of leisure activities increases in line with disposable income and the level of educational attainment. Based on differing positions of market power the increasing flexibility of working hours mentioned above might be expected to accentuate the polarization of the welfare value of leisure time as a function of socioeconomic status, for whereas certain groups of workers are unable to escape being fobbed off with less convenient hours of work, groups with considerable market power will be in a position to bargain for more opportunities of determining the pattern of their use of time.

'DEFENSIVE' HOME PRODUCTION, 'PRIVATISTIC PROPENSITY TO CONSUME' AND 'MODERNIZATION TRAPS'

The following contention about the decreasing wealth value of 'time' is on a different level. Fred Hirsch (1980:91) has pointed out that the goods and services acquired by households can be distinguished according to whether in themselves they provide a primary satisfaction or whether their innate satisfaction equals zero or is even negative. He calls the last-named category *defensive* goods and their use or consumption, *defensive consumption*. The sole purpose of this defensive consumption is to counteract a disadvantage or to correct a worsening in external environmental conditions; that is to say, it only helps to maintain an already achieved level of welfare without raising it. However, if most goods do not bring the end-user any immediate benefit, that does not mean that they are all defensive goods. For example, the purchase of an electric cooker obtains an 'intermediate product' for the household, with the aid of which what are known as 'basic commodities' (in this case meals ready to eat) can be produced. What is significant for our inquiry is whether there is not only a defensive consumption by private households (with its associated costs) but also a defensive household *production*. As households have to spend (ever) more income on defensive consumption in order to avoid welfare reverses, it is just as conceivable that they have to put in more and more unpaid work in order to counteract changes for the worse in the natural, social or technical environment.

At all events, it is inevitable that when market and government organizations reduce or completely terminate the offer of services indispensable to households, forcing them to increase their self-service activities, such defensive forms of use-value production will make their appearance. But far beyond that, our increasingly complex society is stepping up the demands of daily living ('consumption management'), which increase the amount of unpaid work done in households and thereby lead to an extension of defensive production.

The following considerations seem also to be convergent with our initial hypothesis: in the past, market and state organizations have been able to achieve enormous economies of scale and productivity increases through growth in size and centralization. Conversely, a precisely opposite trend has occurred in private households. These have become more numerous and smaller, especially since the Second World War. Thus while the population of the Federal Republic of Germany grew by 14 per cent between 1957 and 1986, the number of households grew by 45 per cent during this period, and this is due in large measure to the increase in the number of single person households, which rose from 18.3 to 34.3 per cent (cf. Federal Statistical Office 1986:186). Naturally this must have resulted in productivity losses (diseconomies of small scale). The less efficient 'mini' organization of household production basically means a waste of time and capital in providing the equipment needed for running a household.

In 1918 Max Weber made the following observation from the First World War illustrating the fact that because of the difference in transaction costs it is 'simpler' to organize business interests than consumer interests:

> Even the current starvation, at least in Germany, has not, or only with great difficulty, persuaded housewives in the mass of the population to accept meals from public canteens, which everybody agreed were beautifully prepared and tasty, in place of their amateur individual cooking, even though canteen meals were much cheaper. (Weber 1924:504)

His impressions provide evidence for the fact that even under really difficult conditions people will forego the advantages of 'socializing' for the sake of maintaining privacy and independence. Although the increase in the general level of prosperity and the concomitant process of social individualization have led to a multiplication of patterns of living and a diversification of lifestyles, this has meant a further 'generalization of privacy as a pattern of living', compared with the first decades of the present century (Mooser 1984:151). This included the trend towards a cultural model of living that Rammert (1987a:321; cf. 1987b) characterizes as a 'consumerist paradigm'. This signifies the adoption of a pattern of consumption that was established in the USA in the 1920s and 1930s, which reached its full development in the Federal Republic from the 1950s onwards as a consequence of the exceptional increases in real incomes (and in association with an increase in the amount of time spent out of the office or factory in the various dimensions). This 'privatistic consumption orientation' results in making production not destined for the market inefficient and is further increased by the change in the size of households and the increase in their number, also brought about by processes of individualization. Because 'the mechanized, highly privatized household obviously satisfies the preferences of many of those concerned' (Zapf et al. 1987a:225), the 'trend to privatistic consumption' must form an important cultural barrier to social innovations which are directed towards more cooperative patterns of supply.

Clearly it is possible to determine whether the (economic) disadvantages of an inefficiently high outlay of working time per household and an inefficiently low loading of the domestic appliances that are accepted for the sake of privacy and self-sufficiency really constitute an impregnably 'rigid' barrier only *if and when* institutional alternatives are available and consequently whether the 'privatistic consumption trend' syndrome is exposed to the opportunity of becoming rationalized in the direction of a partial 'socialization'.

'Privatistic consumption orientation' further implies that households become more closely connected to the markets for labour, goods and services. The increased access to market offers of goods and services brought about by the rise in real incomes has supplanted traditionally self-produced household goods, and household work has increasingly become *consumption* work in the sense that it has concentrated on 'consumption management' and on the 'final stage' of the processing of consumption goods for the act of direct consumption or use. This limitation of the function of households to private (leisure) consumption is complemented by the furnishing of dwellings and by the (public) structuring of the home surroundings. Since the continuing increase in prosperity opens up new ways in which 'privacy' can be established in smaller and smaller household units, the capacities of households to change back to increased self-production are restricted and not necessarily amenable to change by individual decisions. In any event this enormously enlarged panoply of consumer technologies can only be utilized if sufficient funds are available to finance the energy costs, the cost of providing the necessary infrastructure (standing charges), the cost of repairs and specialist knowledge, and so forth. Thus the structural changes described above have ensnared households into a 'modernization trap'.

So if increased amounts of free time can only yield their harvest of welfare in association with improved opportunities for increasing consumption, and are only to a small degree conducive to expenditure substitution, the welfare value of 'time' is greater if it is or can be employed in gainful income-producing work. This increasing wealth differential in the use of time may be responsible for the fact that at the present time employees are not showing such a marked preference for shorter working hours and that in long-term comparisons an ever-decreasing proportion of the growth in distributed profit has gone on shortening working hours and a correspondingly larger share on higher incomes (cf. Hinrichs 1988:163ff.).

THE SPREAD OF 'DO-IT-YOURSELF' ACTIVITIES

Do-it-yourself (DIY) activities provide an alternative way of acquiring ready-for-use production, repair, maintenance or other services; the activities concerned are then performed as ownwork for self-supply or in the context of networks of relatives or neighbours as neighbourly self-help on a basis of reciprocity. The materials, energy and equipment required are purchased in the market in the ordinary way. During recent years the DIY and home-worker markets have shown high growth rates, for the higher the proportion of direct and indirect taxes and wage oncosts included in each hour's work billed by a tradesman selling his services, and the smaller the difference between the net hourly charge of the would-be worker and that of the potential customer, that is the more hours the customer, himself or herself an employee, would have to work in order to 'buy' one hour's work from a commercial contractor, the more attractive does DIY become. In the past these ratios have moved in the direction of making DIY (and other kinds of ownwork) more attractive, thus setting up movement in the interplay between household and market production and causing structural changes within the market sector. But the spread of DIY has been due in equal measure to the increase in the *demand* for such work and the change in the social, skill and technical *preconditions* for DIY as a substitute for bought-in services.

Empirical investigations (cf. IfF 1984, vol. 1:97ff.; Niessen and Ollmann 1987:166) show that the motive 'to save money' is by far the most frequently mentioned reason for doing work at home. A rough calculation shows clearly that this aim is by no means unrealistic, even taking into account the greater productivity in the work of a 'professional' tradesman and the cost of procuring the necessary DIY equipment. If an employed tradesman earns 200 DM gross, the employer has to charge the customer 410.60 DM for work based on this gross wage, including incidental wages costs and value added tax (and this before adding overheads and profit). If the potential customer of the tradesman earned the same hourly wage as the tradesman, he would receive 136 DM (assuming 32 per cent deductions for wages tax and social security contributions) for his hour's work. So in round figures the potential customer can 'save' *at least* his net earnings for two hours of employment if he works the lathe or takes up the paintbrush himself.

This is the position over a broad spectrum of occupational fields, and home workers estimate that considerable amounts can sometimes be saved in this way. A study found that a quarter of the adult population in the Federal Republic were in the 'active home worker' category (in building and home improvement alone) and that they spent at least 30 hours a year at it – an increase of 18 per cent between 1978 and 1983 (IfF 1984). Another 21.4 per cent were 'occasional home workers' (doing up to 30 hours a year). 'Active' home workers put in an average of 92 hours per year on DIY activities, the average for the 'occasionals' being 14 hours.

The predominant reason for the past increase in DIY and its projected future expansion is the growing proportion of homeowners. In 1962/3 only about 30 per cent of households of *employed persons* owned a house and land, whereas by 1983 the proportion had risen to half (cf. Braun 1985:968). Survey findings indicate that 77 per cent of all households would like to live 'within their own four walls' (if possible in a detached one-family house) (cf. EMNID 1983:97). The study cited above (IfF 1984, vol.1:89) made the assumption that by 1990 two-thirds of the net *additions* to the housing stock would be inhabited by homeowners. There is a large potential requirement, particularly among homeowners, for using DIY as a substitute for bought services. The typical 'active' home worker has the following profile: a male manual worker, office employee or official between 25 and 60 years old with a secondary education, having three or four in the family, in his own house in a parish with fewer than 5,000 inhabitants and with a monthly net household income of in the region of 2,500–3,000 DM (cf. Deimer et al. 1983:25; IfF 1984, vol.1:113f.; Keller 1984:172; Merz and Wolff 1988:211ff.).

Not only is DIY practised to a considerable extent in building, extensions and ancillary building activities, but also in (kitchen) gardening and 'around the car'. It is not often that home workers pursue more than one of these activities – and women do so less frequently than men. There are also clear sex-specific 'domains' discernible, and furthermore the amount of ownwork depends on the type of household: single person households are least likely to do ownwork, and complete families most likely. Moreover, with regard to DIY (and more generally in services relating to goods), exchange processes among relations (by far the most intensive) and among friends, acquaintances and neighbours (as a rule less intensive) take place to a considerable and increasing extent, and particularly in regard to house refurbishing, removals and gardening and in building or converting houses – with many hours being spent on the last-named activities. It might sometimes be hard to distinguish this DIY assistance given by non-family members from 'black market' activities.

The increasing number of houseowners, and of households owning one or even several automobiles, the constant rise in the number of households equipped with other consumer durables (provided they can be serviced or repaired by 'unskilled persons') and the continuing above-average increase in the price of the services of tradesmen and other market suppliers are likely to bring about sustained growth in the *requirements* of households for DIY services in the future. At the same time the *arrangements* for meeting the demand in this way are improving. The 'core group' of home workers, namely employed male workers, now has more freely disposable time, added to which a growing number of people have taken early retirement because the average age for retirement has fallen.

Furthermore there is a 'learning curve' in DIY working: 'active' home workers progress in skill and self-confidence and then extend the range of their DIY activities and the time spent on them; they buy more and better equipment and so become even more 'active' and able to make still further 'savings' on bought-in services (cf. IfF 1984, vol.2:5; Niessen and Ollmann 1987:152, 159f., 220ff.).

So far we have looked only at structural factors encouraging more DIY activities; we now turn to cyclical influences. Several surveys have clearly indicated that household production in excess of the norm is not evenly distributed quantitatively over the various types of household, and further that the uneven distribution is not such as to lead to an evening out of the different income levels: 'Ownwork is essentially a middle-class activity' (Merz and Wolff 1988:219). What concerns us here is whether household production is being increased in substitution of market demand when disposable household incomes are falling. Contrary to widespread assumptions, the 'buffer function' of the household is very limited. For example, a survey undertaken in Holland shows that in times of economic recession private households, driven by necessity, rein in their expenditure, especially on consumer durables, yet do not compensate for this by increasing their household production (cf. Ours 1986:430). The findings of the 'welfare survey' also confirm that pensioners, persons incapacitated for work and the unemployed are not in a position to increase their incomes by doing low-paid work in networks; they do not form a larger proportion of such groups than of the general population (cf. Glatzer 1986:34, 36). This agrees generally with Pahl's findings (1988a) that not only do those excluded from gainful employment (whether this is due to retirement or temporary unemployment) typically suffer a drop in household disposable income, but that they miss the workplace as an important forum for contacts and an informal 'labour exchange' (cf. also Jessen et al. 1985, 1988).

Precarious income situation?

As a rule a household's monetary income derives from several sources – the wages and associated receipts of the household members, such as company pensions; social security and other transfer payments; assets and income from assets resulting from earlier savings; money inherited from the older generation and other monetary resources. Since the Second World War the *monetary safety net* thus constituted has increased considerably, and this rise in incomes, unique in economic history, has hastened the processes of social individualization and differentiation (cf. Beck 1986:116, 122ff.). For example, if we plot the course of incomes from work and the associated old age income in the Federal Republic, we find a rise in annual net real income per employed person between 1950 and 1987 of 230 per cent (cf. Statistical Yearbook 1988: table 1.15). Not only were pensioners not excluded from this rise in incomes, their relative position improved. In 1988 the average pensioner with 40 years of insured employment behind him had income from pensions and investments amounting to 64.2 per cent of the net income of a comparable employee; even in 1957 it had been 59.3 per cent. We shall show below, by citing the consequences of the growth of multiearner households (type III) and the results of the past and continuing formation of monetary and tangible assets, that it is quite reasonable to expect that this 'safety net' will be strong enough to provide the vast majority of households (in Germany) with adequate monetary security for the remainder of life. Therefore these households would not have a strong economic incentive to take on *additional* involvement in new systems of moneyless demand satisfaction.

On the other hand, as mentioned in initial hypothesis 3 on page 4, precarious income situations are becoming more widespread, and the number of households that cannot be sure how high and how secure their income will be in the future is increasing. The contingencies that may lead to a temporary or permanent lack of sufficient income include unemployment, (chronic) illnesses, invalidity and divorce. Sociologically precarious income situations are associated with *failed status passages* (such as deviant exit from crises of adolescence, failed education or training, unsuccessful entry into employment or family systems) or with *manifest loss of status* (such as loss of a job, of physical or mental health, of the marriage partner, of creditworthiness, etc.). And although these risks as individual events do not lead to a deficiency of household income, or not to a permanent one, yet if two or more such events are linked, there is a high probability of progressive impoverishment. Data currently available do not permit the present extent and future trend of monetarily precarious states of living to be quantified and correlated with the corresponding figures for households that do *not* fall through the meshes of the safety net provided by the family, employers and the state, and which conversely may even expect their financial situation to improve.

SEVERE UNEMPLOYMENT, MORE MARRIED WOMEN TAKING JOBS
AND THE EXTENT OF PRECARIOUS LIVING CONDITIONS

A further look at the net real earnings of employed persons in the Federal Republic mentioned earlier shows that these increased by a fifth between 1970 and 1986. Yet during this same period average disposable income in employee households rose much more sharply – by 30 per cent – and disposable income per household member in employee households rose by as much as 52.3 per cent. The main reason for this uneven trend lies in the greater number of women taking paid work and the reduction in the size of households. Both these factors contributed significantly to the individualization of careers and ways of life. We shall not investigate further here whether it is the changes in women's career profiles, the need for 'social status' or for a way of satisfying the perceived need for household income that did or does play a decisive part inidividual instances of the shift in family households from type II to type III. At all events the longer and more continuous presence of married women in business during their careers has important consequences for the present level and the social distribution of the available resources of money and also for the *foreseeable* availability of this source of prosperity.

No clear-cut answer can be given to the question whether the increased proportion of married women in employment accounts for the fact that since 1970 incomes have been slightly less evenly divided among private households (cf. Krause and Schäuble 1986:43ff.). But it must have led to both a convergence and a differentiation of incomes in married households of working age. The convergence comes about because, as the net income of the husband increases, the wife does less outside work, both in respect of the proportion of earnings and of the frequency of full-time as opposed to part-time working (cf. Schwarz 1982:211). Conversely the pattern of married women's employment leads to a *differentiation* of income levels because in childless housholds where the husband is in business the proportion earned by the wife is always higher at every income level than in households with children below the age of 18, and hence the household income, which is always higher, is divided between a smaller number of people, namely two. Over against this, households with children are doubly disadvantaged, because they are generally in a career situation in which neither the husband nor the wife (if she is at work) has reached his or her maximum earnings scale: 'A comparison of the material situation of childless families with that of married couples with children turns out to the disadvantage of families with children however long the marriage has lasted' (Schwarz 1980:331; cf. also Berger-Schmitt 1986b:166ff.; BMJFG 1986:42).

More serious loss of income generally ensues if the head of household becomes unemployed. Among multiperson households this occurred far less frequently with married households than with unmarried cohabitants and single parent households. In single person households the unemployment ratio of heads of household was actually twice the average (cf. Zapf et al. 1987b:91f.). One reason for the income losses of this group of unemployed households, which has increased sharply in numbers (type IV) is that it depends on transfer payments, which are lower than earned incomes. These transfer payments, and the disposable incomes of unemployed households, have lagged considerably behind the income growth rates of all private households – indeed there has been a loss in real terms since 1972. Moreover in multiperson households of unemployed persons, it is becoming more likely that another household member or members will become unemployed and less usual for another member or members to be in employment (cf. J. Heinze et al. 1986:35ff.). This doubly disadvantaged situation arises because of the greater likelihood that old and very young persons and the relatively unskilled will be unemployed, and it is intensified in some areas because the marriage partners are usually well matched in respect of age, skill levels and so on.

However, it is hard to judge whether in future the labour market will be able to absorb all would-be entrants, or whether fewer and fewer steady job opportunities will be available, entailing the *expectation* of dwindling disposable household incomes. All the 'serious' forecasts (for instance, by IAB/Prognos, cf. Klauder et al. 1985) believe that full employment will not be reestablished in the near future. Furthermore the divisions in the labour market are likely to intensify. This polarization in society is caused not only by the high rate of long-term unemployment; a change is discernible in the nature of employment relationships that might be described as an 'erosion of normal working relationships' (cf. Mückenberger 1985). Since the criteria for evaluating performance in social insurance are geared to 'normal working relationships', 'new' patterns of work, such as unprotected part-time work, short-term labour contracts, work based on a work contract and illegal temporary outplacement are leading to a widening of the gaps in social security and hence to increased risks of impoverishment (cf. R.G. Heinze et al. 1988:27ff.; Gretschmann et al. 1989). The persistence of slack conditions in the labour market and in particular the rise of unemployment to a postwar high since 1982 have imbued employees with a growing feeling of insecurity both regarding the safety of their own jobs and their chances of finding alternative employment should they become unemployed (cf. Zapf et al. 1987b:54ff.).

INCREASINGLY CONFIDENT EXPECTATIONS OF SOME
HOUSEHOLD TYPES BECAUSE OF INCREASING ACCUMULATION
OF MONEY AND TANGIBLE ASSETS

In addition to state and company pensions, which cannot be altered by individuals, some private households in the Federal Republic have voluntarily formed *additional* assets which they can utilize either freely or within the framework of contractual agreements. Thus in 1983 66.8 per cent of households had taken out life insurance as a further 'pillar' of provisions for old age; in employed households the proportion was even some 10 percentage points higher. Furthermore private households have accumulated substantial assets in other forms of investment such as savings accounts, securities, etc., through restricting current consumption. Between 1970 and 1986 net monetary assets held rose by 340 per cent, appreciably faster than the disposable incomes of private households, which rose by 190 per cent (cf. Bedau 1987:527; Müller-Krumholz 1987:518). It should however be remembered that these 'gross' figures conceal the differing amounts saved relative to disposable household income and the correspondingly dissimilar distribution of assets, and they do not reveal that in 1983 at least 5 per cent of households had no monetary assets and a further 8 per cent owed money to banks (apart from building loans and mortgages). Thus 'of the households with positive money balances . . . the "poorer" half possessed one-tenth of the assets recorded, and the "richest" 10 per cent of households possessed 45 per cent of total money assets' (Bedau 1986:357; cf. also Euler 1985:415f.).

Although the distribution of monetary assets and the income they bring is *even less uniform* than the distribution of household incomes, two further findings are noteworthy for the purpose of our inquiry: (1) The changes in the pattern of money investment have revealed a trend to long-term investment with a higher return. At every level asset formation is moving in the direction of investment not tied to an immediate objective and hence different from 'saving up' for the purchase of indivisible high-value consumer goods. This trend reveals the increasing importance attached to thinking ahead so as to obtain more income by investing. (2) In future an increasing number of households of older persons will be able to enjoy this additional investment income, for between 1973 and 1983 households in which the household head is aged 45 or over have increased their monetary holdings more than those in other age groups. This age differentiation of assets holdings is the logical result of the 'life cycle' of households, since the comparatively lower incomes in the 'younger' households have to be spent (almost) entirely on furnishing the house and on current living costs or the purchase of household equipment. But not only do monetary receipts form an increasing proportion of the 'older' household income; a redistribtuion occurs during the following decades from the concentration of financial resources in these 'older' households. For when these asets are passed on, they bring about an improvement in the income and/or assets situation of the 'younger' households. But this future improvement in the resources owned by today's 'young' households will not be evenly distributed. Owners of houses and land are predominantly households with average household incomes or above.

To sum up, the number of (multiperson) households with several earners has risen in the past and is expected to rise further. These households have acquired not only more financial resources but also the expectation of a steady, unchanging flow of income. This is partly because a growing number of households have more than one source of income, and cumulations of earned income and/or (various) employment substitution incomes and investment income will be much more frequent in future. Such families may enjoy stable employment, several incomes in the household, house ownership, old age pensions from the state and the employer, productive assets and preferential access to informal procurement sources. These factors, reinforced by the intergenerational transfer of assets that will be more frequent in the future, give rise to a 'Matthew effect':[8] some households, starting from a favourable position, rise to higher levels of prosperity and are distanced from an 'underclass' with insecure employment, a greater risk of incapacitation, intermittent periods of unemployment, lower current income and a corresponding insecurity of outlook on the future. Moreover these relatively disadvantaged households have very little prospect of improving their position through inheriting assets.

Growing dependence of welfare upon money?

Even though some private households will in future have a higher, steady level of income and the prospect of its continuance, this does not necessarily mean that they should look forward with confidence to greater overall 'prosperity'. Income and welfare would begin to diverge if it began to cost more simply to *maintain* a given standard of living; in that event a constant level of welfare and supply would cost more in monetary terms. This would doubly disadvantage households that had to expect their income stream to level off or even to fall or fluctuate unless they had other opportunities of meeting their needs that could be exploited without the expenditure of money.

In talking about the increasing dependence of welfare upon money (hypothesis 4 on page 4) we are not referring to the well known fact that inflation causes an overall rise in the price that has to be paid for a constant basket of goods and services. What we are referring to are four effects which, though they impinge jointly and are intertwined, can nevertheless be clearly distinguished analytically. They are

- *Structural* effects, meaning that both household and neighbourhood structures change in such a way that more expenditure becomes necessary per person per unit of benefit achieved;
- *Substitution* effects, meaning that goods and services that hitherto did not have to be bought but could be obtained in some other way can now only be had for money;
- *Price* effects, meaning that the prices of certain goods that are important to the maintenance of the level of well-being are escalating at a rate far beyond that of general inflation; these price trends, far in excess of the general run of prices, are observable especially for services, and have been correlated with the limited extent to which such 'intangible' goods can be produced more economically;
- *Quantity* and *quality* effects, meaning that either because of a change in cultural styles, patterns and levels of discrimination, the type and quantity of a component of well-being are raised and/or that suppliers succeed in eliminating the lower quality goods and services from the market by 'trading up' and thus imposing higher standards of quality upon the buying public.

The individualistic privatization of lifestyle is intimately bound up with the market as the dominant system for supplying wanted goods and services. 'Individualization signifies market dependency in all dimensions of the conduct of life' (Beck 1986:212). This dependency does not refer only to the labour market, on which the performance of work is exchanged for income and status; it also refers to markets for goods, when alternative channels of supply become exhausted because of suppliers' strategies and changes in the requirements of the demanders (consumers). In what follows we shall illustrate this growing dependence of well-being on money from the trend of expenditure on the consumption of leisure goods and household durable consumer goods. Then we shall turn our attention to 'niches' in the production of well-being that exist or have reappeared, in which services are performed based on informal network relationships, in substitution of others financed by individuals or the community.

LEISURE IS BECOMING INCREASINGLY 'EXPENSIVE'

The pace at which disposable incomes of private households in the Federal Republic of Germany increased from the beginning of the 1950s created completely novel degrees of freedom in the utilization of these incomes and led to a shift in the weighting of the structure of private consumption. The dissolution of lifestyles specific to one level in society and of class-oriented patterns of consumption is seen most clearly in the areas of expenditure on leisure goods, housing and travel. In these areas conspicuous consumption can be indulged and 'positional' lifestyles literally 'staged'. After 1970 expenditure on leisure goods expanded at a faster rate than individual net incomes, from which we may conclude that a 'quality effect' was being sought. Unless the additional leisure were structured in a money absorbing way it would not be experienced as an increase in well-being; on the contrary, many people would find leisure 'boring' if the only outlets were those provided by the prevailing institutionalized distractions. In particular the increased availability of consecutive 'blocks' of time during recent decades has presented a considerable challenge for expenditure intensive use of the time, because in the nature of things it opens up a wide variety of choice. This explains the fact that although total free time expanded by only some 16 per cent, expenditure on leisure activities rocketed.

In all three types of households investigated in the 'current economic statistics' by the Federal Statistical Office, expenditure on 'holidays' amounted in 1987 to just one-third of the money spent on leisure goods (cf. Angele 1988:582). There are few discernible limits to the increased expenditure on leisure spent away from the home locality, and to stand still is to lose ground in this more than in almost any other area of consumption. When the good 'holiday travel' has become one of the normal prerequisites of households, this betokens a transition to higher quality, that is, to (increasingly) more expensive foreign travel, and/or to the growing habit of taking more than one foreign holiday each year. Both variants can be verified from statistics on expenditure on holidays and the intensity of travel (cf. Hinrichs 1988:193f., 200ff.).

Tourism is not the only leisure activity expected to make the leisure market one of the fastest expanding sectors of private consumption. New facilities such as tennis and squash courts, swimming pools, saunas, fitness gymnasiums and so on are increasingly taking over from leisure activities hitherto self-organized (in clubs or associations) and from municipal facilities such as open-air or indoor swimming pools, and are replacing these 'cheap' facilities altogether in some subsectors. It is likely that, in future, supplier strategies aimed at satisfying (latent) needs of consumers with regard to the way they spend their leisure will link households' feelings of well-being even more strongly to the expenditure of money *and* the financial resources for leisure consumption. This gives the advantage to those households with more freely disposable income. Because of the 'visibility' and the high 'social exchange value' of such money-dispensing leisure activities these households act as *consumption exemplars* and intensify competition for social position.

But not only is leisure becoming increasingly 'expensive'; the capital costs of lifestyle are increasing. It has already been shown that as households come to contain fewer and fewer members, everyday tasks in the home become less and less 'profitable' owing to the negative scale effect. Conversely these 'diseconomies of small scale' mean that the per capita cost of running a household is constantly on the increase as a structural effect. But money is needed not only for the *purchase* of consumer goods.

It is becoming increasingly impractical for users to repair faults in or undertake maintenance of their technically advanced household equipment, while many small items simply cannot be repaired and have to be replaced at once if they fail (the quantity effect). However, this trend does not prevail across the board; there are many practical openings for ownwork, for example in building and renovating houses, which can be opened up to non-specialists through appropriate supplier strategies. But then again, households can only achieve gains in well-being in so far as they have money available. Money is needed for investing in the equipment that will save money.

'OLD' AND 'NEW' NETWORKS LIMIT THE GROWTH OF DEPENDENCE ON MONEY

When 'individualization' is under discussion it is said that the decay of traditional patterns of living in industrial societies is bound up with increased *social* mobility. But by the same token it is connected with an increase of *regional* mobility (see for example Beck 1986:125f. and 138). When traditional links become more tenuous, time has to be spent on *forming* contact networks that are sought because of their potential for increasing well-being – and this need increases *pari passu* with regional mobility. Where contact cannot be made with such networks or where they remain ineffective on account of fluctuating membership, the individual then has to satisfy any requirements he may have through the market. So the less contact there is, on account of mobility, with such groups the more dependent are individuals on having money of their own to make such purchases.

On the other hand, if there were not some remnants of more or less stable associations, the prospects for novel systems of meeting demand beyond the level of the household would be extremely unfavourable. The temptation to generalize too strongly about the growing dependency of lifestyle on money because of increased spatial mobility should be tempered by the observation that regional mobility – defined for our purposes as movement within the country beyond municipal boundaries – has *decreased*, not *increased*, in the past. In 1955 64.5 per thousand of the population changed residence in this way, but by 1970 this had fallen to 48.1 and by 1986 to only 41.5 (cf. Federal Statistical Office 1955:3; Proebsting and Fleischer 1987:615). These figures exclude moves within municipal boundaries; and changes in parish boundaries may also deflate this measurement of mobility. At least two plausible reasons can be advanced for the greater 'immobility'. The increase in home ownership makes for stronger roots and indeed often results in employees giving up opportunities of promotion. Since, because of the increase in the number of type III households, a move is increasingly likely to involve *two* job changes, this can only strengthen the propensity to stay put. Even though, objectively, people are less tied to one place (because of cars, telephones, family-owned consumer durables) and changes in lifestyle are less and less hampered by long-term decisions on location, at the same time the subjective linkage to local social contact networks such as neighbours, friends and acquaintances has increased, or at least has remained constant, as in the case of relatives (cf. Data Report 1985:457; Böltken 1987a). Whether the increasing importance of 'small networks' is explained as an aspect of the 'retreat into privacy' and supported by survey research (cf. Piel 1987), or whether the constant oscillation in society between 'what is public' and 'what is private' currently favours the private in terms of well-being (cf. Hirschman 1982) is not important for our purposes.

It is however critically important that the majority of private households have relatives living not far away from them, and that this constitutes a social resource in that they are available for day-to-day assistance and special problems. This applies in large cities almost as much as in smaller localities (cf. Böltken 1987b; Lüschen 1988; Diewald 1986). For example, in the mid-1970s 46 per cent of children up to three years old, whose mothers were in employment, were looked after by grandmothers, who were thus making it possible for their daughters or daughters-in-law to take paid employment (cf. BMJFG 1986:84f.). (Grand)parents also give many kinds of tangible and intangible assistance, especially to 'young families'.

Conversely, by no means all old people are alone and isolated, and where social contacts exist health problems do not in most cases have a serious influence on their enjoyment of life (cf. Zapf et al. 1987b:78ff.; Lehr 1988). Nor is it altogether correct to equate 'old' with 'in need of care'. There is no doubt that after the age of about 70 the proportion of sick people and those in need of care rises and complexes of interacting problems increase, but only rough indications of the absolute number of persons in need of care and assistance exist. A study on social data has shown that there were in 1978 between 1.6 and 2.5 million old people in the Federal Republic needing care in private households; the findings of its socioeconomic panel stated that 4.2 per cent of households were 'assistance households' (cf. Thiede 1986), though welfare survey findings show the figure as 9 per cent. Despite these uncertainties it can be taken as established that the great majority of old people in need of care are looked after by relatives (about 90 per cent). Care in an old people's home appears generally to be only the last resort compared with the preferred alternative of the maintenance of an 'independent lifestyle' for as long as possible. Most persons in need of care are looked after by their spouses or by daughters or daughters-in-law, either in the same household or outside it. It is widely agreed that long-term care of people who need such help generally results in overloading the carers (who are nearly always women) and also endangers the stability of the whole family (cf. R. G. Heinze et al. 1988:117ff.). Such overstrain of the potential help occurs especially when there are other unavoidable claims on the helper's time, such as outside work, in addition to the subjective obligation to assist a family member.

As was mentioned above, it is clear that *neighbourly* ties have grown and exchange relationships have been strengthened. However, neighbours generally assist with goods rather than personal services. Where there are serious and persistent problems neighbours are not expected to help as much as the family – and friends give assistance of a personal nature intermediate in quantity between that of neighbours and that of relatives. Neighbours are more likely to help out occasionally and in less time-consuming ways, such as doing errands and small household tasks.

All in all this means that *informal networks* of relatives and neighbours (and friends) give services of a personal nature to a large part of the population. Quite obviously, however, 'the potential for personal and social self-help is largely bespoken' (Blosser-Reisen 1988:165). Already these network relationships are insufficient by a wide margin to make up for deficient household care and to supply what is lacking in the services provided by the welfare state. In particular, households consisting of one elderly person (typically, widows of manual workers) tend to be insufficiently looked after.

It is likely that lacunae of this kind will become more numerous in the future. On the one hand, because of the changed age structure of the population more persons are needing care; also the number of persons willing to undertake complete personal care is dwindling, partly because so many more married women are entering employment and fewer and fewer households are suitably constituted to provide long-term services of this kind. This being so, the consequences of progressive individualization and the pluralization of living conditions mentioned at the beginning of this section are likely to result in an increasing number of persons being unable to rely on adequate supporting services and incorporation into primary networks.

Some conclusions: the connection between formal economic supply systems and deficiencies of supply

It has been shown that *supply side* strategies (both in markets and with suppliers of public services) frequently result in formalizing economic supply systems that had been informal; in other words, they convert help, self-supply, etc., into services that are bought or else financed out of taxation. In this way continual product innovation in many categories of goods depresses the relative use-value of products created in ownwork and devalues the skills involved or discourages people from acquiring them. By their very complexity, technically advanced products often can no longer be serviced or repaired at home (they are not 'user serviceable'). The same applies to services and their professionalization. 'Socially technocratic' expert knowledge (for example in areas such as socialization, care, health and nutrition) discredits and supplants traditional lay knowledge and dissuades people from acquiring the relevant skills of self-help and diagnosis. Commodification and/or professionalization impair the basis for communicative relations (cf. Jessen et al. 1988:79; Ostner and Willms 1983:219).

Such considerations readily fit into wide-ranging contemporary diagnoses by social scientists and critical evaluations of the pathologies and problems resulting from modernization processes. One need only cite influential works by Lutz (1984) and Habermas (1981) as examples of this. Lutz draws a picture of the social and economic history of the dynamic development of industrial societies of the West in the twentieth century, in which he makes use of a central thought from Rosa Luxemburg's theory of imperialism (1913): that capitalism, by no means only in its early phase, but as a whole, bears the imprint of a logic of 'territorial advance', that is to say, continual expansion into a non-capitalist environment. If a sufficiently comprehensive view is taken, two subprocesses can be distinguished in this 'territorial advance': 'external colonization', that is to say the drive towards dependent modernization of important parts of the Third World and of regions of the world not yet penetrated by capitalism; this is then continued in an 'internal colonization' or 'colonization of the lifeworld' (Habermas). In Lutz's economic and sociological analysis this corresponds to the gradual undermining and decimation of what he himself describes as the 'traditional sector' within the capitalist economies. He says that this sector is characterized by the fact that 'in it, the separation of work and family life, business and home, is at least partially complete' (1984:125) and that important elements of a 'strongly intensive household production' (p. 128) and of the mode of subsistence dependent on it can still be encountered. He explains the phase of growth and sustained prosperity in the West German economy after the Second World War as a last 'territorial advance': it applies particularly to the 'traditional sector' as a whole, that is to say both to the (mainly female) workers bound up with it, who are taken up into the employment market, and – closely connected with this (p. 213) – the goods and services produced in the traditional sector, which are now substituted by industrial and professional products; both the workers and the products of the traditional sector have been 'sucked up by the industrial market sector' (p. 217).

This description of the trend connected with this last 'territorial advance', which we adopt here without going more deeply at present into the experiences of alienation and hypotheses of conflict to which Habermas gives prominence, leads to the conclusion of the 'inevitable ending of postwar prosperity in Europe' – precisely because the territorial advance now completed was the last conceivable one and there are no more areas into which expansion and penetration can take place. We should like to supplement this chain of reasoning, which rests particularly on the gaps that have appeared in full employment since the mid-1970s and the forecasts that they will persist at least in the medium term, with a second argument: the social and economic problems of the underemployment of the working potential of society cannot be overcome by reliance on a *spontaneous* revitalization of the 'traditional sector', precisely because, to continue the metaphor, the territory 'occupied' during the process of modernization under market economy industrialism during the postwar boom has become so structurally changed and disorganized that this line of retreat would appear to be cut off.

Elsewhere we have characterized this situation as the 'modernization trap' (Offe and Heinze 1986:473ff.) which is intended to emphasize both aspects: on the one hand the traditional development patterns of industrial capitalism have reached an impasse, and on the other hand in their course and as their result they have at least to a large extent blocked the exits that might have been available in the form of 'traditional' modes of economic life and subsistence as emergency aids and escape options in earlier phases of development. The consequence is that endeavours to dispatch those sections of the population that are affected by the crisis symptoms of the labour market and the welfare state to look for ways out of their difficulties in family, neighbourhood, community and relationship circles, and to conjure up the charms and effectiveness of precapitalist ways of life with the conservative-romanticizing outlook of many protagonists of 'new subsidiarity' are likely to prove fruitless and misleading (cf. Berger and Neuhaus 1977).

Such an attempt would be hopeless and misleading above all because the 'objective' socioeconomic changes that the process of modernization in industrial society has brought with it are paralleled by 'subjective' attitudes, expectations and criteria of what constitutes a 'normal' and 'appropriate' lifestyle. Consequently, 'territorial advance' has its precise mirror image on the *demand* side. This is manifested in (a) what we described earlier as the individualistic privatization of the mode of living and consumption. This mode of living looks to the market as the dominant economic supply system and often meets all arrangements for the 'common' use of articles of everyday use or the exchange of articles of consumption between households with the suspicion that these can be at most second-best emergency and substitute solutions, because they entail limitations on individual freedom and infringements of a sheltered sphere of privacy and intimacy within the household. Then (b) there is a strong preference rooted in the consumer culture, and it has probably been particularly marked within the Federal Republic of Germany, for high standards of quality, for 'high-class work', for the 'genuine' products of 'specialists' and 'specialist firms', of craftsmen and professionals, in comparison with which all supply systems operating at a lower level of quality are not regarded as acceptable second-best options but as quite unacceptable 'junk', 'trash' and 'botched work'.

Of course, we should not overlook contrary trends and destabilizing factors liable to lessen the importance of the privatistic, quality conscious and market oriented concept of well-being. These are: (a) new forms of *poverty*, which are making it impossible for growing sections of the population to participate in the 'quality intensive' markets as purchasers – they have to content themselves with mediocre or low quality levels; then (b) cultural patterns of a *'new moderation'*, unpretentiousness and self-limitation on the part of some of the new middle classes in the towns lead to similarly deviant, often 'ecologically' motivated patterns of consumption and lifestyles ('changed values'); but probably the most important is the fact (c) that skilled services exhibit the tendency, often noted, to introduce excessive *price rises* and hence, as can best be demonstrated in the proverbially 'cost explosive' area of health and nursing care or in repairs by craftsmen, take on a literally exclusive character, because they can no longer be financed nationwide and 'for all' via the market, insurance systems or taxation.

Opposed economic and cultural trends like these give rise to a strong economic motive for using (and hence for providing) 'subprofessional' and 'informal' arrangements for economic supply. Naturally the professional and commercial suppliers do their best to inhibit as far as they can this competition from products produced under self-help conditions by making use of government legislation and administrative regulations.

The economic and cultural modernization of modes of consumption and habits affecting both the demand and the supply side causes lacunae in supply and qualitative suboptimalities in the functioning of the system. Three aspects of these relative and partial defects of supply should be distinguished; they are (1) a growth in self-service requirements, (2) a growing exclusivity in commercial supplies, and (3) a decrease in self-help capability.

1 *Requirements for 'self-service' and the burden of 'coping' in private households*   A new trend of rationalization has now become well established in the production and distribution of goods and services in the formal economy. Comparatively undemanding ancil-

lary operations needed to ready the articles for use are increasingly being sidelined from the formal economy and – on the pattern of 'self-service' (cf. Gershuny 1978) – handed over willy-nilly to the purchasers or customers. The automobile is perhaps the first and most important piece of technical equipment in the modern material culture that is wholly adapted to supplementary 'self-service'. The same pattern is being followed by cases of self-medication in pharmaceuticals, individual study from radio and television programmes of the 'college of the air' type and by self-service in the retail trade. Many technical aids now in widespread use in private households incorporate the concept of self-service and are designed in such a way that users can employ their own relatively modest capabilities and skills in putting the finishing touches that convert the 'pre-products' they have bought into ready-for-use products.

In addition to these price incentives for user households to perform these self-service functions, there is a trend particularly in public services to *compel* users to perform certain operations themselves: for example, by the curtailment or total elimination of services they are made to stamp rail or bus tickets themselves, to collect parcels from the post office, to obtain the information needed to make applications, and so on. Indeed it would seem that the amount of additional self-service chores passed on to private households by way of administrative and commercial rationalization measures has become so large that they clearly result in *social selectivities of the level of supply*. The coincidence of self-service demands with unevenly distributed self-service capacities inevitably leads to gaps in supply. The best-known example of this is to be found in the personal social services. Scharpf (1985:18), for example, finds a developing 'extreme shortage of supply of personal nursing and care services for young, sick and old people that cannot be overcome by equipment or supplied efficiently on a mass basis'. Another category of 'underprivileged persons' is, for example, those in an 'automobile oriented' city, where public transport is sparse and infrequent, who have only limited access, or none, to the use of an automobile.

One might also say in a transferred (but by no means only metaphorical) sense that individuals, with any needed support from their private partnership, friendship and above all family relationships, are compelled to deal with a whole host of contingencies of life by 'self-help', to cope with their residuary burdens and to procure the necessary remedies from their own resources. It is central to current thinking about the sociology of the family that the family is conceived as the all-purpose source of help of last resort, where 'problems and crises for which no specialized and professionalized system of security . . . feels itself to be responsible, finally . . . land

and emerge as an appeal for or an obligation to help that cannot be turned aside' (R. G. Heinze et al. 1988:118).

This 'privatization of problem solving by passing it on to the family' (ibid.:120), making it the first repository for stress factors such as problems and needs of family members arising from the school, the labour market, the job, provisioning, mental and physical health, social deviance, nursing, assistance, regeneration and advice, is exactly analogous to the self-service tasks which, as mentioned above, are unloaded on to private households in the context of the modernization and rationalization processes in society. And just as in the other sphere, so in this one families exhibit differing degrees of ability to cope with problems depending on their structure and the material sociocultural 'basic equipment' of the individuals, households and families concerned.

2 *Exclusivity of commmercial and professional supplies*   And yet in nearly every case in which 'normal supply' has been converted to self-service intensive procedures, the traditional methods of supply which make the fewest possible demands on the end-user have remained in existence. This is symbolized at filling stations in the USA, where there are two rows of pumps to choose between, one marked 'service' and the other 'self-service', giving customers the choice of being served at a higher price or serving themselves and saving the difference. Here, as with many other personal, social and professional services, visible provision is made for a 'complete' service for more demanding customers who are able to pay for it.

3 *Declining self-help capability*   The processes of modernization and urbanization in society unquestionably result in a lack of such arrangements for satisfying demand, with the consequence that potential gains in welfare remain unachieved. For these processes both lead to a lessening of the capacity of private households to help themselves and also destroy the conditions whereby a compensatory network of service relationships between households might have been developed. The survey by Jessen et al. (1988) clearly reveals the extent to which the capacity for moneyless self-supply through the formation of non-market networks stands and falls with the confluence of very specific preconditions of social structure and social space. Typical preconditions for the emergence of such networks are: house and land ownership, to promote demand for such services while also providing an ambience in which the relevant skills can be developed; stable relationships with relatives, friends, neighbours and colleagues at work, not interrupted by mobility and anonymity; and finally the participants must be strongly integrated into the labour market, since

this provides the informal network both with human capital and with capital goods that can be used on loan. It is therefore not surprising that it is the milieu of specialist workers in rural communities, with a clearly defined social structure, that proves to be specially fruitful ground for the development of a network of self-supply activities. This finding is also illuminating in that conversely it indicates the extent to which in (nearly) all other kinds of social structure there is an *under*supply of opportunities, incentives and resources for households to form a network of help and cooperation.

To sum up, these considerations lead us to the following conclusion about defects that exist in the level of provision and the uniformity of the supply of goods and services constitutive of welfare to private households in modern social structures. Households and their members have the task of dealing with 'self-service impositions' and 'coping' passed on to them as a side-effect of technical, professional, bureaucratic and business rationalization strategies; besides being structurally weakened in their (markedly unevenly distributed) capacity for self-help and informal ability to cope, they have to pay a higher monetary price wherever this weakness makes them manifestly unable to deal with problems of self-help, and this gives rise to distinctly regressive distribution effects.

3

Value Problems and the 'Cooperation Circle'

The problem of criteria

Among the tasks of this study is to see what approaches have been made at other times and in various places to the problem of converting 'time' available to individuals (understood as an abstract measure of the totality of beneficial activities they are in a position to perform) into values of well-being, that is specific benefits, without the prior need to convert this time into money income as paid working time or as independent economic activity. The study further addresses the 'constructive' problem of how, with the benefit of experience gained at other times and in various places, solutions to the problems can be thought up and tested that would enable useful services to be produced without the intermediary of money, even in the conditions of a 'modern' social structure such as that existing in the Federal Republic of Germany. This does not imply an attempt to sketch out a wholly 'different' economic order or economic constitution; that would be beside the point, both in theory and practice. What we are looking for are limited supplementary, compensating mechanisms well within the bounds of the scope for political reform available both in government policy and in other problem areas.

If we ask what are the normative criteria for the various arrangements made in society for balancing supply with demand, we encounter three requirements that these arrangements must satisfy. These requirements are reciprocity, freedom and equality. Each of these criteria of value stands as such in a close affinity with *one* of the three well-known principles of management – which can be summed up as community, the market and the state – though generally at the cost of violating or at least understressing the other two criteria. Elsewhere (cf. Offe and Heinze 1986:485ff.) we have summarized these interrelationships in the following way.

Wherever and whenever they are in operation, *community* (joint) arrangements for the production of well-being maximize the criterion of *reciprocity*, or mutual obligations, but have little effect on the values of freedom and equality. In this context, at least at the level of the interpretation of interactions and the expectations that accompany them, reciprocity means the absence of relationships of exploitation or domination. 'Community' social entities typically function without formalized rights and duties and without monetarized relations of equivalence between their members. Instead, by virtue of shared standards, symbols and identities, they foster the belief that every contribution made by a member to the welfare of the community will be repaid sooner or later by contributions from others, without the need for a formal settlement either in money or by rote and rule. In any event the members place such a high value on belonging to the community that any net losses in the internal ratio of performance and counterperformance are considered insignificant in comparison with loss of the association itself.

One important structural characteristic of such associations is that they are not formed for a limited period. It is assumed that the interactive relationship and hence the opportunities for balancing out will continue to exist for an indefinite period, so that it is not open to any member to accept the services of others while reserving his own until a final date that can be calculated, and thus exploit the community. The moral obligation to do things for the community does not even need to be buttressed by the expectation that those who do the good deeds will themselves reap the rewards. They may have in mind others (for example grandchildren) as beneficiaries of the moral claim to 'counterbenefits' that are due on account of what they have done and sacrificed; Boulding (1981:31f.) has termed this relationship 'serial reciprocity'. The mechanism of bringing together by the expectation of continuity, of which the social arrangements of the nation and of marriage could be cited as examples, functions not only anticipatively but also retrospectively and hence is self-stabilizing. If a person in reliance on future reciprocal acts has 'saved up' a certain 'credit' in acts performed for the community, it becomes increasingly irrational to leave the community, since only within the community does the prospect of compensation for what the person has already done exist.

Of course this does not mean that non-reciprocity does not in practice occur within a nation, a marriage or other association, and that all contributions are finally repaid. All it means is that such communities only endure for as long as the subjective confidence of their members in the long-term reciprocity of performance and consideration continues. This confidence enables guarantees of equivalence to be waived and allows the contributions of the parties to appear as a formally unconditional 'present', 'sacrifice' or 'inheritance', the performance of which only binds the recipients more closely together in bonds of obligation. As long as this trust exists, it would be quite out of character to insist (as is done in markets) on an equivalence between performance and consideration with a time limit, or to embody the rights and duties of membership in formal rules. It is often assumed in political philosophy (Rousseau) and in more recent sociologically orientated treatises on systems theory that such arrangements for balancing supply and demand are encountered only in small social entities, or at least in relatively simple ones; but in fact it appears that historically they have been successfully utilized as well by large social movements (such as the workers' movement), assurance systems in social policy (the 'compact between the generations') and especially by nations at war ('death for the fatherland').

Thus while communities both depend on and generate the expectation of reciprocity, they are quite unsuited to embodying the values of freedom, equality and universalism. Community arrangements conflict with values of freedom because by their standards the 'exit' option is invalidated and moreover makes less economic sense the longer they endure. And communities cannot be universalistic and egalitarian precisely because their inner reciprocity is generally based on standards deriving from the exclusive ethos of their membership and their 'special' collective identity which marks them off from the surrounding world.

Market arrangements for balancing supply and demand exhibit similar functional strengths and weaknesses. A characteristic of market relationships is their reference to a point in time. They are governed by a universal presumption of discontinuity with reference to the future. Every seller must bear in mind that the customer may buy elsewhere next time, and only if he constantly gears himself to this eventuality will he gain a 'steady' customer. The same applies with reference to the past. No shared identity or common life history is needed in order to enter into a commercial relationship. Because of this singular abstraction from past and future the market can claim to be the only medium which (in the form of the world market) can set up global relationships between actors on a long-term basis. This abstraction also extends to standards of domination or cooperation. One party to a transaction can ignore the feeling of the other party that he or she has been exploited or overreached at least for so long as the conditions of the unequal exchange, and hence the compulsion on the dominated party to conform, continue. Either party may terminate the arrangement – *if* he or she can find more favourable terms elsewhere. This undisguisedly 'unbrotherly' functioning of market relationships, with few prior imposed standards, provides a maximum of formal *freedom*, but at the same time exhibits the often described seamy side, in that it leads to the erosion of harmonious relationships and has a desocializing effect. In the same way the inherent operating mode of markets offends against universalist and egalitarian criteria of value. At best markets provide equal opportunities, but not equality of outcome or even the same share for all in a minimum standard of enjoyment of welfare values. Moreover the strict time-relatedness of market interactions and their exclusive reference to the money medium ensure that a large number of unequally distributed non-monetarizable social costs and disregarded claims on the future are created.

The advantage of *state* provision for coordinating supply with demand lies in its capacity for generalization, that is, in its ability to lay down similar living conditions and frameworks of action for the generality of citizens and in a variety of material respects, and to stabilize them over time. The modern welfare state was not the first to have as its distinguishing characteristic nationwide regulatory functions of this kind and highly specific universalizations. These were pioneered by the constitutional state of the nineteenth century, which at least claimed to create a cumulatively increasing amount of accountability, predictability and (both social and military) security. Traditionally the incompatibility of this universalizing, standardizing and provident activity of the state with demands from freedom has been seen to be that the state, by intervening in the market with the proceeds from taxes and other dues, reduces both the volume of resources available for investment in the market and also the freedom of the economic actors to dispose of them. More recently criticism has been directed specifically at the loss of freedom in developed welfare states – the increasing monitoring and supervision, the institutional incapacitation and the decisions arbitrarily taken by others affecting clients of the welfare state. On the other hand, the conflict of values between the universalism of the welfare state and community reciprocity is less frequently in evidence. Some say that comprehensive state provision and regulation by law tend to level out those special characteristics and collective identities that previously served as a basis for community forms of welfare creation. There is also apprehension that the development of systems of provision and participation by the welfare state may deprive the small networks of solidarity at the level of the family, relatives, neighbours, the local community, etc., of their opportunities for action and self-affirmation by creating a climate in which everybody can rely on the fact that everyone else's needs for provision and help will somehow be met through appropriate entitlements to care and administrative services provided by the state.

The upshot of this brief outline of the three traditional guiding principles of regulatory policy (the community, the market and the state) is that each of them is specialized on a particular criterion of value (reciprocity, freedom or equality) but that because of the way they operate they tend to infringe – seriously in some cases – the other two values in which they do not specialize. In practical terms this means first, that whoever recommends 'more market' (or more community or more state) is in effect proposing one step forward and two steps back at the same time; but this course would be rational only if (contrary to the premises introduced above) it could be demonstrated that the equivalence of the three values was debatable and so it was acceptable to sacrifice the two values that were being submerged. Secondly, it means that if we do not wish to take such a course we shall have to seek a solution to problems of regulatory policy along the lines of a complex interlocking and an association between these three 'primary' regulatory principles, rather than maximizing one of them at the expense of the other two.

We should like to broach a solution to our problem of criteria by this second route, that of interlocking the three guiding principles. As we have explained at length, under the social and economic structural conditions existing in the Federal Republic of Germany and in other comparable countries, the possibilities of using time 'productively' while bypassing the money medium are severely restricted if not entirely absent. On the one hand these limitations – from the viewpoint of the productivity of the overall economy – lead to the economically irrational or at least suboptimal wastage of factors of social well-being and hence to a lower standard of provision than that which is theoretically possible. On the other hand, seen from the standpoint of distributive justice, with which we are just as much concerned, they lead to another outcome, well substantiated by research, that is unacceptable from the standpoint of political morality. This is that people in precisely those sections of the population, socioeconomic categories and stations of life where they have (a) unused time resources that could be used and (b) owing to their general standard of living most urgently need to convert this available time into 'use values' are least able to do so. For this reason a workable institutional system of non-monetary communal use of time might open up the prospect of a more equitable structure of the distribution of opportunities in life to at least the same extent as the proposals for *monetary* redistribution of income and assets under discussion in political and academic circles might be expected to produce.

From a 'social engineering' viewpoint one might compare the principles we hope to develop here with the problems now facing power engineering, which is similarly challenged to bypass (physical) conversion processes in order to avoid energy losses. Such a comparison may highlight the structural problem involved. We are looking for social 'technologies', that is to say for socioeconomic institutions that will exploit activity potentials at present lying unused, by eliminating conversion stages and introducing new methods of utilizing available resources, thus bringing about an improvement in the quality and levels of provision – and this *outside* the money nexus of taxation or the market and also *above* the level of the restricted exchanges between households and/or families.

The function of the money medium and the markets which it makes possible is to bring together people, their economic activity and its results in long chains of effect, constantly renewing a complex network of (material, time and social) relationships between them, in other words to 'socialize' individuals economically in this way. Units of time and the activities corresponding thereto that are not channelled via the market and valued in money clearly do not exhibit a 'socialization potential' comparable with the money medium. The use I make of my money affects almost every element in a global economic society, at least in the aggregate effect of the demand and price signals which it triggers; but the way I spend my (unpaid) *time*, in the limiting case of the enjoyment of leisure purely as a consumer, affects only myself and also, in the opposite limiting case of large charitable organizations to which I 'devote' my time, only the many specific opposite numbers with whom I may come into contact while performing this work. Based on this difference, a 'global' effect might be ascribed to money, contrasted with a 'local' effect for the above activities.

Clearly, in order to solve the aforementioned problem of social policy (under its dual aspects of production and distribution) it is necessary to 'invent' institutions that will permit a certain socialization of the time medium. Time would have to be treated *like* money, yet without being *traded for* money. To put it in a paradox, the 'local' effect of time would have to be mobilized over a large area and, so to say, nationwide.

The solution to this problem, which has been repeatedly advanced ever since early in the nineteenth century in many different variants and tried out in many a practical endeavour, often utopian and sometimes positively naive, consists in the introduction of a time currency or an 'hourly fee' that would be exchangeable only for services measured by the time expended on them, thus putting time into circulation. In this way it should be possible to transfer services, not indeed at their money value as determined by the market, nevertheless *in the same way as* in markets, between persons 'unknown' to one another, between different types of goods and between different points in time.

Proposals and concepts of this kind have both an egalitarian and a libertarian thrust. They contain the thought of equality in two variants: on the one hand they seek to institutionalize the equality between workers and types of work; differences of talent and skill are intended to make no more difference than variations in the intensity of demand for different types of goods. 'An hour is always worth as much as an hour.' On the other hand this would enable workers for the first time to organize their lives in a different way from that of paid labour, which implies subservience to the power of the purchaser of labour, thus weakening the power of the latter which would be, as it were, running in neutral. Ideas of this kind for overcoming class divisions in society, as espoused by Robert Owen, Johann Carl Rodbertus and others, clearly smacked of utopian socialism. At the same time there were clear references to the value of freedom; the situation of the poorer sections of society should not be determined by collective provision or the mechanical attribution of a standard handout that was the same for all: instead it should be provided in a market-imitating way, in that each participant in this alternative economic system should freely decide how much work he or she would do and of what kind, and on which consumer goods he or she wished to spend the time certificates received in return for the work.

The 'cooperation circle' pattern

What applies universally to projects of reform in economic and social policy and innovative proposals also applies to the system we shall now briefly delineate, and which we provisionally name the 'cooperation circle'. With good reason, today's proposals for reform no longer consist of 'grand designs' and grandiose visions such as proliferated during the eighteenth and nineteenth centuries. Instead they rely on the persuasive power of small steps that can win support from, or at least be tolerated by, those motivated by many different outlooks, that are not inimical to the *raison d'etre* of any important interest in society and that can be achieved by a relatively slow, gradual process of reform, in the course of which the object in view may if necessary be modified or the approach redirected.

The 'cooperation circle' model is a concept of reform in this modest sense, made up of the following components:

1 It is suitable for the exchange of services *between households*. It might embrace from a few dozen to perhaps 500 participating households; this would ensure both that it was definitely a 'local' arrangement, far below the regular distribution radius of ordinary markets, yet also capable of neutralizing to a large extent the diseconomies of small scale and the high per capita capital costs of modern households which were described in detail earlier. The effect would be that at least rudimentary skilling and specialization effects and growing economies of scale could be achieved, and these in turn could lead to time being saved on individual household activities and/or money being saved on market purchases of the needed goods.

2 Exchange would be based on the *principle of equivalence*, but would be mediated not by money but by a special currency of certificates or vouchers, not convertible into money. The equivalence principle makes possible transactions even between 'strangers', that is to say between persons who have no reason, whether of family, friendship or other bond, to give, ask or receive favours. Such equivalence is a necessary condition for achieving the structures and functions of scale enlargement.

3 The exchange-based transactions would take place *between* private *households*. This characteristic implies on the one hand that goods and services provided internally by households are excluded, removing any threat of interference with the sphere of privacy and intimacy. But what is more important is that, on the other hand, only households and not firms or other corporations could become members, so that the exchange system would be free from the strategic interests in earnings, profits, etc., proper to such entities.

4 The choice of the *'time basis'* for the currency has several implications of practical relevance and attraction as a standard. To begin with, it would largely inhibit price formation mechanisms and the profit motive encountered in the business world. Secondly, the purpose of choosing the hourly basis is to abate the material inequalities built up in the market economy to some extent by the fact that they enable those groups of persons who, although they have 'plenty' of uncommitted time but little money, can apply this abundant resource to transactions from which they will receive counterpart services that will enable them to save a part of the expenditure of their 'scarce' commodity of money. The advantages thus accruing to these groups should generate integration effects desirable in terms of social policy. For this reason the term 'reskilling' of time is used to describe this effect. Thirdly, to the smoothing effect on the social profile would be added a possible smoothing of the career profile; for by 'time banking' it would become possible to neutralize that vexing characteristic of time, that it 'runs away', meaning that it

cannot be saved up. In this way it would be possible to transfer time to the future – to originate a claim on the future work of others by investing one's own time now, a claim that could be 'cashed in' later when one's own time was at even more of a premium.

5   The currency and the exchange network are suited to and concentrate on the exchange of *services performed in the neighbourhood of the family, personal care, the household and its environment*. With this emphasis it can be expected that the necessary equipment and skills (being the material and human capital of the households) will already be to hand in a certain quantity and variety, with the result that the economic advantages of exchange circle relationships, if they can be achieved, would be immediately recognizable and spontaneously used by the members. On the other hand this emphasis does imply the limitation that speculative, 'responsible' and professional services would be largely excluded from the exchange, though this would also to some extent prevent conflicts from arising with market suppliers of such services, and their associations. Limiting the range of services has the further advantage that specialist services for a special clientele (such as social casework or welfare) would not be exchanged (if they were, it would inevitably result in mismatches between supply and demand), but rather a broad, flexibly adjustable range of 'everyman's services' for 'everyman's needs'.

6   'Cooperation circles' organized in this way are adapted to the *conditions of the social structure and the social culture* typically to be found in urban residential areas of mixed social composition. By this we mean conditions with a certain anonymity and mobility, but also with widespread and common problems of household, time and consumption management. Since membership of a cooperation circle and each individual transaction within it would be based on a voluntary 'purchasing decision', these are morally undemanding interaction relationships, which under such conditions seem appropriate precisely because in the strongly individualized conditions prevailing in modern life and society strong links of association and obligation can scarely be taken for granted. Because of this the conditions of membership and participation are deliberately made low key, and this should have a beneficial effect on membership and 'turnover'.

7   For reasons that become clear in the analysis of case examples and practical experiments in part II, exchange circles and networks of this kind cannot be expected to form and maintain themselves spontaneously, particularly in places and among population groups where a considerable increase in welfare and equality might be expected from such moneyless 'parallel markets' at neighbourhood level. They are obviously public goods (as are city fire brigades or other service organizations) which nobody expects to be formed on

the basis of private initiative and dedication, unregulated by the authorities; on the contrary it is only the state or municipality that sets up and regulates such bodies. The conclusion is that cooperation circles can come into being only as *the result of supportive, pro-motional initiatives by provincial or municipal authorities or other sponsors.*

A possible objection against this way of proceeding by experiment and construction runs that it should not be made the business of the state, muncipalities or scientists to 'invent' social arrangements for welfare and the supply of necessaries, but that it should be left to the spontaneous ability of individuals and social groups or associations to come up with solutions to specific situations of demand and need by using the moral and material resources available to them at the time, converting and adapting their consumption, production and living praxis as best fits their purposes. Such a viewpoint, with its conserva-tive or libertarian overtones, overlooks an important consideration: it was precisely in the course of those market economy and statist-professional processes of modernization that gave rise to the problems we are now confronting that there was also a partial loss of the sociocultural abilities and dispositions that are the sociological pre-requisite for the spontaneous discovery and utilization of patterns of joint self-help and ownwork, and hence for the emergence of informal networks. In so far as this diagnosis is relevant to structurally and socioculturally rooted lacunae in self-help, themselves the results of processes of individualization, bureaucratization and modernization, there is clearly little point in holding up traditional social virtues, such as the ethos of voluntary service, of good neighbourliness or of universal benevolence as examples for emulation, and in advocating political abstention and non-intervention into the bargain.

PART II

Local Moneyless Exchange Systems in Historical and International Perspectives

4

'Useful Activities': An Overview

In this chapter we shall first try to give a systematic enumeration of the many different kinds of 'useful activities' that are performed in modern societies outside gainful employment organized in businesses. We shall note any specific limits imposed on the extent of these activities and any current endeavours to remove such limits or to extend the boundaries of action.

1 *Home work within the family unit* In this area there is an ill-defined boundary between 'purposeful activity' and 'relationship' or 'caring' work, at least as we perceive it when we do this work. Not working towards a goal envisaged and deliberately pursued, but performing a multitude of tasks based on sympathy, love and caring is the characteristic of these activities – and the special burden they impose. In sociological theory (Parsons 1954) the family is distinguished from all *formally* organized transaction systems by the fact that specific activities within families are described as 'functionally diffuse' in contradistinction to the 'functionally specific' way of acting found in businesses, associations, administrations, etc. This distinction has the advantage of revealing a 'rule of the distribution of the burden of proof': in families (and other communities) the rule is that the *addressee* of actions, requests and incitements to interaction of all kinds must provide justification if the demand in question is not met, whereas in all other circumstances the *agent* is responsible for addressing requests for interaction 'correctly'. (For example, if I go into a restaurant intending to buy stamps, it is *I* who have mistaken the door; but if Johnny's parents will not give him the bicycle he so much wants, they must convince him it is because they fear for his safety in the heavy neighbourhood traffic).

Thus family work is functionally diffuse in the sense that the services performed are of such a nature that they are accepted by the family members as diffuse duties which for material and/or moral reasons cannot be substituted by outside services. This 'total responsibility' constitutes, from the standpoint of business organization (mentioned here but not really pertinent), a first structural disadvantage of family work, because the advantages of specialization based on acquired status (as opposed to generation or sex status) remain unused.

A second disadvantage lies in the extremely small radius of distribution characteristic of family households. Only members of households are potential recipients of services, and some of these are simultaneously performing services. To a limited extent such services and help can also be based on relationships of the neighbourhood, friendship, relationship or collegiality type, but with the difference that in the context of such relationships services and help are requested and supplied for individual cases and ar not (or at least not without an agreed equivalent requital) available as routine duties of those performing the services.

2 *Do-it-yourself services* Like family work, DIY is also confined to households but here 'purpose use' predominates over 'process use', whereas in family work both categories of use merge into one another without distinction. The object of DIY activity is to do inhouse something which is fully available out of house, thus not only saving expense but also achieving recognition for the type and quality of the work done. The inherent limitations of this kind of activity lie in the discrepancy between the equipment, space and skills deployed and the desired level of quality in the finished articles, (for instance, in making and repairing articles). Manufacturers and dealers have tried to exploit a market for 'home work' that is constantly expanding, by offering for sale products designed to mitigate this discrepancy, claiming that in this way home workers will be enabled to achieve usable and satisfying results with 'simple tools' and 'without special training'. Yet it is questionable whether DIY offers real savings over outside purchase, either of finished goods or craftsmen's services, when all the costs of the working time spent, and the usually vastly underused equipment, not to mention the risks of accident and botched work, are taken into account; if it does not, then the loss must be subjectively compensated for by 'intangibles' such as prestige, process utility, the value of leisure and pride of workmanship. There is a further limitation in that DIY activities are associated with certain modes of life, sex role definitions, income and age groups (see above) and hence are by no means potentially an 'across the board' form of activity.

3 *Hobbies* Although similar to DIY, hobbies give much more prominence to process utility, which is experienced in the very act of doing the work. The value of the result is either identical with that of the process (as with the principle of amateur sport that 'taking part is what counts') or else is not judged by direct comparison with the work of professionals (examples are arts and crafts, music in the home, etc.).

4 *Associations and self-help groups* These are similar to hobbies, except that the process utility is created and enjoyed in a group, that is to say with a much enlarged radius of social distribution, in any event going beyond the household. They also make more efficient use of such goods as expensive sports equipment and installations, and services such as instruction by means of lectures accompanied by transparencies, etc. This enhancement of the collective character of the activity and its appeal to shared values as compared with the hobby of an individual corresponds to the greater formalization of the interaction in such matters as the law of associations, the rights and duties of members, offices within the association, etc.

Self-help groups exhibit similar social structures to associations, principally because they concentrate on the interests and needs of their members, though they are generally less formalized and have a different field of activity, centred on psychosocial and health assistance and advice for members of the group. They appear to originate in quite specific sociocultural conditions: 'All the empirical studies on the subject point out that the potential benefits peculiar to self-help groups can only be appropriated by sections of the population that possess certain social capabilities. Participants must be able to initiate or sustain intensive group processes' (R. G. Heinze et al. 1988:132). The praxis of self-help groups is often based on a self-understanding that is critical of the professions and in this sense emancipative. It could be summed up, rather on the lines of Alcoholics Anonymous, as the view that 'we' can help one another better, with less discrimination and more cheaply than members of the caring professions and the authorities who organize those services are able to do. Certainly one internal limitation on the self-help movement has to be that its members might pursue this theory beyond reasonable limits, with the result that (a) professional help and services are refused even when they could and should be used, and/or (b) the pronounced social selectivity of self-help activities and their social catchment area militate against the implementation of criteria of equity such as that of community-wide care and the universal availability of the basic rights of a welfare state. In other words, within limits, self-help networks benefit those who 'go along' with them, but in practice they are not open to everybody and moreover (on account of their mainly inward-looking concern) are in no position to exert a favourable influence on the situation, chances in life and care of non-members, because this could only be done by political and administrative activity.

5   *Activities based on duties formally laid down*   By means of laws, regulations and compulsory by-laws households can be made to perform unpaid services in favour of non-members of the household or of the general public, even where there are no links of association between those concerned as there are in an association (an example might be local by-laws enjoining snow clearance or the sorting of household waste). Similar contractual obligations or formal agreements may also exist between owners with condominium arrangements; in such cases their duties extend not only to pro rata payments for the purchase and maintenance of jointly owned property (for example a sailing boat) but also to contributions in the form of the obligation to perform specific tasks (for instance, the duty of cleaning the staircase used in common).

There is also a 'tributary duty' in the form of contributions in kind for 'public goods' in compulsory military service, in liability for jury service and in legal obligations to go to the assistance of others in such circumstances as traffic accidents. These have their counterparts in historical social or labour services including industrial conscription and/or forced labour for convicts and on occasions for recipients of social assistance, some of which will be referred to later on in the discussion.

One inherent limitation on the effectiveness of formal obligations of this kind may be that – at least in large and anonymous social contexts – the quality of the services suffers from the way in which they are performed: when work is done only under compulsion there is an inclination, or at least a temptation, to skimp it, and the costs of recruitment, training, monitoring and inspection for quality control of the output are correspondingly high. This explains why such activities are carried on mostly in 'total institutions' such as prisons and military units, and even there are often confined to proverbially simple, undemanding and easily monitored tasks. In the civil sphere, such as a compulsory year of socially beneficial work for young women, the counterpart to military service for men, they have little to recommend them: 'Since the groups of persons liable for compulsory social service the performance of which they were bound to regard as time "wasted" which prevented them from pursuing other objectives which as individuals they rated more highly, problems with motivation and hence also quality were only to be expected' (R. G. Heinze et al. 1988:177). In normal circumstances it would seem that only the presence of local monitoring (for instance, by neighbours, as is the case with activities laid down in house rules) or the support of strongly ingrained standards and values of bourgeois life (ecological awareness or a moral obligation to help in emergencies) ensure that duties laid down will be fulfilled to an acceptable level of quality and reliability.[1]

6 *Honorary positions* Choirs give public concerts, the voluntary fire brigade makes its services available in the case of fire or other emergency, the members of local associations of welfare agencies or parishes perform social services voluntarily – and all this without any motivating cause based on legal obligations and/or material incentives and rewards. It would seem that this case, of special interest for our purposes, and which has attracted some attention in discussions about social and political reforms (cf. among others Fink 1986; Sachsse 1986; Hegner 1986b; as an overview R. G. Heinze et al. 1988:133ff.), generally exhibits one or more of the following characteristics:

1 The individuals or associations offering voluntary services of this kind belong to a clearly defined and demarcated social milieu or a community that makes a practice of taking on voluntary work and which affords social prominence to those who assume these duties; depending on the strength and the degree of formalization of such obligations and the intensity with which they are scrutin-ized they can be regarded as transitional forms between 'honorary positions' and statutory obligations to perform a given activity (for example, jury service).

2 Persons undertaking voluntary work benefit from 'selective incen-tives' and advantages; these might range from financially attractive 'expense reimbursement' to the expected furtherance of career plans, business and ideological interests through suitable contacts and communications, or to improving or gaining the prospect of public aid by voluntary 'prepayments' in the service of the public.

3 In connection with these two views of the motivation structure of honorary work and association activity there could be a certain tendency to 'homologous client selection', that is to say preferen-tial 'servicing' of the group of a local, confessional, regional, age or other category, to which the persons doing the voluntary work themselves belong (sometimes going so far as to confine the 'service' to group members). Such cases represent a grey area between honorary and self-help activities.

All in all it is a characteristic of voluntary forms of activity that they are based on an amalgam of formal obligation, calculation of advantage and selfless commitment in favour of some or all of the members of a larger community.

With regard to voluntary activities a distinction should be made between those that have an organized connection with the activities of associations, societies, churches or public authorities and those that are carried on outside formal organizations of that kind as voluntary work by individuals and as assistance given to particular persons. This distinction is important because it can help to reveal opposing tendencies in the 'old honorary class' which is associated with large organizations and the 'new honorary class' of unorganized individual helpfulness. The latter is characterized as follows (with implicit recourse to sociological categories such as individualization and change of values): 'Unconditional devotion to the social task and renunciation of the satisfaction of a person's own needs and interests is nowadays being replaced by a freely chosen commitment that can be adapted to the worker's strength and potential contribution and is not qualitatively beyond them' (R. G. Heinze et al. 1988:138).

There has been a shift in motivation. The old type of such organizations (for example, charitable bodies) are finding it increasingly difficult to find replacements from the younger generation for their present supporters, many of whom are ceasing voluntary work because of age; at the same time there is a growing potential of readiness for the 'new honorary activity', but this does not feel at home in the existing organizations and hence does not encounter 'demand', that is, the opportunity of expressing its benevolent impulses, and in consequence often remains untapped. This shift must be regarded as a constraint on voluntary activity.

7 *Paid occasional work below the tax threshold* This category covers services performed for money between private persons, but which are too low in value to be assessable for tax purposes. They do not give rise to an employer/employee relationship, being similar to an occasional transaction involving work. Examples of this are paid help with housework and caring services, paid help from neighbours, private lessons, etc.

8 *Ilicit work or illegal employment* These types of paid work come one step nearer to the formal economy. For the most part they do not just represent occasional or part-time work by those concerned, but give rise to an illegal working relationship. The attractions and disadvantages of such work, and hence the reasons why it is illegal, are well known. The workers involved, often recruited from among the unemployed and groups on the fringes of

the labour market, forego their protection and other security rights and dodge the contributions and tax they would otherwise have to pay. The illegal employers (who feature only where illegal *employment* is involved) are able to operate more exploitatively and gain unfair competitive advantages, besides saving money on social security contributions and tax. The downside for them is that they are likely to be employing relatively unskilled and possibly unreliable workers, and purchasers of their products have to set against the lower price the fact that the goods carry no guarantee and are often substandard. There is a wide consensus in the promotional, trade association and scientific literature that although such practices may bring short-term advantages to some, in the long run they result in serious disadvantages for the perpetrators, their clients and the industry generally and are therefore justifiably prohibited by law (cf. Burgdorff 1983).[2]

9 *Independent alternative businesses* These too occupy an intermediate position, in that externally they operate as a component of the formal economy but in their internal relations (for instance, between the owners of the business and the workforce) they establish a quasi-household type of relationship with little formality or clear functional demarcation. This implies a demanding reciprocal obligation to work conscientiously and to deal responsibly with the firm's assets and earnings, besides maintaining standards of social behaviour. The disadvantages of a somewhat informal structure with little emphasis on hierarchical relationships may sometimes be offset by the fact that members of such firms are content to work for low wages or that they are subject to an urge of 'self-development' (cf. Benseler et al. 1982; J. Berger et al. 1985; Kück 1986).

Dimensions and boundaries of the concept of work

All the types of useful activity briefly touched on above are situated in a grey area between the purely consumptive *use of time* (such as going for a walk or visiting a cinema) and *formal gainful employment*, in which work performed, or its practical results, are exchanged for a monetary earned income. For a long time the social sciences and other disciplines have encountered considerable problems of delimitation, not to mention actual boundary disputes, in this grey area (Anthony 1977) in which, as is natural, considerable social interests are at stake. This is so because only activities whose practitioners can successfully lay claim to be doing 'work', as a social and moral seal of quality, also enjoy the respect and recognition deriving from such activities (on the concept of work cf. among others Bahrdt 1983; Dahrendorf 1983; Offe 1984; Clausen 1988; Guggenberger 1988; Hegner 1988; Pahl 1988b; Gorz 1989).

The women's movement that has emerged since the late 1960s in new political and ideological formations gave a powerful impetus towards enlarging the meaning of the concept of work to embrace activities outside the sphere of paid employment, beginning with the demand for 'wages for housework' that was widespread for a time but then retreated into the background. Researches by social scientists into the time budgets of private households have also identified a greater number of activities which people feel have to be performed if, under the conditions of modernized living, household relationships with the markets for goods and services, the authorities and the professions are to be considered adequate and satisfactory, and if proper attitudes *vis-à-vis* political agents and the housewife's own personal environment, culture and plans for living are to be achieved; and these activities are tending to preempt an increased share of time. New and unaccustomed concepts such as 'relationship work', 'care work' and 'consumption work' emerged in the 1970s and helped to highlight the inadequacy of a merely twofold division of the areas of living into 'work equals paid employment' and 'leisure equals purposeless idleness' and to replace it by a triad of paid work, unpaid work and the use of leisure. It may be that the emergence of non-institutional forms of politics, social movements and citizen's initiatives and self-help groups has helped to awaken the realization that there is an area *between* 'work' and 'leisure' that has qualitative and quantitative significance, together with the realization that the single dose of socialization and education received during the first two decades of life is no longer capable of providing a sufficient 'store' of attitudes and competences for the entire course of life. Workers' skills need constant honing and updating through instruction and reskilling throughout their careers. Furthermore, government policies have increasingly come to target activities located in that no man's land such as illicit work, the informal economy, self-help and own-work. This is partly in order to combat their real or supposed deleterious effects, as in the case of illicit work and several kinds of criminality, but more often to look for ways of escape from the bottlenecks caused by crises in public finances and the functional weaknesses of bureaucratically organized state social services, seeking to open up possible lines of escape for 'superfluous' sections of the labour force in times of persistently high unemployment. Against the background of these very mixed motives, expectations and developments it is pleasing to note the emergence of what is already known in the USA as the 'third sector' of voluntary activities, which are not formalized and therefore (or so the optimistic expectation goes) likely to be unalienated and 'independent', making for a healthy situation in the culture of society, in government policy and in the social sciences, too (cf. among others Levitt 1973; Balbo and Nowotny 1986; Powell 1987; Ronge 1988; also Berger and Neuhaus 1977).

For all that, it would be a mistake to reinterpret the concept of work too widely or to overstate the potential for 'independence', 'disalienation' and solidarity of forms of activity intermediate between the market and the household. For in the first place, with all due credit to the many different kinds of utility creating activities outside the sphere of gainful employment, an activity can only be described as 'work' if it is directed towards an objective that is both *premeditated* and also *regarded as useful not only by the worker but also by others*, and accomplished with a reasonable degree of efficiency and technical productivity. By these criteria of efficient purposefulness and social validation of the objectives by others, a good proportion of activities conducted as 'hobbies' would fail to qualify as 'work', and would have to be classified as leisure occupations, in so far as either a historically achieved normal measure of productivity is not equalled (as for example with fishing for sport, usually a highly unproductive method of obtaining fish) or else the product is of a highly personal and idiosyncratic nature, that is, not a socially validated one (as in the case of many people who go in for watercolour painting and other artistic activities in their spare time). Similar considerations would exclude from the sphere of what can be usefully described as 'work' the activity of maintaining personal relations in everyday life and dealing with conflicts arising in them, 'hard work' though this can undoubtedly be, because in it the 'process' can scarcely be distinguished from the 'result'. Wherever the process utility of an activity satisfying to its practitioner clearly exceeds the potential use-value of the results of the activity to other people, it is hardly appropriate to employ the concept 'work', since that concept clearly presupposes both the 'social' – that is, socially validated – nature of the objectives and the susceptibility of the activity to criticism in respect of its efficiency and productivity. If these limiting definitions were applied to the activities described above under the headings household, DIY, associations and so on they might well exclude a considerable portion of them from the sphere of own 'work'.

Moreover some caveats are in order with respect to the oft-praised (cf. Gorz 1982) unalienated, independent and self-determined nature of the activities taking place in the indeterminate area between the market, the state and the household. These caveats relate to the price that has to be paid for these undoubtedly attractive social and moral benefits of unpaid employment from the overall viewpoint of government policy. This price consists both in the potentially serious infringements on formal liberty and on equality and evenhandedness. Formal freedom and the protection of the privacy of the individual are under threat wherever the above-mentioned kinds of informal work are elevated to the status of quasi-community obligations, under which the participants 'cannot defend themselves' against their mutual pretensions and which otherwise (for instance, on the presumption of market conditions) cannot arise. Even if, as in the case of self-help groups of the Alcoholics Anonymous type, privacy is protected to the greatest extent possible, it is not possible effectively to prevent, over the whole spectrum of voluntary, honorary and unpaid charitable work, the occurrence of infringements of personal privacy and serious intrusions of allegedly informal obligations on the area of private freedom. Just because informal modes of cooperation of this kind are neither public service administrations nor markets nor families, they have to rely on the mobilization of 'communal' forms of social control, which are at least potentially in conflict with the rule of private independence (and for this very reason are frequently avoided).

Another dark side to most kinds of non-formalized work that should be noted is that in most cases they generate a pattern of provision of social space that is markedly less equitable and has more gaps than appears desirable in the light of the welfare state principle of 'parity of living conditions'. Only in certain levels of society, subcultures, city districts, networks of relations, age groups and occupational groups – by no means in all of them – does it prove possible to establish informal systems of supply and to keep them viable over long periods, because the 'cultural capital' needed both for the establishment of such networks and for their use by individuals is very unevenly distributed.

Three conclusions emerge from this review of types of non-market work and the critical discussion of their efficiency and their implications for social policy; they are conclusions which appear to constitute determinative criteria for helpful political action in this area. First, such projects should be concentrated on and confined to the area that can be unequivocally classified as 'work', because it satisfies the criteria of 'use values for others' and 'adequate productivity'. It follows that government initiatives should not be directed so much towards the encouragement of leisure or help in the cultural and/or psychosocial aspects of living as towards remedying the deficiencies in provision that many private households are unable to overcome by themselves, either because they are too small or for other reasons, leaving gaps that either cannot be filled at all or, if they can, only by outside supply via the market or the state. The second requirement is to minimize the dependence, the obligation to give and receive services and hence the loss of formal personal freedom, that is often endemic in informal services and reduces their attractiveness, by bringing about a degree of formalization and institutional ballasting of informal work. Quasi-market arrangements would seem to be best adapted to this end, as they involve arms-length bargaining for the exchange of goods or services. Thirdly, an important criterion is that population groups and people in certain contexts of social space who, for the above reasons, are not in a position to make use of the special productivity of informal work through already existing networks, community and neighbourhood associations (cf. Pahl 1984) should be given access to such arrangements for informal self-supply.

5

Historical Excursus

The type of solution explored in this research report, the introduction of moneyless systems of exchange, is by no means an 'invention' of the 1980s. A backward glance at the history of the early socialist movements of the nineteenth and twentieth centuries reveals a wealth of original, unorthodox proposals in which this thought plays a central part. Some of these more or less fully worked out plans were given a practical trial, though there were also very many activities whose inception is not easy to trace back to a dogma-based source.

A good framework to use as a basis for examining the great variety of types of examples from the past is provided by asking what arrangements the various schemes made for organizing exchange operations. The answers to this question enable the proposals and projects to be arranged along a schematic continuum ranging from those in which exchange relationships are based on principles of social solidarity, and which have developed almost like natural growth,[1] to plans and schemes of utopian social reformers, technical high fliers or members of other elites for effecting a just distribution of goods by means of government allocation and military compulsion.[2] Those cases in which, although an organization and the institutionalization of moneyless exchange relationships was considered necessary, the voluntary principle was definitely to be preserved, fit into the broad middle ground between these two extremes.

The purpose of this section is to provide a series of snapshots affording an overview of this continuum and a description of the historical examples to be encountered in the middle ground, and of the thinking behind them. We begin by outlining the experiments with moneyless exchange systems that were initiated for highminded reasons of social reform in British and French socialist circles during the first half of the nineteenth century (1 and 2). Next come some of the proposals and projects born of the poverty of the 1930s in an

effort to combat unemployment, to improve the lot of the unemployed and/or to influence events in the economy by way of credit
policy through the establishment of small-scale exchange and payments communities using an 'alternative' currency (3 and 4). Third
and last comes a look at the history of the unemployed self-help
movement in the USA which for a short time underwent spectacular
development and which furnishes a rich field of historical experience
as to the effectiveness of exchange systems set up spontaneously in
a situation of great privation to combat its effects (5). An analysis of
the reasons for the enormous difficulties faced by such experiments,
and the failure of many of them, is also important both in discouraging premature optimism regarding the prospects for the type of
solution proposed here (see part IV) and also perhaps for avoiding a
repetition of mistakes made in the past.

(1) *Robert Owen* (1771–1858) is reputed to have inspired the early
consumer cooperative movement in Britain in the 1820s and 1830s.
Owen's adherents in these circles relied on the theory of work value,
only sketchily developed, that they had adopted and adapted from
the writings of Ricardo. In his 'Report to the County of Lanark' in
1820, Owen had written that the value of any goods could be
calculated only from the time needed for their manufacture, and
consequently the producers were entitled to the full revenue from
their work. As Owen saw it, the 'defect' in the capitalist economic
system was a problem of value, in that instead of the natural measure
of value, that of human work, an artificial, fictive measure, money,
was used as a basis for calculating all economic transactions, and this
gave rise to a problem of distribution consisting of the fact that
capitalists and other 'idlers' retain profits and withhold from the
workers as the real producers the full revenue from their work. To
solve this problem of value and distribution Owen proposed the
creation of a moneyless system of exchange and supply – a market
in which all products should be exchanged at their average labour
value, that is at their prime cost price.
    Ideas of this kind, propagated by Owen and other socialist theor-
eticians, provided the breeding ground for the foundation of consumer cooperatives from 1828 onwards in many places in Britain.
These cooperatives of artisans or labourers and their families
organized joint purchase of goods and uniform distribution to their
members in return for weekly contributions. Owen himself had
different plans in mind from those which, after his return from
America in 1829, he found being practised in the consumer cooperatives. In the model which he preferred (the 'equitable labour
exchange') the organizational structures of the consumer cooperatives

were bound up with the idea of a currency covered by goods.[3] The equitable labour exchange was a market on which workers exchanged their wares in their dual capacity as producers and consumers. Each worker received for his goods a recompense in the form of 'labour notes' representing the value of the raw material and the average working time needed to produce the goods, and with these notes he could purchase his requirements at any time from the warehouse of the exchange. The value of the goods was determined by assessors appointed for that purpose. A labour note for sixpence was the equivalent of an average hour's work. To cover running costs a brokerage fee of 8.33 per cent was levied on all the goods sent in. The labour notes in circulation were supposed to correspond exactly to the value of the stocks of goods.

The first equitable labour exchange was opened in September 1832 in London with financial and organizational support from Owen. Next year branches were opened in Birmingham, and probably also in Liverpool and Leeds, and there were plans for other localities. At that time there was no state monopoly of the issue of currency, so that there were no formal obstacles to the issue of labour notes. It appears from Owen's correspondence and from articles in the periodical *Crisis* published by him and his son that at first the London exchange was extremely successful and had a large turnover. However, no business documents of the exchange have survived, so that the information, as to which there is some conflict of detail, cannot be checked. The exchange was initially operated by shopholders and individual traders, and later on by artisans and their organizations. These active members did not, by any means, have only the far-reaching objectives of their theoretically experienced promoters in view; their concern was to make an immediate economic profit. Payments difficulties began to surface in the autumn of 1833, and efforts were made to overcome them by concentrating on purchasing in the ordinary market high quality raw materials for members' production of urgently needed goods. But the initial euphoria and the confidence in the viability of the system had evaporated, membership fell rapidly, and no more labour notes were issued after 31 May 1834. Owen had drawn his own conclusion after the first year's operation – that the labour exchange was 'a drop in a bucket' compared with the many more soundly based social experiments, and a trifling affair in view of the total potential of the workers' movement for social reform (quoted from Garnett 1972:141f.).

The defects in organization that dogged the translation of the original concept into practice – a too hasty start without sufficient preparation, financial resources or competent organizers, competition from speculators trying to exploit the exchange, and financial bottle-

necks through sudden demands for payment for which Owen had
not made provision – could in principle have been avoided; but there
were also two structural reasons largely responsible for the failure of
the experiment. First, it soon became difficult to balance supply with
demand as regards the *type* and *quality* of goods. Luxury articles
piled up in the warehouses, while the craftsmen's main object was
to obtain urgently needed foodstuffs in exchange for their goods.
Owen had not provided any market smoothing mechanism to counter
any disequilibrium in the market. Ever the optimist, he had assumed
that if a gap in supply appeared one simply hhad to call on producers
of the goods in demand and the problem would be solved.

In the second place, revaluation of the goods was difficult, complicated and by no means as just as Owen had thought it would be. A
price of sixpence an hour made it attractive for everybody who was
earning less on the open market to join the exchange, while it was
hard to attract those who were earning more. Also, workers who
had to produce their goods under less profitable conditions were hard
put to it to cover their costs at the average prices, and accordingly they
complained. Owen thought that contretemps of this kind were just
teething troubles and that the assessors were having difficulties they
would overcome before long, thus concealing the Achilles' heel of
his system, which was that the value of one piece of work would
never be exactly the same as another, unless the two were produced
under identical conditions. Karl Marx in his polemic against the early
socialists repeatedly placed his finger on this sore point. In 1847
(1969:84) he wrote: 'In exchanging these two quantities of working
time you are by no means exchanging the mutual situation of the
producers or altering the respective situations of workers and manufacturers in the slightest degree.' As long as the method of production
was left unchanged, moneyless exchange experiments only repro-
duced the prevailing market conditions. The early socialist theory of
labour value was nothing more than the 'scientific expression of the
economic conditions of contemporary society' (ibid.:98).

(2)   The French socialist *Pierre Joseph Proudhon* (1809–1865) investigated – as did many of his contemporaries in socialist circles – the
legal rules governing the economy, developing a rather imprecise
theory of labour value and fiercely attacking the propertied classes,
or more accurately their unearned privilege of deriving claims against
third parties from their titles of ownership. However, what distinguishes Proudhon from other socialist theoreticians, including Owen,
is that his practical proposals for solving the problem he had analysed
relate not to the reorganization of work but to the reform of the
money and credit system. Money and interest were to be abolished

and credit transactions were to be organized on the basis of mutuality and exchange: that was Proudhon's proposal, which he disseminated in the politically eventful years of 1848–9 in the periodicals *Le Représentant du Peuple* and *Le Peuple* which he published.

In his articles he sketched out the model of an 'exchange bank' (*banque d'échange*) which provided an organizational structure for the principles of a lending system based on the natural economy. One of its most important characteristics was that exchange certificates (*bons d'échange*), like Owen's labour notes, should take over the function of money as a medium of exchange, and these certificates were to be issued to members of the exchange bank association only on sight of what were called 'realized values', meaning goods and services actually delivered to the bank. Anybody who agreed to observe the rules of the exchange bank could become a member. Another characteristic was that members should always be given credit free of charge or interest. Proudhon maintained that in a system of natural economy credit was no longer a privilege of those who owned money. All producers gave one another credit; when interest had been abolished, credit would come to mean the same thing as exchange (cf. Proudhon 1973:I.212ff., III.63ff.; Diehl 1968; Denis 1896; Lichtheim 1969:92ff.). Under such an arrangement money was no longer in use as a medium of exchange, but continued to be a measure of value for determining the prices of the objects to be exchanged. Unlike Owen's system, this one did not foresee a revaluation of the goods and services delivered at the exchange bank. Proudhon believed he had found a solution to the problem of money and interest, but he excluded from this claim the problem of value that was discussed widely and at length elsewhere. How the values of the goods and services were to be determined justly – that is, in accordance with the only standard common to them all, that of labour – remained unresolved.[4]

After the response to the publication of his proposal for an exchange bank had proved less than overwhelming, Proudhon initiated on his own account a practical attempt to found such a bank, though he had no starting capital whatsoever. In the autumn of 1848 he published the statutes of the 'People's Bank' (*Banque du peuple*), which differed slightly from the original version. These included the stipulation that – at least during the initial period – money would also be permitted in exchange for circulation certificates (*bons de circulation*) and that a low rate of interest (2 per cent) was to be charged on loans. The intention was that the part money played should progressively decrease as and when the bank was doing enough business and had a sufficiently large membership. Furthermore the prudent stipulation in the exchange bank proposals that certificates were only to be issued against *concluded* transactions was dropped in favour of a general formula under which the products must be *delivered* to the bank without any guarantee that a taker for them would be found among the membership. In other words, the bank was not to assume the functions of a selection instrument against potential suppliers; rather it would guarantee unrestricted outlets and in this way generate additional wealth.

On 11 February 1849 the bank was opened in Paris and in some provincial cities. This time there was a huge response, and the membership grew rapidly. After about a month (19 March) members numbered 1,613 independent master craftsmen and entrepreneurs, 8,699 workers in a wide variety of trades and more than 30 workers' associations that had become corporate members. But before the bank could open for business it had to be dissolved, because Proudhon had been sentenced to three years in prison. Proudhon and his colleagues parted in dispute, because not all deposits could be repaid to the depositors immediately owing to an insufficiency of reserves.

But even though the idea was not tried out in practice, there remains considerable room for doubt as to the viability of the exchange or people's bank concept. The internal market created in the model was no different from the formal market with regard either to the organization of labour or to the price sysem, and so was prone to the same defects and dislocations it was expressly designed to help overcome. For Proudhon it was not so much the establishment of an exchange community with its own payments system as the 'magic ingredient' of interest-free credit that was to provide a starting point for reforming capitalism. However, both the desirability and the practicability of the side-effects to be expected from the introduction of such measures would appear to warrant some scepticism. In the last resort credit would be granted even under the exchange bank concept only to a limited circle of credit-worthy persons, able to provide reliable guarantees and securities. Thus the privileged borrowers, hardly likely to include those on lower incomes, would benefit from the reduction of interest, besides being able to produce at lower cost – say with an interest rate of 5 per cent – and so be better placed at the outset. Secondly it is unlikely that interest-free credit could be granted for an unlimited period, because there would be a run on the bank, especially by people who could offer some guarantees but were not immediately in a position to produce the corresponding exchange values with their certificates. Furthermore Proudhon's system provides no guidance on procedures to be followed when quantitative and qualitative mismatches between supply and demand were to be anticipated. It would at least have been easy to incorporate the stipulation that the bank would only accept the goods on commission and that certificates would not be issued until they had been sold. But even a safety arrangement of that kind would scarcely have been sufficient to overcome this structural problem of moneyless exchange in the long term.

(3)   The rather weird financial theorist *Silvio Gesell* (1862–1930), founder of the so-called 'free economy theory', proposed a different way of solving the economic problem. Money was not to be sidelined from its function as a medium of exchange by recourse to the exchange of goods facilitated by money substitutes, as proposed by Owen and Proudhon. Instead the money circulation should 'regain its health' by diminishing the natural advantage money has over goods that, unlike them, it does not 'deteriorate', but is durable and hence can be hoarded. This would be achieved by building an automatic decrease in value into the money system.[5] 'Thus if money is not to have any prerogatives over goods, like them it must rust, go mouldy and rot, must be eaten away, get sick, run away, and when it's all gone the possessor has still to pay the fee of the guarantor' (Gesell 1922:8).

Gesell designated this new kind of money to be created, which through its property of constant devaluation would give its possessor no incentive to hoard it, 'free money'. It was intended to replace metallic and paper money entirely in its functioning. Gesell proposed that free money should lose 1 per thousand of its purchasing power weekly, making 5.2 per cent annually. The money had to be 'revalued' by affixing stamps equal to the loss of value, otherwise it would be completely unusable as a medium of payment. The expected result of this measure was that each individual would try not to pay the loss in purchasing power out of his own pocket and would spend the money or take it to a savings bank as quickly as possible, where it would be stored without interest but also without loss of value (in other words, it would be restored to the money circulation in the form of an interest-free loan). In this way money would be in a state of forced circulation, according to Gesell, and the only way a 'currency office' would be able to influence the money circulation was by acts of monetary policy, thus controlling the economic process according to the principles of the quantity theory.[6]

Michael Unterguggenberger was also an adherent of Gesell's 'free money theory'. He became mayor of the municipality of Wörgl in the Tyrol in December 1931. Faced with the desperate economic situation in his community,[7] he had a resolution passed in the local council to introduce emergency money in the form of work confirmation certificates. In accordance with Gesell's theory, this money was subject to constant depreciation and hence was forced into circulation. The commune had notes to the value of 32,000 schillings printed, and deposited the amount spent during the period of the currency experiment (totalling no more than 12,000 schillings) with the local Raiffeisen bank as collateral. These notes, which were not valid until stamped at the mayor's office, lost 1 per cent of their face value each month, making 12 per cent annually. The devaluation had to be made good on the last day of each month by the holder, by affixing a stamp equal to the devaluation. The money was placed in circulation by the commune, who had the consent of its labourers and officials to pay their wages and salaries in this medium as to 50 per cent of what was due, later raised to 75 per cent. The work confirmation certificates could be encashed by paying an exchange fee of 2 per cent of the face value in ordinary schillings. This experiment with a devaluing money lasted for over 14 months (from July 1932 to mid-September 1933) and involved a group of some 6, 000 persons living in Wörgl and on the surrounding farms.

The real 'gainer' from the emergency scheme was the commune, which received additional income both from the sale of the 'devaluation' stamps and from the exchange fee, and which also collected substantial amounts of tax arrears, since the inhabitants and traders of Wörgl had every incentive to get rid of the shrinking money by paying their local taxes at the end of the month. The work confirmation certificates could be used only in the local area. All the shops in Wörgl accepted them, so they could be used for all the immediate necessities of life such as food, clothing and rent, but not for federal taxes or for postal and rail charges. By using the money received by the communal coffers, and with the help of provincial subsidies, the commune succeeded in implementing planned investments in road-building and tourism, thus providing work for some of the unemployed.

The population made no difficulties about going along with the currency experiment. No disadvantages, for example from price rises, appeared; people got used to affixing their stamps at the end of the month, and it was seen as a boost to morale that quite unconventional countermeasures against the economic depression proved feasible. On the other hand, reports that the population was wildly enthusiastic about them are to be treated with some reserve and perhaps put down to the promotional zeal of the mayor. The Wörgl experiment attracted a great deal of attention, and the little commune in the Tyrol became a 'Mecca for free money enthusiasts', who took the depreciating money back home with them as souvenirs, so that in the end the volume in circulation had seriously diminished – an unexpected form of hoarding. Neighbouring communes planned to issue their own emergency money on the pattern of Wörgl.

Others too had reservations and objections. For the retail traders of Wörgl, accepting the currency was a decidedly two-edged affair. For while they gained from a certain increase in turnover connected with the issue of emergency money, the wholesalers from whom they obtained their supplies, and who had greater market power, were not so keen to take the money. This led critics of the experiment to assert that by accepting the 'disappearing' money the retailers were in effect having to pay a hidden tax on turnover, since they could not really use the money for their business transactions. On top of that, the Social Democratic Party in the Tyrol made difficulties for the mayor and pressured him to give up the experiment, which did not feature in the party manifesto. But the main opposition came from the Austrian National Bank, which regarded Wörgl's declaration of independence as an infringement of its monopoly of issuing notes and feared, with good reason, that the experiment might be followed by others. So the bank obtained a court order in September 1933 forbidding the commune of Wörgl to issue constantly depreciating money.

It is not easy to determine what in fact were the successes of the currency experiment, because several factors were working in conjunction. The healthy flow of tax payments into the communal coffers was due more to the restricted usability of the emergency money and the high fee for exchanging it than to the devaluation of the certificates. And yet it did result in receipts of tax arrears that otherwise would have been lost. The attraction of the 'miracle of Wörgl' had the favourable side-effect of stimulating tourism. Other sources of finance were also tapped for the investments in the commune. The velocity of circulation of the money remained low, which is not very surprising since the money, being paid out to labourers and clerical workers, went almost exclusively into the relatively constant circulation of money for consumption. All in all, then, the Wörgl experiment was an emergency measure that was successful in the short term, but its success almost certainly owed virtually nothing to its inbuilt characteristic of constant depreciation. Therefore it does not furnish reliable conclusions as to the practicability of the 'free money theory', because after all the only principle borrowed from Gesell's plans was that of forced circulation through constant depreciation of the money. For the rest, the issue of the new money was always confined to the immediate neighbourhood; acceptance was voluntary; two monetary systems were functioning side by side, and the local currency was only of subsidiary importance. (On Wörgl see Muralt 1934; Gaitskell 1936:399ff.; Hornung 1934 is critical, on an empirically reliable basis; also Novy 1986:372f.).

(4) During the 1930s many unorthodox proposals were advanced for overcoming, at least in part, the enormous economic problems. In 1933 *Emil Lederer* proposed the creation of small domestic markets for the production and distribution of products of the natural economy. The workless were to be given opportunities of working in factories that had been shut down and paid with work certificates instead of money. With these certificates they could purchase the goods produced in their sector. Surpluses were to be distributed among the unemployed who had not yet found work. Lederer regarded this strategy of the creation of 'islands of social economy', in the telling phrase of Klaus Novy (1978:246ff.), as no more than relief operations of limited duration, which might help reestablish unemployed workers in gainful employment. Successful self-help, he wrote, was better than looking on and doing nothing.

The American *Frank D. Graham* put forward a similar proposal in 1933. He advocated the creation of an 'emergency employment corporation' to rent unused factory premises for the employment of those out of work. His plan, too, envisaged the creation of an internal market in which the unemployed should exchange goods and services in their dual capacity of producers and users. As an internal payments system Graham proposed the introduction of certificates that would lose 5 per cent of their purchasing power monthly in order to prevent hoarding. Projects for the unemployed based on the models of Lederer and Graham were established at some places in Germany and Austria (see Novy 1986:376f.). Graham's plan was also taken up by the self-help movement of the unemployed in America, whose activities will be described separately in section 5 below.

In the *Netherlands* unemployed workers inspired by the ideas of the utopian socialist Edward Bellamy (1850–1898) established small production cooperatives between 1938 and 1941 called 'Werkgemeenschappen van en voor werklozen "Door Arbeid Welvaart" (DAW – 'working groups of and for the unemployed "Welfare through Work"'). Groups of this kind existed in Deventer (1939–41), Dordrecht (1938–40) and Hoorn (1939–41); very shortlived attempts were begun in 1939 at seven other places. The members grew agricultural products and were mainly active with repair workshops and small shops. Work done was remunerated with points or coupons that could be traded in for needed goods and services. Membership was handled in a very selective way; discussions about religion or politics were forbidden, and members who infringed the principles of the association could be rigorously excluded. The Ministry of Social Affairs monitored the activities of the projects with extreme suspicion and 'made life difficult for them'; for example, members were not exonerated from work obligations laid on them by the state. Those projects that were still in existence when the Second World War began had to cease their activities in 1941, when the German occupation troops tightened their grip (see IISG, Archief Door Arbeid Welvaart).

Walter Zander's proposal for the introduction of 'railway money' in 1934 represented a way of mobilizing unused productive workers by means of credit policy. Zander maintained that the problem was that whereas the receipts of German railways were constantly decreasing, orders from the railway were urgently needed in order to stimulate economic activity, yet these could only be financed by incurring risky new indebtedness. A possible format for solving the problem was to build in such a way that the railways would place orders (for instance, for new signal lamps) to be paid for not with legal currency but in credit notes that could only be honoured at railway offices. In other words (to keep to this example) the railway would be exchanging the signalling lamps for its own servies, namely the transport of passengers and goods, without using legal tender which it had yet to acquire. The suppliers of the signalling lamps could pay their freight charges with the credit notes, as well as partly remunerating their own employees with monthly season tickets or holiday travel. The railway simply undertook to accept the credit notes at their face value, but not to convert them into money. This simple arrangement would help to avoid excessive fluctuation in the value of railway money, because a loss in their value would be an incentive to make more use of them, as the user could get more miles for his money, with the result that the exchange value of the certificates would rise again because more would flow back into the coffers of the railways. At the same time the railways management would take care not to grant too many fare reductions, thus avoiding an uncontrolled, inflationary issue of the credit notes. Zander believed that a plan of this kind could be applied to all enterprises that provided important public services, such as the Post Office, shipping companies or local public transport undertakings.

(5)   During the 1930s a broad *self-help movement of the unemployed* arose in the United States. It built up a large number of networks for the exchange of goods and services that members could not obtain on the formal market, and these networks experimented with 'alternative' methods of payments clearance. The networks were by no means organized on a uniform pattern; they also varied considerably as to size, membership structure, area of operations and effectiveness. The first such self-help organization, called the 'Unemployed Citizen League', was founded in July 1931 in Seattle, Washington State. It was followed by many more, especially during the summer

of 1932. The movement peaked in the spring of 1933 with more than 400 groups and a membership totalling some 75,000. In 1934 the financial situation of the unemployed was improved by state assistance payments, and the number of these exchange associations fell considerably. During the next few years more and more producer cooperatives were formed, some of which lasted until well into the 1940s. It is estimated that by the end of 1938 no fewer than half a million families were active in some 600 organizations in 37 federal states.[8]

In 1932 and subsequent years, two different types of exchange cooperatives were to be found: there were organizations that exchanged their own goods and services for products from outside; and those that besides the external exchange relationships also arranged the exchange of goods and services among members within the organization. Organizations of the former type ran a warehouse that was filled with the products used to remunerate members for their work; they distributed these products among all the members on the principle of need. They did not generally charge membership fees and did not need any full-time staff. In organizations of the second type distribution of the goods and services was governed by the 'work input' of each individual and was settled by means of a moneyless exchange medium. Organizations of this type generally charged membership fees and had an administrative staff appropriate to their size.

An example of the first of these two categories is the Unemployed Cooperative Relief Association. It was an umbrella organization formed in the spring of 1932 and by March 1933 it covered 45 local groups ('units') in Los Angeles County. The local units, which operated comparatively independently, organized an exchange of surplus products with farms, enterprises and welfare organizations against work done by their members, for example fruit and vegetables for agricultural labour. They distributed these foodstuffs to their members or exchanged them for other urgently needed products with other units. Every member who fulfilled the required quota of work – usually two days' work per week – earned the right to supply hemself and his family from the stocks held by the organization. Since no provision was made for the exchange of goods and services between members, all mutual services of help being credited to the hourly budget of the member, there was no need to introduce a medium of exchange. Everybody who subscribed to the principles of the organization received a membership card for which no charge was made. Any necessary administrative work could be done by members and credited to their budget of hours. The local authorities supported the organization by making available engine oil and gasoline, 'the elixir of life of the self-help movement' as it was called, without which the organization would not have been able to operate its transport vehicles. A well-functioning basic group or unit with about 500 active members (plus families), consisting mainly of trainees and unskilled workers, performed an average of 1,700 hours 'budget' work a day. Exchange organizations of this type were most heavily concentrated on the Pacific coast, where the climatic conditions permitted agricultural work all the year round, thus enabling the self-help groups to produce a wide range of goods not only in the summer.

In Los Angeles there were four more exchange organizations of the second type, of which the Los Angeles Cooperative Exchange with 5,600 members was by far the largest. This body organized an exchange of goods and more especially of services among its members with the help of a medium of exchange called 'credit transfers'. A central office recorded offers and requirements (supply and demand), kept account of the services exchanged and made addresses available. Members had an account book in which credits and debits were recorded. They themselves negotiated the prices for their services, and payment could also be made in money. There was a firm rule that work owed to the organization must be performed within one month. A brokerage fee of 10 per cent was levied on each transaction. The administrative staff of the organization who were doing the bookkeeping at headquarters were also paid in performance credits. Anybody could join by paying the entrance fee of one dollar and agreeing to abide by the statutes of the organization. Nobody had a claim to a particular service if the organization was not in a position to offer it. A basic prerequisite for the operation of the system, in addition to accurate bookkeeping, was the capital of confidence that the members themselves contributed to the organization, their goodwill. To cover any necessary monetary outlays by the administration, such as telephone charges, it was planned to form a reserve fund from voluntary gifts. Most of the members belonged to the higher occupational groups, so that the organization was in a position to offer a broad range of quite high value services, which included repair services, caring services, language and music teaching; a restaurant was operated, and the list even included life insurance.

From 1934 onwards a large number of self-help organizations came into being with the primary aim of setting up a system of limited 'own production'. Those employed in them were remunerated with 'alternative' currencies and exchange relationships were supposed to develop only around these 'production units', as the nuclei around which this self-employment system crystallized were called. The Washington (DC) Self-Help Exchange, formed in July 1937, is an example of a well-functioning organization of this type. The object of the organization was to create a supplementary system of supply particularly for groups of persons on small incomes that would enable them to use their 'free time' (in most cases compulsorily free) for the improvement of their standard of living and in addition to become members of the organization's production units operating with a system of credit notes, and thus acquire new skills. Because these were the objectives, considerations of efficiency and cost had as far as possible to be subordinated to the social concerns both of individuals and of the group as a whole in the organization's production units and arrangements. The very mixed membership worked together successfully for years and received support for many of its activities from outside sources including charitable contributions from churches and other bodies, government money and voluntary services from students at a nearby university.

In the early phase the initiative for founding the exchange associations came primarily from the unemployed themselves, sometimes with help from socially committed individuals, less frequently from trade unions. The municipal authorities were usually well disposed towards them, but were by no means always prepared to give practical suport to the initiatives in cash or kind. The products exchanged, especially in organizations of the first type, consisted almost entirely of foodstuffs, wood for fuel and, less frequently, repairs to houses in return for a rent rebate. Usually the groups were very careful to insulate their internal exchange marts from the formal markets, so as to avoid both competitive campaigns and price undercutting, and hence conflicts with trade unions. But this was not always possible, if only because they were at the same time trying to obtain steady work in the formal economy for as many of the their members as possible. Generally speaking, members were satisfied with the performance of their organization. Local retailers sometimes opposed the introduction of moneyless methods of settlement, on the grounds that a closed system of payments would adversely affect their profit margins which, unlike those of the wholesalers, were pared down.

There were many kinds and denominations of circulating media: 'due bills', 'goods certifications', 'credit transfers', 'vouchers', 'exchange checks', 'tokens', etc., which can all be covered by the term 'scrip'.[9] In the federal states of California and Colorado the use of local currencies or credit notes was forbidden by law, so that the organizations were compelled to resort to 'points accounts' and 'performance credit certificates' (as in the Los Angeles Cooperative Exchange above). The only cover for the exchange media were the goods and services of the members. The Natural Development Association at Salt Lake City in Utah created a sort of guarantee for the scrip by introducing a 'skilled membership' category: specially reliable and experienced people were awarded this distinction and then had to pledge themselves to pay up to 1,000 dollars if any defects or lacunae were found in their performance, to be paid in money or work. The newly created means of payment were not always handled very carefully, and the financial situation of several groups must have been very delicate. Usually the initiatives were started up without elaborate conceptual preparation and then adapted to any awkward circumstances by trial and error.

Without doubt the self-help groups succeeded in improving the welfare of their members in the absence of a government social security network. The members were able to employ their unused capabilities in doing something useful, thus improving their prospects of obtaining employment in the future, of 'rehabilitating themselves economically', as it was put. The aim of economic rehabilitation was especially prominent in those organizations that still existed or were formed at the end of the 1930s. Yet it must be emphasized that the organizations had to contend with considerable difficulties. Very seldom was full self-supply achieved; in particular, high-grade food-stuffs suitable for storage could be procured only under favourable climatic conditions, which were rare, and·this constituted a serious gap in the supply structure of the unemployed. Furthermore the organizations remained dependent on the money system, because they urgently needed money for the maintenance of their infrastructure and seldom received this in sufficient quantity from the state. There were also management problems, such as poor bookkeeping, slackness in the operation of 'alternative' clearing systems, consistent overtasking of members as regards their social situation and their skill capabilities, etc. The 'free rider' problem also came up at times, when individuals tried to exploit the group system. Nevertheless the self-help organizations succeeded in institutionalizing structures of a multilateral exchange of goods and services despite extremely unfavourable surrounding conditions. Yet arrangements of this kind, made in spontaneous response to those conditions, were still unmistakably a makeshift remedy in an emergency situation with high unemployment and a disastrous supply situation. It was from the outset doubtful whether they would survive 'in good times', and only a very few of their begetters can have intended that they should do so. A contemporary observer summarized the experiences in the following pertinent words:

> The possibilities of a system of distribution outside the regular cash channels of trade are a matter of opinion. It may be said, as regards the exchange groups, that unless a store is operated at which the

member may obtain what he needs, the advantage of the association is very limited. For commodities and services are not easily balanced in value, and direct barter arrangements require an amount of contact work, an ingenuity of planning, and an expenditure of thought and energy far beyond the inclinations and possibly even the abilities of the average person. Such arrangements are utilized in an emergency, lacking a better system, but their continuance in good times is doubtful. (Anon. 1933, no. 6:239f.).

6

Canada's 'Local Employment and Trading System'

The account that follows is based on an interview and subsequent correspondence with one of the organizers of this initiative. In addition, we have analysed a lengthy description of the project (Petersson 1989), and we were also able to examine a large amount of written material which was produced by the initiators of the project as aids to organization, for publicity purposes and for training. We also studied an economic appraisal of 'The second economy and the social welfare system' written by Professor A. Rotstein for the Policy Analysis Division of Health and Welfare of the Canadian government (Rotstein 1985).

The socioeconomic and social space context

The Local Employment and Trading System (LETS) project came into being in 1979 on Vancouver Island, off the west coast of Canada. It was adopted both in similar forms and in many variants in a number of localities in the region, including the small town of Courtenay in Comox Valley (50,000 inhabitants) in British Columbia. It was to have been extended to the regional capital Vancouver in 1985, but was a palpable failure from the outset. The fact that the project had its origin in the social space conditions of an island is of interest in as much as island communities in other places also appear to provide fruitful ground for innovations in the sphere of informal work, as for example the islands of Guernsey (see Grubiak and Grubiak 1960) and Sheppey (cf. Pahl 1984; also Rotstein 1985:38) in Great Britain. However, a more important trigger for the mounting of such projects than the island location seems to be the fact that the local population is suffering under a severe economic depression, either one of long standing or a recent one.

Thus until the early 1980s the town of Courtenay in the Comox Valley was mainly dependent on two employers, a local US Air Force base and a timber mill that provided raw material for the paper industry. Following a decision taken elsewhere, the American base was transferred to another province, while the timber industry went into recession. These two events resulted in a drastic rise in unemployment, which caused some of the able-bodied inhabitants to emigrate and made a large proportion of those who remained dependent on public assistance. According to a number of reports, the initiative for starting up the LETS project was due to a practitioner of remedial exercises, motivated partly by the fact that as a consequence of the shrinkage of the local economy and in the absence of adequate social security and health insurance, many of his patients could no longer afford his services. Consequently he had a personal interest in seeing an alternative system of exchange organized.

Main features and characteristics of the LETS system

The system differs from others described in this report in that exchange within the local economy is based not on 'work money', time credit notes or similar money substitutes based on time quanta, but on a 'subsidiary currency', the 'Green dollar'. Another interesting point is that this supplementary currency has no material basis at all; it does not circulate in the form of coins, notes or certificates; balances and credits appear only as figures in bank accounts. The currency does not represent an independent measure of value for work done, as does for example 'time money', but remains closely integrated into the system of market prices, maintaining a relationship with the 'official' dollar (see pages 92–5 below).

The system works through four communication flows. The first of these communication flows goes via an advertising leaflet that is sent free of charge to all households in the township (see document 1). This leaflet contains brief descriptions of offers and requirements, arranged according to types of goods and services, which prospective participants in the system wish to bring into the exchange process. Prospective suppliers pay a moderate fee of 30 cents per advertising line for publication of their offer. Besides a short description of the commodity of service offered, the advertisement contains the name and telephone number of the would-be suppliers and the inquirers. There is also a logogram for the place of residence and (by some suppliers) an indication of the 'currency proportion' (see below).

The second communication flow runs between the purchasers of goods and services and the bank. Immediately after each transaction

LETSystem COMOX VALLEY 576 ENGLAND AVE., COURTENAY 338-0213/0214

OFFERS MARKED + + AND REQUESTS MARKED - - CURRENT LISTINGS . . . 10/01/85

CLASS	DESCRIPTION	PHONE
000 TIME, LABOUR, SERVICES, ETC.		
003 + +	SPINNING CLASSES, PART GREEN, BEG. OCT.	338-6090 CO
004 + +	BELLY DANCE LESSONS 80% green	335-2569 CO
004 + +	MUSIC LESSONS	336-8429 CU
006 + +	FRENCH TUTORING & ENGLISH TUTORING	336-8429 CU
006 + +	RUSSIAN - - LESSONS AND TRANSLATION	339-3881 CX
010 + +	ADOLESCENT, CHILD AND FAMILY COUNSELLING	MV
010 + +	PHONE OLIVER	337-3375 MV
011 + +	PROFESSIONAL DIETITIAN $20 GR./HOUR	338-6877 CO
011 + +	IRIDOLOGY READING $6 FED/$6 GREEN	337-6460 HV
021 + +	ROOFING	335-0750 HI
029 + +	DENTISTRY, 15%-25% GREEN	336-2133 CU
031 + +	MASSAGE THERAPY, REIKI	338-1522 CO
035 + +	BABYSITTING	338-7824 CO
041 + +	RUG SHAMPOOING	338-7824 CO
041 + +	HOUSECLEANING & WINDOW CLEANING	336-8259 CU
051 + +	SEWING AND ALTERATIONS, CALL VILMA AFTER 6	337-5368 BC
061 + +	TYPING	337-5368 BC
061 + +	GENERAL TYPING 100% green	336-2010 CU
062 + +	BOOKKEEPING, INCOME TAX	337-5368 BC
074 - -	PHOTOGRAPHER FOR WEDDING, OCTOBER 20,85	338-1340 CO
078 + +	GERMAN TRANSLATIONS 100% green	336-2010 CU
083 + +	PIANO TUNING, $35 FED. $15 green	338-1432 CO
085 + +	SIGNS - - PAINTED OR CARVED	339-3881 CX
090 + +	GENERAL LABOUR, $10/HR PART GREEN	338-0892 CO
090 + +	SKILLED GENERAL LABOURER	338-9560 CO
090 + +	DO HOUSEWORK, GARDENING, YARDS, WINDOWS ETC	338-8250 RO
090 - -	GENERAL HOUSE MAINTENACE AND REPAIRS	338-5888 CO
100 TIME, LABOUR, SERVICES, ETC. CONTINUED		
113 + +	CARPENTER	338-9560 CO
113 + +	CARPENTRY	334-3443 CO
113 + +	CARPENTRY	338-0558 CO
113 + +	CARPENTER: COMPETENT AND FULLY QUALIFIED	CX
113 + +	REASONABLE RATES	333-3465 CX
117 + +	FORM & CONCRETE WORK, FLAT OR VERTICAL	338-0558 CO
121 - -	INSTALL NEW WIRING FOR TRAILER	338-8815 CO
124 - -	GLASS INSTALLER FOR TRAILER	338-8815 CO
131 + +	HOUSE PAINTING	339-3881 CX
135 + +	CERAMIC TILE SALES AND INSTALLATION	757-9341 BO
146 + +	TREE PRUNING	338-8891 CO
150 + +	HOME AND YARD MAINTENANCE	338-9560 CO
150 + +	ROOF AND GUTTER CLEANING	338-8891 CO
150 + +	CAT AND BACKHOE WORK	336-8336 CO
151 - -	CAT LEVELLING	338-8815 CO
163 - -	SOMEONE WITH TRUCK TO HELP MOVE-URGENT	337-8097 MV
168 + +	BICYCLE REPAIR	338-0558 CO
200 LOCAL PRODUCE AND FOOD PRODUCTION		
200 + +	FIREWOOD - - $70/CORD	338-0558 CO
200 + +	FIREWOOD TO SELL, LEAVE MESSAGE-OFFICE	NI
200 - -	SEASONED FIREWOOD WANTED	335-2569 CO
200 - -	WANTED FIREWOOD-CASH AND GREEN	336-8871 CO
200 - -	WANT TO BUY FIREWOOD, ALL OR PART GREEN	339-0162 CX
220 + +	VEGETABLE TRUCK FARM-PRODUCE - - FRESH, AND	MV
220 + +	FOR CANNING AND FREEZING 50% CASH/50%GR	336-2357 MV
222 - -	+ + GROUT'S GARDENS-NORTH ISLAND	CO
220 - -	HIGHWAY + + WILLING TO BUY PRODUCE FOR GREEN	338-0724 CO
221 - -	GARDEN VEGETABLES AND FRUIT WANTED	339-0162 CX
223 - -	WANTED, HAY AND SOME GREEN	336-4336 CO
223 - -	LAMB, PORK, BEEF, CHICKEN OR FISH WANTED	339-0162 CX
236 + +	FRESH APPLE JUICE, pasturised, $3-2 Litres Please bring	CO
236 + +	your own containers	338-1914 CO
274 + +	CULINARY AND MEDICINAL HERBS: TARRAGON SAVORY, THYME, COMFREY, AND MORE . . .	334-3677 CO
291 + +	CHICKEN FEEDER	338-7824 CO
295 + +	GOAT KIDS FOR MEAT, 2 DUCKS, CHICKENS	338-7824 CO
297 + +	RABBIT CAGES AND EQUIPMENT	338-7824 CO
297 + +	RABBITS: BREEDING STOCK, PETS AND MEAT	336-8336 CO
297 + +	SATINS, CALS AND DUTCH	
300 LOCAL GOODS MANUFACTURED AND REPAIRED		
310 + +	DISPLAY BUTTONS, 2-1/4", MADE TO ORDER YOUR	CO
310 + +	DESIGN - - OR WE DO ART WORK	938-7972 CO
322 + +	ORG. MECH. UNIVERSAL CLEANER 10LB./$10	338-5582 CO
336 + +	WOVEN TAPESTRY RUGS, TABLE RUNNERS, PURE	CO
336 + +	WOOL	336-1010 CU
371 - -	CEMENT BLOCKS	338-8815 CO
381 + +	PORTRAIT PAINTING	939-3881 CX
386 + +	EARRINGS, MADE TO ORDER	337-5368 BC
391 + +	STONE CARVING	338-4764 CO
395 + +	DOUGH DOLLS	335-2569 CO
398 + +	BELLY DANCE PERFORMANCES 60% green	339-7494 CO
399 + +	WOODEN TULIPS FOR SALE 2/3 GREEN	

CLASS	DESCRIPTION	PHONE
400 SHELTER, LAND, ACCOMMODATION		
470 - -	STRUCTURE, BIG OR SMALL	338-8815 CO
600 TRANSPORTATION		
610 + +	MECHANICAL WORK	338-9560 CO
616 + +	AUTO BODY WORK	338-9560 CO
616 - -	TRUCK TO BE MADE READY FOR PAINT	338-8815 CO
621 + +	CAMPERIZED BUS	338-7824 CO
622 + +	RAMBLER CAR FOR GREEN DOLLARS	339-5437 CX
625 + +	THREE RUNNING FORD VANS, SOLD SEPARATELY	CO
625 + +	OR AS A LOT	338-8815 CO
625 - -	FORD VAN OR PICKUP WITH BURNED OUT MOTOR	338-6426 CO
677 + +	UTILITY TRAILER, HOLDS 1 CORD FIREWOOD	338-6815 CO
678 + +	4 14 RADIAL TIRES FOR '69 VW VAN ♦100gr	339-5884 CX
700 BUY, SELL AND TRADE, ETC.		
722 - -	4L ICECREAM PAILS & LIDS $.25 FED. OR GR.	338-5582 CO
722 - -	CANNING JARS	339-3744 CX
724 + +	FOUR-SLICE TOASTER $20 GREEN	338-7366 CO
724 + +	TWO-SLICE TOASTER $15 GREEN	338-7366 CO
727 - -	PROPANE RANGE-GOOD WORKING ORDER WANTED	339-3465 CX
728 - -	SMALL FRIDGE - - 36 INCHES HIGH	337-8279 MV
729 - -	SMALL FREEZER	339-3202 CX
739 - -	LUGGAGE, LARGE PIECE FOR GREEN WANTED	339-3465 CX
741 - -	SOFA AND LOVESEAT	339-3202 CX
744 - -	WOODEN DESK FOR GREEN (MESSAGE)	338-5371 CO
746 - -	USED WASHER & DRYER, CALL VILMA AFTER 6	337-5368 BC
748 - -	VACUUM CLEANER WANTED	339-6461 CX
749 - -	USED PICTURE FRAMES FOR GREEN	338-7124 CO
751 + +	AMP DC PORTABLE WELDER $300/268gr write PO	CO
751 + +	BOX 3658 COURTENAY	CO
752 - -	LAWN MOWER, CALL VILMA AFTER 6	337-5368 BC
758 + +	1940 GIBSON TRACTOR W/ FRONT END LOADER	338-5888 CO
758 + +	AND VARIOUS ATTACHMENTS	CO
758 + +	5-10H.P. OUTBOARD MOTOR, URGENT, BUY OR	CO
759 - -	LEASE, FED. OR GREEN. 339-7766	287-3255 CR
761 - -	3- OR 5-SPEED BICYCLE, MESSAGE AFTER 6	337-5368 BC
768 - -	CHAINSAW 10-25 HP OUTBOARD, 1/2 CASH-1/2 GR	339-0424 CO
776 + +	BEIGE BATHROOM SINK BASIN, $10 GREEN	339-0162 CX
776 + +	BATHTUB, TOILET, WALLMOUNT SINK, AND	CX
776 + +	PROPANE HOTWATER HEATER	339-3465 CX
778 + +	WOOD STOVE	338-7824 CO
781 - -	GOOD SLR CAMERA	339-3202 CX
782 - -	SMALL TENT 14 GOOD SIZE	338-7366 CO
783 + +	DAUST ROLLER SKATES, MEN'S SIZE 6, VERY GOOD	CO
783 + +	CONDITION, $50 GREEN	338-6877 CO
783 + +	PAIR SKIS-FISCHER RC4 160'S, TYROLEA 80	CO
783 + +	BINDINGS, $120 CASH/$30 GREEN	338-5588 CO
784 + +	HAMMOND ORGAN MZ/LESLIE SPEAKER-SUITABLE	CX
900 COMMERCIAL		
907 + +	ROLLING PIN KITCHEN SHOP - -	CO
907 + +	LINENS, POTTERY, COPPER, ETC.	CO
907 + +	SELECTED ITEMS 30% GREEN	334-2642 CO
912 + +	TRUCKING, BACKHOE SERVICES	337-5738 MV
913 + +	JUMBO CHIMNEY SERVICE	DI
913 + +	PROFESSIONAL INSTALLATION	DI
913 + +	CHIMNEY SWEEPING	339-5122 DI
923 + +	+ + GROUT'S GARDENS-NORTH ISLAND	CO
	HIGHWAY + +	CO
923 + +	LOCALLY GROWN GRESH VEGETABLES AND	CO
923 + +	IMPORTED FRUIT, $10 GREEN FOR $50 CASH	338-0724 CO
923 + +	BREAD & BUTTER PICKLING CUCUMBERS WHILE	CO
923 + +	STOCKS LAST, PRE-ORDER, 100% GREEN	338-0724 CO
924 + +	NEW LEAF WHOLE FOODS, NORDIN AVE. COMOX	CO
924 + +	10% GREEN ON MOST ITEMS	339-5911 CX
927 + +	'PIZZA GALORE' AT THE CARDBOARD HOUSE	HI
927 + +	BAKERY ON HORNBY ISLAND, FRIDAYS ONLY 5PM	HI
935 + +	TO 9PM 50% GREEN	335-0733 HI
935 + +	WOODEN TOYS & CHILDREN'S FURNITURE	338-9647 RO
936 + +	COUNTRY UPHOLSTERY, SPECIAL TRUCK	MV
936 + +	BENCH SEATS $130, MATERIAL FED.	MV
936 + +	LABOUR 1/2 + 1/2, CHECK ON PRICES FOR	MV
936 + +	TRACTOR AND HEAVY EQUIPMENT REPAIRS	337-8897 MV
938 + +	BUD'S CUSTOM WOODWORK	BC
938 + +	FULLY EQUIPPED CABINET SHOP	BC
938 + +	QUALITY WORK ONLY	BC
938 + +	CABINETS, COUNTERS, DOORS, WINDOWS, ETC	337-8093 BC
941 + +	FUTON DESIGNS-PART GREEN ACCEPTED	338-8022 CX
950 + +	RENT-ALL EQUIPMENT CENTRE-TOOL HIRE	334-3678 CO
962 + +	REID'S COURTENAY ESSO, ISLAND HWY N. 4%	CO
962 + +	GREEN ON GAS, OIL, ACCESSORIES, CONTACT	CO
962 + +	LETS OFFICE FOR DETAILS	334-3844 CO
976 + +	BRIAN'S SECONDHAND IN ROYSTON	CO
976 + +	WIDE VARIETY OF MERCHANDISE	338-7198 RO
993 + +	INSURANCE, LIFE & WAGE, 1/4 GREEN	336-8613 CO

Document 1. Advertising leaflet of the LETS system in Comox Valley, Canada (reduced)

the purchaser informs the bank which services he has received from whom and what amount in 'green' dollars is to be credited to the performer on account of the service. This communication flow is organized cheaply in that these communications are usually recorded on an answerphone. (It must be assumed that this telephone call is usually made in the presence of the seller/creditor, who can then satisfy himself as to the accuracy of the data relating to him). The purchaser is also debited with a fee of 30 cents for each transaction, and in this way the costs of the – pared down – administrative work can be covered. Communications between purchasers and the bank, and also 'search communications' between buyers and potential sellers (which, though not a formal part of the system, are assumed to take place) benefit from the tariff structure of North American telephone companies, under which local calls are not individually recorded and charged but are covered by the standard charge for a telephone installation.

A third communication flow consists of communication between the bank and all persons or households who have taken part in a transaction during the preceding period (of one month). This feedback from the bank to participants consists of an individualized (named) list of the transactions completed and a collective (unnamed) one, and the account balances resulting from them. The individualized listing informs each participant of the transactions he/she has completed and the balance of the account. This shows the recipient whether his/her account is in balance or has a credit or debit balance. The collective feedback shows whether the system as a whole is in balance or whether and to what extent it is out of balance. Disequilibrium would at least indicate a dangerous situation if a considerable number of participants showed a 'high' debit balance; such a situation would give good grounds for withdrawing confidence from the system, because every participant would be bound to suspect that a significant number of 'free riders' was using the system unfairly without making any contribution to it. Thus the individual part of the account lets each individual know whether he or she is *himself or herself* a net debtor (and if so honour-bound to step up efforts on the 'seller' side); the anonymous collective listing indicates whether *all the others* have been behaving conscientiously, or whether a large number of participants have not done so. Hence this regular balancing of the accounts performs the function of documenting the extent to which the system is financially sound and trustworthy.

This purpose is also served by a fourth possible communication, which acts as a fallback. Before entering into a transaction the seller can obtain information as to the creditworthiness of the buyer and, if he or she finds that the potential partner is a considerable 'net debtor', can withdraw from the transaction. In other words, there is no banking secrecy; on the contrary there is a perpetual positive facility for obtaining information as to the trustworthiness of the prospective buyer in the common interest that the payments system should be in balance. This at least makes it more difficult to abuse trust. There is also the ever-present possibility that 'members simply choose to ostracize those who are not pulling their weight by selling into the system' (Rotstein 1985:41).

The initiators of the system believe that the automatic nature of the creditworthiness checks built into the third and fourth of these communication flows renders the introduction of a credit line unnecessary. In other words, everyone knows that he or she can incur as much debt as he/she likes, as this facilitates the 'credit financing' of purchases and to that extent increases the turnover; but everybody also knows that everybody else can incur as much debt as they like, and that this entails a danger of exploiting the system and weakening the currency; and lastly every participant knows that he or she must exercise personal vigilance against 'exploitative transactions' and that, thanks to the 'goldfish bowl' accounts this can be done, and conversely each participant expects 'everybody else' to be on the lookout where he or she is concerned, since all transactions are completely voluntary. So far, the initiators of the system appear to have been justified in their original basic assumption that this ingenious automatic mechanism for ensuring trustworthiness will maintain the system on a steady course of expansion.

The supplementary currency system differs from normal banking not only by the absence of banking secrecy but also the fact that interest is neither collected nor paid. Consequently it 'costs' nothing to run a deficit, so long as it is a moderate one; as we have seen, 'excessive' debts are sanctioned not by the payment of interest but by the expectation that a seller who feels he or she has grounds for suspicion will refrain from doing deals with the buyer. Conversely, the advantage of not paying interest on credit balances is that there is no sense in simply 'holding' a credit balance, because it brings in no income. The cumulative result of these two functions is to provide a rather mild stimulus to transactions on the principle that 'each person is his neighbour's bank' (Petersson 1989).

Resources and basic ideas of the initial phase

The organizers of the LETS project believed that the dynamics of a parallel economy fuelled by 'green' dollars would develop in accordance with a series of assumptions and principles (though they have proved to be only partially viable in practice, see below):

1 A high degree of technical and managerial efficiency in the administration, organization, recruitment of members and public relations of the projects. Advanced products of the modern communications and information industry were installed in order to minimize the cost of maintaining the system. These included automatic answering machines for recording transactions, computers for compiling individual and group balances, the dispatch of computer diskettes with programs for initiating similar projects in other places, the use of video films as training aids and the networking of local mainframe computers via the telephone network. This high degree of technical rationalization made it possible to deal with all the administrative work (mainly decoding the tapes from the telephone answering machines, printing and dispatching the extracts of account and the lists of offers and demands) in a working time of eight hours a month. This expense was partially paid for in 'green' currency.

2 A high degree of commitment on the part of the small group of initiators and organizers, absorbing much time over a long period. These people work either on an honorary basis for partial remuneration in 'green' dollars in administering, initiating and propagating projects of this kind, and they represent an important ideological and moral resource for them. Most of them apparently come from the 'alternative' spectrum of green and liberal political leanings; they are distinguished by a pragmatic, experimenting turn of mind and operate outside the ambit of the regular political parties.

3 Instead of making demands on government authorities, municipal bodies, owners of capital or social organizations the initiators base their methods on an important principle of policy that only the self-interest of normal people, properly understood, can lead to the discovery of the best way to secure their livelihood and harmonize supply with demand. Following this line of thought, which is not untypical of movements and initiatives of social innovation in Anglo-Saxon countries, grants and subventions are not sought for meeting the expenses of starting up and running the project; instead contributions are collected from the prospective beneficiaries themselves. These contributions consist of membership fees (in the Canadian case under discussion, a single joining fee of 25 dollars per household and 200 dollars for firms), and the payments for advertisements and for administration mentioned earlier. Resources of 'ordinary currency' are needed in order to pay external costs such as post and carriage. The outgoings are said to be 2 dollars per month for each active member.

4 One of the main reasons for believing the project will succeed and continue to expand is the expectation that 'normal people',

especially when grappling with serious economic disadvantages and high unemployment, will recognize the potential advantages of the project from a sense of their own immediate self-interest and will help it to snowball. To this end it is considered neither necessary nor helpful for the project to be targeted on particular groups of persons, political subcultures, already existing associations and the like. Indeed the promoters are convinced that if it were restricted to certain groups and cultures (for example a local 'alternative scene') this would only be taking on a deadweight of political ideology or culture, which would prove counterproductive by investing it with an aura of exclusivity.

5   However, conscious and careful note is taken of the fact that a whole series of habits and fears as well as prejudices and misunderstandings may hamper the development of the enlightened self-interest of the 'normal human being' (see below). From this the conclusion is drawn that such mental obstacles must be dismantled by patient, careful, realistic and relatively long-term explanatory and promotional activities; towards this end a panoply of professional techniques for social and adult education (such as plays, demonstrations, video films, planned games, etc.) is employed. With a 'populist' flavour the project is directed not at particular elites, groups or subcultures, but relies on the fact that its advantages will become apparent to the enlightened common sense of all normal citizens in all walks of life, age groups and social classes, when once the barrier thresholds of mistrust and the habitual 'fear of debts' have been overcome, and that such enlightenment can be actively pursued.

Praxis and problems of the parallel economy

Our researches did not result in an unequivocal and conclusive assessment of the success of LETS and similar projects from the experience gained so far. On the plus side is the statement that in the Comox Valley project there were 600 members after it had been running for two years and a turnover of some 500,000 dollars. Naturally this figure represents only the 'green' proportion of the transactions, which varies according to the nature of the service and could not be reduced to an average. If the average ratio between 'ordinary' and 'green' currency is put at 80:20, on this hypothesis the recorded 'green' turnover of 500,000 dollars would indicate an additional 'ordinary' turnover of 2 million dollars. Another point in its favour is that projects of this sort multiplied; according to an apparently well attested statement, by the autumn of 1988 some

40 recorded systems of this type existed (meaning that they were maintaining irregular contacts and exchanges of experience). Most of them were in Canada, the USA, Australia, New Zealand, England or Wales. The system is in practical operation, with many small variants, in many Anglo-Saxon countries; in the USA alone there are said to be several hundred functioning exchange networks of this kind (Rotstein 1985:73; Battelle Institute 1984:18ff.). There are some less rosy though disputed and variously interpreted reports of stagnation and abrupt collapses of some of these systems, and of the difficulty they experience in attaining 'critical mass' to become self-sustaining and capable of further diversification.

The special feature of LETS projects, which immediately distinguishes them from all other organized forms of interhousehold networking of ownwork, consists in their close integration into the formal economy, whose prices and price formation mechanism the system, as it were, adopts. A basic rule is that in principle there is equivalence between the 'official' and the 'green' currency (also expressed int he fact that debts incurred in 'green' currency can in principle be repaid in 'official currency' – even though this is not obligatory, since there is no strict credit line). According to one's point of view, this bypassing of the principle of 'work money' so dear to 'alternative economies' and cooperatives, which entails the *egalitarian* valuation of all work and services measured in units of time, represents an advantage or a disadvantage. The disadvantage is that participants in this parallel economy renounce the egalitarian ideological principle of an 'association of equals' and instead launch themselves into the currents of market price formation driven by scarcity relationships. Conversely there is the advantage that this economy no longer remains confined to a comparatively narrow spectrum of subprofessional and semiprofessional services and commodities, but that in principle the alternative currency can be used over a very large part of the local economy.

Under the rules of the formal economy every purchasing decision presupposes an implicit agreement between buyer and seller regarding the price of a given commodity. By means of the conscious *splitting of the currency*, which is usable over a very large proportion of locally produced and distributed goods and services, this (under normal conditions) single transactional dimension of the price (for a given quantity, quality and so on) is supplemented by a second transactional dimension, in which agreement must also be achieved. This could be conceived as meaning that after agreement on the *level* of the price has been reached in a 'first round of negotiation', a second negotiating round follows in which agreement has to be reached as to *the proportions in which* the sum now fixed as the price has to be settled in one currency or the other (the 'currency proportion').

Thus the special conditions of a split currency complicate the calculations made by both parties in that a second negotiating dimension is brought in. In negotiating the currency proportion the seller is influenced by the comparative *usability* of the parallel currency, and the buyer by its *acceptability*. The less the restricted usability of this currency means to the seller, objectively and subjectively, the readier will he or she be to accept a larger proportion of the price in the parallel currency; and conversely, the greater the 'procurement advantage' the informal economy offers the buyer for his or her income requirements, the more interested will he/she be in receiving a high proportion in the parallel currency. So if the informal economy – in this case the economy trading with 'green' dollars as a medium of circulation – grows, and hence the quantity and diversity of the services and commodities it offers and the work required of it grow, the parallel currency proportion of the average transaction will likewise grow, and vice versa.

This arrangement has the considerable advantage that the boundary between the formal economy (in which transactions are mediated by conventional money) and the informal economy (in which mediation is by credit notes or similar devices) is not sharply drawn, but is manipulated *variably* and *made dynamic*. The currency proportion varies from transaction to transaction, and this variability

> allows persons to recover immediately at the time of the transaction whatever fraction of the worth of the good is only available in the outside economy. For example, a person may offer to drive people or to move goods with their time being valued in green dollars and the value of the gasoline being accounted and paid for in conventional dollars. LETS will only record the green part of the transaction, leaving the matter of the conventional dollar balance entirely to the members involved. (Rotstein 1985:43)

The term 'making dynamic' means that, as with the mechanism described in development economics as 'import substitution', as the market becomes more diversified the local parallel currency will gradually become suitable for procuring goods that formerly had to be paid for in conventional money. The reason for this is that in terms of the calculation described above an increasing number of sellers will have good reason to accept a similarly increasing proportion of the prices of the goods or services they sell in the parallel currency. Of course it is hardly to be expected that the average proportion of the local parallel currency (or in the analogy of development economics, the 'national currency') would ever come close to the 100 per cent mark, unless the economy was a closed, autarchic – which means a very primitive – one. For even if the informal economy had a strongly expansive dynamism, cost components such as energy, taxes, freight services, many raw materials and preproducts procured externally would still have to be paid for in conventional currency. But it is quite possible that *some* of these prior services and other cost factors might be replaced by *local* products, and that would increase the usability and circulation volume of the parallel currency.

In theory the expansionary thrust of the parallel currency might be expected to give rise to structural effects, favouring import substitution (as in the example of Wörgl, chapter 5) and also increasing the share of services (especially those with a small number of manufacturing stages). Such hypothetical structural effects also differentiate the LETS model from the other models that rely on certificates. The difference is that in this case a more 'offensive' strategy in economic policy comes into the realm of possibility, whereas the other models may be said to have the disadvantage that structurally they are confined to the role of 'stop-gap' programmes and makeshifts for particular population groups and types of services. This distinction is based on the fact that the 'second price ticket' (the possibility of making the proportions of the two components of the currency dependent on the service involved) enables the system to be extended practically to the whole area of local value creation, and any raw materials and preproducts procured externally have to be paid for in the official currency pro rata to their proportion of the value of the final product.

However, the data and reports of experience so far available indicate that practical results up to the present fall far short of attaining such demanding objectives. Yet there is no doubt about the structural advantage of the system. It offers both the unemployed and everybody else the opportunity of transforming their labour power or working time (even small, unevenly distributed amounts of the latter) into 'purchasing power' *without* the necessity of either working for an employing firm or of possessing capital, which is a *sine qua non* of earning a living by self-employment.

In view of this extremely innovative arrangement, ideally suited, it would appear, to the socioeconomic circumstances in Comox Valley, its potential appears to be vastly underused. The services principally transacted through the system appear to be almost entirely those attributable to the domestic sphere of ownwork and activity in the immediate surroundings of the residence. They include: vehicle maintenance, woodcutting, carpentry and joinery, teaching, hand-made toys, craft manufacture of ceramics, jewellery, candles, children's clothing, payment of rents, gardening, therapeutic services, trade in used household goods and leisure activities (cf. Petersson 1989; and see document 1 above). The *de facto* limitation of the system to these kinds of service activities is all the more remarkable in that interviewees stress the high process utility gained through participation: people make new acquaintances, discover unsuspected talents, experience the pleasures of cooperation and enhanced self-esteem. Hence these enhancements of social life and experience, so much appreciated by those taking part, must be added as a additional bonus to the fact that by taking part they can save part of their regular monetary outgoings and can afford to buy items that would otherwise have been beyond their limited budgetary means. So why is it that, despite all this, they clearly confine their purchases rigidly to the kinds of services described?

Based on the facts and reports we have, there seem to be two possible, and complementary, answers to this question. One answer relates to objective structural characteristics and vulnerable points in the system. These are that it is not proof against two kinds of 'exploitation'. One variant of such exploitative relationships is obvious and has already been mentioned earlier: nobody can be quite sure that *nobody else* will seize an advantage at the expense of the group by running up large debts and then opting out or perhaps even moving out of the district. The thought that this might possibly occur engenders a cautious attitude in all potential participants with the result that such transactions are undertaken only to a limited extent, only in case of need and/or with trustworthy partners. The net result is that the expansionary thrust of increasing the services on offer is throttled by the motive of caution. Clearly, on the other hand, the 'confidence-building measures' mentioned earlier, such as the publication of individual and group balances, are of little avail because they take effect only at the level of the *service* decision, but not at the prior level of the *participation* decision.

Another, less visible, exploitative relationship to which the system is susceptible would come into play if the two transactional dimensions distinguished earlier (the price, and the currency proportions) became *interactive* and consequently transformed the rigid one-to-one relationship between the two currencies into a market relationship with variable 'rates of exchange'. This could occur if the convertibility advantage of the regular currency (the fact that such goods as airline tickets and other 'external' goods can be purchased with appropriate amounts of it) were played off against the 'limited utility' of the local parallel currency with the result that buyers who have nothing to offer except 'green' currency as a payment medium, *had to compensate for this disadvantage by offering a higher price.* This arrangement would of course enable sellers of goods who accept part of the selling price in the parallel currency to exploit buyers who, owing to lack of a regular earned income, are unable to pay the full price in ordinary currency by increasing the price as a function of the currency. To illustrate: a bakery sells bread for 100 dollars in regular currency and for 110 dollars at a currency proportion of 80:20; in consequence, the owner of the bakery would have a claim through this 'supplement' on free services from customers unable to pay in normal currency. The application of this arrangement (even the anticipation that it might be applied, a contingency against which no institutional safeguards are possible) will very quickly lead to the parallel currency coming into disrepute as a 'poor people's currency' liable to exploitation, hence unattractive to hold.

But the organizers and partisans of the project believe that there are much stronger reasons than these *objective* factors why it has so far failed to live up to their expectations. They point to *subjective* factors such as inhibitions, lack of understanding, conventional habits of thought, mistrust and so on, that originate not in the characteristics of the system but in the attitudes and dispositions of those who might otherwise take part, with the implication that these attitudes could be overcome by education, public relations, consciousness raising and advertising. They mention especially 'fear of incurring debts', which could be countered by a painstaking campaign of economic information about the stimulating effect and the 'collective productivity' of credit creation. Despite the undoubted difficulty of changing ingrained habits of thought, people must be brought to see that contracting debts can actually be altruistic, since as debtors they are providing others with a claim on their own future services and giving them the opportunity of earning income without becoming employees. No doubt it is difficult to inculcate the realization that in a debtor–creditor relationship it is the *latter* who should be the favoured one (naturally without any payment of interest from the debtor) in an economic culture in which the poorer sections of society often regard getting into debt as having the moral status of (a) an undisciplined temptation to excess which, if not withstood, (b) will have to be paid for dearly with more abstinence. Reservations of this kind are mentioned as a considerable hindrance to the operating viability of the arrangement: 'People are reluctant to spend in many cases because they find it hard to believe that they have anything to offer in return' (Rotstein 1985:42). The project's proponents try to counter this attitude by a trick of wordplay, so as to avoid the concept of 'debt' with its negative connotations: 'LETS proponents insist that the term debt be dropped in favour of commitment to the community' (Rotstein 1985:42).

Although the LETS model has received considerable public exposure (on popular television programmes) and despite the extremely committed activity of politically motivated organizers and advertisers, it appears that the attempt to transvalue debts into good deeds (as it were a 'micro-Keynesian' attitude, sometimes called 'do-it-yourself Keynesianism') finds very few takers among debtors as a whole. On the other hand, reports we have seen appear to indicate that objections against the two objective possibilities of exploitation are less serious. Other moral and cultural reservations and fears mentioned include the suspicion that goods and services procured from the parallel economy may not be of satisfactory quality – though this is countered by saying that liability problems of this kind could be settled through channels open to any buyer, including the law if necessary. The other objection relates to the fear that transactions in which the parallel currency is used might be open to the suspicion of involving at best semilegal 'black market goods'. The project initiators counter this suspicion – and its consequent fears of conflicts with the taxman – by pointing out that 'green' income has to be declared for tax like any other income and hence such transactions should not come under the stigma of illegality.

The LETS scheme and economic and social policy

Not only its initiators but also qualified economists (Rotstein 1985) believe that the LETS model has the potential for bringing about a general increase in prosperity, a fact that brings it within the purview of government policy. This prosperity effect is twofold:

1   In conditions of structural economic weakness, negative or stagnating growth and correspondingly higher unemployment, the LETS model, by giving rise to a parallel or supplementary economy, enables a certain volume of economic subsistence goods and services to be produced that otherwise would not be produced – at least, not within the framework of a formal money economy:

> The importance . . . of a secondary currency lies in its facilitation of production and exchange which would otherwise not take place. In situations of persistently unused capacity, or what Keynes called 'underemployment equilibrium', the creation of such a 'second economy' is a new approach which has not previously been considered. (Rotstein 1985:20)

And from a dynamic viewpoint there are two further advantages, in addition to the subsistence providing effect. One is, as already mentioned, that if the model is suitably designed it is not unreasonable to expect that stimulating effects will radiate from the expansion of the economy brought about by the parallel currency, effects that could reach the formal economy as well, somewhat on the lines of import substitution, in the wake of which further 'domestic' employment would then ensue. Moreover there is the second consideration that there should be no occasion to fear that a local parallel economy of this kind would under *all* conditions solidify into a 'grey area' of economic activity and persist as a permanent 'foreign body'; for a sudden upsurge of investment and demand for labour would be bound to result in a flexible thawing out of the parallel economy as a result of the comparatively better opportunities available in normal employment and the much wider usability of the income derived from it, so that the parallel economy would be reduced anticyclically to a remnant, and a small one at that. So it is rather like a bypass operation in the case of a heart attack, which is useful for relieving arteries that are blocked but does not necessarily have to do permanent duty for them once they are healed.

2   A second advantage claimed for the system is that the subjective consequences and effects of unemployment – the 'process losses' of structural weaknesses in the economy, as it were – can to some degree be made good by the fact that the system offers unemployed workpeople the opportunity of reassuring themselves of the value of their own labour power, of gaining recognition by others and partially overcoming the financial hold-ups in their living conditions:

> The informal economy may not meet the economist's strict criteria of 'efficiency' or high productivity, but its justification is self-evident. When we recognize the enormous waste and loss of income that mark periods of high unemployment, then traditional criteria of efficiency must take second place. Nor can we neglect the human factors: the demoralization, frustration and hopelessness that accompany forced inactivity. (Rotstein 1985:14)

This, too, is reinforced by a somewhat longer-term consideration. According to numerous theoretical papers and forecasts about the future of social security and the social services, it is likely that the purely bureaucratic provision of the necessary services by the state and professionals is not destined to be the pattern of the future, whereas on the other hand far-reaching privatization and commercialization of these services would be frustrated in most countries owing to the serious reservations arising from the forseeably regressive distribution effects of such a strategy. In this dilemma there is a widespread call for a planned change in the structure of the social assistance, services and safety net, often heard as a demand for a change 'from welfare state to welfare society'. It is by no means impossible that the LETS model, or even more the 'service credits' system (see chapter 7 below) which has a similar basis, might represent *one* potentially viable answer and thereby possess a justification for its existence in terms of *social* policy even in the perhaps unlikely event that its function in terms of *economic* policy were to become redundant because of a renewal of full employment.

These two categories of beneficial effects in both economic and social policy were advanced in political discussions in Canada as a basis for the demand that the exchange network based on a local parallel currency should be assisted by government policies. We shall give detailed consideration to the prospects for such demands in chapter 14. At this point we will only touch on the proposals advanced by Professor Rotstein of the University of Toronto in his report copiously cited above. They relate to four points:

1 An employment oriented policy of shortening working hours at all levels and of job-sharing will be easier to implement and justify to the employees affected if they can be shown a well-organized, reliable exchange network up and running outside the formal economy as a 'further option for sustaining productive ability' (1985:72).

2 The considerable need for advertising campaigns and public information activities which experience shows to exist, especially in the initial phase of projects of the LETS type, and the limited effectiveness of the initiators and organizers hitherto available for the task justify the use of limited public assistance for introducting the model through courses and start-up aid. At the same time the extreme sensitivity of such projects to state intervention, sponsorship and regulation should always be kept in mind.

3 One important obstacle to the rapid growth of exchange networks of this kind appears to be that workless citizens who might join them have reason to fear that if they become active participants this might jeopardize their legal claim to receive unemployment benefits. And in fact the upper limits for tax-free subsidiary income in the Canadian unemployment insurance systems are so tightly drawn that there is good reason for this apprehension. Therefore the report calls for a significant raising of this threshold or for incomes received by the workless in 'green' currency to be disregarded.

4 This would have the further advantage that if these thresholds in

unemployment assistance were raised it might lead to several categories of employees temporarily or permanently forsaking employment in the formal labour market, claiming unemployment assistance and then increasing their real income through active participation in the parallel economy. Were this to happen, it would obviously amount to a reduction in the supply of labour, desirable in some circumstances, and consequently a better equilibrium in a – shrinking – labour market.

7

The 'Service Credits' System in the United States

On account of many of the economic, social and historical characteristics of its origins and development, the United States of America can be described not only as *the* homeland of the typical institutions of industrial, commercial and financial capital, but also as the fruitful and innovative field of experimentation in 'alternative', anti-capitalistic and non-capitalistic, ways of organizing production, distribution and consumption. The fecund tradition and continuing vitality of experimentation in economic organization in this country are due in no small measure both to the unique cultural, ethnic, religious and political heterogeneity and fragmentation of American society and to the absence of strong political institutions making for uniformity and regimentation comparable with those found in social and welfare states in Europe.

Although in recent years scientific and political circles have experienced a strong upsurge of interest in those forms of economic and welfare activities that are known in the United States as 'third sector' or 'voluntary sector' (cf. Powell 1987; Ostrander and Langton 1987; also Harman 1982), there is as yet no reliable system of classification for recording those economic phenomena that can be sited within the triangle between private households, the capitalist market economy and the state administration of welfare, and which in the USA display an astonishing vitality. Here we shall not embark on a systematic survey of all the projects, models and economic practices in the USA that are of interest in connection with our subject-matter; instead we shall concentrate on the example of 'service credits'.

Our present purpose is to use the 'service credits' model (SC) to investigate whether the *synthesizing of altruistic, efficient exchange and public interests* which is the enlightened aim of the theorists and initiators of this project appears likely to lend itself to durable implementation. The 'test case' of SC is particularly well suited to an examination of this question, because no other unconventional sociopolitical innovation has in recent times generated such a large amount of theoretical support, private and public promotion, assistance in legislative and administrative circles and media attention as this model.[1]

Theoretical and normative foundations

It was Edgar Cahn who did most of the preparatory and concomitant theoretical work on the SC model. He set out his ideas in a series of lecture papers, consultative opinions, working papers for committees of legislative bodies and so on (see especially Cahn 1986, 1987a). Since the mid-1960s Cahn has worked in the institutional triangle between academic jurisprudence (as Professor of Law at Florida International University, and having been *inter alia* co-founder of the famous Antioch School of Law in Washington), reform-oriented authorities in the American federal government (including working in the Office of Economic Opportunity of the Johnson administration and its 'War against Poverty') and social and civic rights movements (for instance, self-government for the Navajo Indians). The specific theoretical and normative thrust of the ideas Cahn has developed and actively introduced into the political process derives from this scientific and political context. He summarizes the brief antecedents of the reform project in the following words:

> The original proposal developed in 1980 was general in nature: why not create a 'special purpose' local currency to put people and human needs together? In 1983 and 1984, a paper entitled 'Surplus People: A Modest Proposal' received limited circulation, some encouragement and much scepticism. The first applications began to emerge in 1984 and 1985 in the context of the elderly and the manifest need to expand the available supply of home- and community-based care as an alternative to nursing-home care. Legislation was enacted; programs were planned; and by 1986, several experimental efforts were under way. Problems encountered in these first pilot programs were treated as practical issues to be 'worked out'. By and large the problems were resolved successfully on an *ad hoc* basis. (Cahn 1987a:2)

The starting point for this was the critique of society, particularly common in the USA, that the economic arrangements in capitalist societies lead systematically to the existence of unmet needs alongside unused human labour power that *could* fully meet those needs and yet is *prevented* from doing so by the dominant but insufficientl effective distribution pattern of the monetary market economy and the political and administrative apparatus that serves it. The introduction of an alternative and supplementary medium of distribution, that of 'service credits' (based on the same 'bypass operation' principle as that of the Canadian examples cited earlier) is proposed as a remedy for this structural problem. It provides for the introduction of an alternative, supplementary medium of exchange, the 'service credits'. Individual holdings of SCs and the value, that is the purchasing power of the voucher currency, are to be recorded and underwritten by regional bodies (municipalities or federal states). This would enable needed services in the area of 'subprofessional' social services mainly (though by no means exclusively) for elderly and aged citizens to be provided. Traditions and power relationships in the American political system have led Cahn to present his ideas in the form of a defensive front against the state executive, which must be presumed to have a strong aversion to (a) confronting voters and taxpayers with social reforms that are going to cost money, and (b) relinquishing their own bureaucratic and professional functions and responsibilities to agents and groups outside the established system of the social services. Besides the corporative self-interests of the state authorities and their staffs mentioned in the last point, which result in fierce prejudice against self-help and ownwork, three factual objections are also discussed and refuted. These are: (1) the 'problem of quality'; (2) the 'problem of supply', and (3) the 'problem of the withdrawal of altruistic motivations'.

(1)　First as regards the problem of *quality*, the obvious objection that the unskilled labour that has to be mobilized under the SC system is not suitably qualified to meet the needs and demands of the clientele has to be dealt with. There are three counterarguments to this objection: In the first place there is the idea that there must be a strict 'ceiling' to the spectrum of the services in question – that they must consist only of simple services and of performances calling for skills that can be quickly learned. Secondly provision is made for relatively stringent quality assurance procedures which include training courses, detailed rules of conduct (cf. document 2), sample checks, client surveys and so on. These ideas point to a markedly hierarchical trait in the system, so much so that in practice (see below) it shows some disquieting signs of becoming an 'alternative bureaucracy'. In the third place the objection of inadequate quality receives a riposte in the form of a counterproposal that the monopoly powers traditionally claimed by members of the bureaucratic professional service administrations should be 'experimentally' challenged. It is argued that the 'deprofessionalization' of part of the personal social services under the SC system would 'provide an

---

CODE OF ETHICS

The Service Credit Volunteer shall NOT:

1. Use the service recipient's car;
2. Use the service recipient's telephone for personal calls;
3. Burden the service recipient with one's personal problems.
4. Attempt to impose one's religious beliefs or political beliefs on the service recipient;
5. Solicit or accept money, gifts or tips from the service recipient;
6. Bring friends or relatives to the service recipient's home;
7. Consume alcoholic beverages or use medicine or drugs for any purpose other than medical reasons in the service recipient's home or prior to service delivery;
8. Breach the service recipient's privacy or confidentiality.
9. Consume the service client's food or drink.
   (Volunteers may eat their personal lunch in the service recipient's home and use the service recipient's bathroom facilities.)
10. Smoke in the service recipient's home unless prior written approval has been given by BOTH the sponsoring agency supervisor and the family caregiver.
11. Discriminate or treat with less care and concern on account of race, color, national origin, sex, physical condition, handicap or age.

Document 2. The 'Code of Ethics': extracts from very extensive documentation on the rights and duties of those taking part in SC projects for the Workshop on Service Credit Projects, Miami, October 1987

ongoing test of whether each function must be discharged by a fulltime, qualified staff person rather than by an unlicensed, part-time, non-professional' (Cahn 1986:18). This opens up the prospect of an arrangement (always seen as complementary to a considerable 'residuum' of genuinely professional services) within which lay assistants replace professional social workers at an equal, if not higher, level of competence and because of the resulting potential cost savings present at least a partial challenge to the professionals' claim to a monopoly.

Moreover the anti-bureaucratic cast of the model and its critical attitude to the professions rests on the optimistic assumption that the computer technology now available can be used to make management functions simpler and more democratic. Whereas previously the task of identifying the 'suitable' treatment and the 'correct' way to apply it was one that could only be undertaken by trained staff members backed by wide knowledge of the rules and professional experience, nowadays thanks to special computer programs 'matching' can be done by anybody. By utilizing this technology it is possible to effect dramatic economies in administrative (and indeed marketing) transaction costs with equal or even enhanced accuracy, because the computer makes available at the touch of a button knowledge and experience formerly the preserve of professional service-providers:

> A user-friendly, computerised management information system is now fully developed and field tested with the capacity to run on a centralized or decentralized basis, to operate on any scale from PC (with hard disk) to mainframe, and to track credits earned and spent, to permit persons earning credits with one organiation to transfer those credits or spend them with another organization, to maintain quality control reviews in response to complaints. The system has the capacity to match volunteer availability with client requests for service and can do so based on availability, zip code proximity, language ability, special hobbies or skills, mobility problems, smoker- or non-smoker preference, and a host of other variables. . . . It takes less than five minutes to input a comprehensive personal profile of each volunteer, seconds to match any request, and seconds to update the 'bank account' status of each participant. (Cahn 1987a:68)

(2) The *problem of supply* arises from two causes. On the one hand, the service exchange under the SC system cannot be organized comprehensively for *all* clients in need of it, because the effectiveness of the system obviously depends on particular conditions of culture and social space; and on the other hand the target group of older clients is precisely the one that with advancing age will be least able to contribute services into the exchange. Clearly these two circumstances imply the likelihood of considerable gaps in supply, and Cahn thinks that these should be overcome by integrating the service exchange into traditional forms of charitable and philanthropic voluntary work.

For such a tie-up to be effective it is essential that the vouchers earned by giving help and care should not be used solely as consideration for the 'purchase' of other services, but should be equally capable of being gifted to individuals or donated to corporations such as clubs, parishes, trade unions or, in the German context, welfare associations. This would make holdings of vouchers, in other words claims on goods or services, also transferable otherwise than by way of direct exchange. It would mean that family members prevented by such factors as living conditions or distance from giving caring services to elderly relations could be enabled to do so indirectly by earning vouchers where they live, by providing different kinds of services, then making the vouchers available to their needy relatives. Alternatively the vouchers so earned could be transferred to associations as above, which could then use them to provide 'free' services within the ambit of a potentially fully comprehensive network of voluntary lay helpers. This highlights the concept at the heart of the SC system, which consists of systematically combining altruistic motives of voluntary assistance with motives of self-interest; it is designed to make the provision of help capable of circulation, as it were. Good deeds would not only be their own reward – they would earn the further reward of a claim on the services of others.

Cahn believes that the supply potential of SC networks could also grow through the psychological advantage that the equalizing effect of using a time unit for settlements (1 hour of service = 1 hour of service, of whatever kind) would eliminate any 'class distinction' among service providers. The assumption is that under these conditions those taking part would be prepared to perform tasks which, if they had to perform them professionally, they would never undertake because of their 'menial' and 'underpaid' nature, with the implication that the voucher currency would have the effect of neutralizing 'loss of status'. 'There is no loss of status in accepting a form of compensation that is valuable but expressly incomplete. Price represents a "market judgement" of worth; service credits are non-judgemental except to the extent that they confer social approval of an unquantified and unquantifiable amount' (Cahn 1987a:24).

(3)   This appreciation also contains a counterargument against the objection that the provision of personal social services in the form of an exchange is bound to lead to the further *erosion of altruistic motivations*. In the American context this objection is advanced in particular by opponents of the SC system who, like the Red Cross or the charitable organizations of church parishes (see below), call on charitably and philanthropically motivated work by volunteers and use it on behalf of their particular clientele. These organizations are obviously afraid that SC networks might constitute unwanted competition for them, which would as it were entice away what hitherto had been available as potential charitable 'unpaid labour' by offering payment in the form of vouchers for such services. This also came up in our interviews with representatives of German welfare organizations. Normally this fear is cloaked in concern that arrangements of this kind would only result in giving an impetus to an egoism that was in any event widespread, thus aggravating problems of supply in the field of simple personal social services instead of

overcoming them. However, these fears and concerns do not really hold much water because, as has just been shown, it is not the altruistic motives as such that are weakened and, as it were, declared to be 'superfluous'; rather what is weakened and sent into decline is the institutional separation between the 'market' and 'society', between self-interest rationally pursued through exchange and moral obligations communally fulfilled.

The consequence of this 'undifferentiated' principle of the SC system is that it is immaterial whether assistance was given by the helper because of his/her interest in earning vouchers and the return they bring or from a sympathetic obligation in respect of the needs of the recipient – or whether in a given case these two motives are intertwined. Thus the helpers employed by the various clubs and associations are quite free to decide whether (and in what proportions) the credits they earn are to be used for themselves or donated to these organizations, which thus assume the character of a 'bank' for services. From the recipients' point of view this arrangement seems to have the advantage that they are not obliged to feel beholden – often somewhat humiliatingly – to others for the 'goods deeds', but can regard themselves as at least partially the possessors of valid claims on assistance, even if these claims are not on account of their own payments, whether purchases, insurance premiums or taxes, but on account of assistance given previously, claims transferred by others or indeed consideration which the helper himself or herself can claim at a future date. 'To the extent that services are purchased with credits earned, service recipients may perceive themselves as consumers rather than donees' (Cahn 1987a:24). For this reason a 'synergy of altruism and self-interest' organized in this way (Cahn 1986:27) might do more than make donors more willing to provide services; it might also make recipients more willing to call on these services and to accept them even from 'strangers'.

Thus the 'qualitative', 'distributive' and 'moral' objections against the SC system can each be rebutted at the theoretical level with comparatively convincing arguments; but the Achilles' heel of the system remains – and it is a 'political' objection. It rests on the fact that the system could be used as a reason and excuse to run down still further welfare services that have already come under heavy pressure for retrenchment, and to substitute for them an allegedly spontaneous replacement by self-help arrangements in the form of an exchange. The by no means unrealistic political fear that the proposal to supplement inadequate *state* welfare services by *social* welfare services might be taken, either in a spirit of naive liberalism or one of open cynicism, as a means of justifying even greater reductions in the social services is leading in the USA (and similarly in Western Europe in principle) to a dilemma of reform strategy from which there seems to be no easy escape: 'Reasonable solutions would be easy if there were a consensus that the national government could be trusted to reward rather than to exploit voluntarism' (Cahn 1986:34).

This dilemma exists because of the coincidence of three factors. Bureaucracies and professions, including the trade unions and associations within them, defend their common corporative self-interest in their traditional fields of activity and the corresponding monopoly powers attached to them and, as mentioned earlier, they oppose any proposals for partial 'despecialization' and 'communization' of their functions. This opposition, understandable from the viewpoint of their sectional interests, can also be justified by the rationale that it is in the 'best interests' of their clients. Liberal left politicians and social theorists, with their egalitarian leanings, are not well placed to oppose such a stance, and not only because they have much in common socially with the state and municipal officials, professionals and trade unionists involved. For in addition defence against this stance meets with scepticism because the utopian ideology of the social and liberal left lacks credible images of social common interest groupings that could underpin 'social welfare' arrangements by filling out and supplementing the formal welfare state. Whereas the conservative political classes rely on the family, the neighbourhood, the parish or congregation, the 'community' and so on as traditional bulwarks against the sociocultural pathologies of the modernization process in general, and against 'regimentation by experts' in particular (cf. Berger and Neuhaus 1977), the political left is notorious for being unable to 'offer' any equivalent that is both convincing and proof against the very criticism it advances to such good effect against the particularistic, patriarchalist and other 'antiquated' characteristics of conservative concepts of order (cf. Sandel 1988). The left is hard put to it to find an answer to the demand for 'unslanted' forms of social organization that could serve as connecting links for a nonparticularistic 'new subsidiarity' (R. G. Heinze 1986) and ultimately as a leading idea for a 'socialist civil society' that at present can only be formulated as a paradox (cf. Keane 1988). There is a third component to the dilemma in which strategies for reform are caught. In the USA, as in most of the countries in Western Europe, the shift to the right in the balance of political power that occurred during the 1980s provides strong grounds for apprehension that – as the last quotation from Cahn implies – every step 'forward' in the direction of organized *social* readiness to give help and accept responsibility carries the risk of being followed, at least in the short term, by an equal step *backwards* in *state*-organized provision and services: and this circumstance is put to good (that is, bad) use as an alibi and excuse by those on the left who would like reform but are trapped in a conceptual dead end.

How the SC arrangement works

The actual arrangement can be represented by a (rather large) number of communication flows between individual and collective agents. Figure 2 shows these agents and their communication interrelations. In the centre of each network is a 'sponsor' organization, which might be a local welfare association, a parish, a trade union, an organized ethnic group, a hospital, etc. This organization functions as a 'bank', from which the circulation of the service vouchers originates. During an initial phase of its activity the organization receives grants from an external source such as a local council or a private institution to cover its administrative and promotional costs. In addition to the organization and its administrative staff there are three categories of persons taking part in matching needs with services in this exchange network; they are the 'donors', the regular participants, and the 'recipients'.

'Donors' are persons who give voluntary social services as traditionally understood, without receiving vouchers in return – at least not to the full equivalent of the hours they donate. To the extent that they waive remuneration, they are in effect making available 'capital' to the organization in the form of a corresponding number of vouchers, and this capital can then circulate in the exchange network itself. The 'donors' are motivated not only by philanthropic and altruistic considerations; other interest-oriented motives also come into play. Most of them receive, for a very limited period, very modest expenses refunds paid for from the external funds received by the organization. They are also given an induction and training course in which they can acquire elementary skills and knowledge in the social sciences. This human capital formation is at the same time offered as a basic qualification for subsequent occupation in regular social service posts, and the use of public funds for this purpose is justified on the grounds that it promotes the entry or re-entry of persons so qualified into vocational careers. A further inducement is that those taking part in these courses are paid, not indeed in money but in vouchers which (or some of which) can in turn be made available to the organization. For each hour of instruction, students are credited with half the value of an hour of service ('learning credits'). At the end of this training programme an examination is held, and those who pass receive a

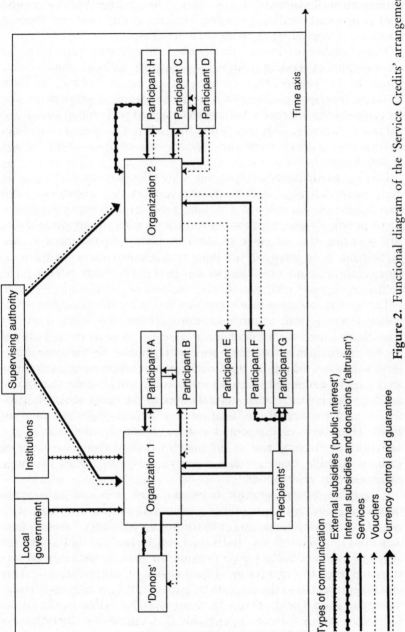

Figure 2. Functional diagram of the 'Service Credits' arrangement

Types of communication

External subsidies ('public interest')

Internal subsidies and donations ('altruism')

Services

Vouchers

Currency control and guarantee

certificate. 'Donors' may also be attracted by the idea that as students or trainees they are taking part in courses which consist partly of the performance of voluntary social work. The sponsoring organization is of course interested in engaging workers of this kind and topping up its own 'capital stock' with their services.

Thus, while the 'donors' participate in the 'capital formation' by a net surplus of services rendered over services utilized, the converse is true of the 'clients'; they do not (yet) possess a credit in the form of saved vouchers, enabling them to make claims on services, or else they are unable for reasons of health or age to perform an equivalent volume of services. This means that they are net recipients of services and receive services from the 'donors' allocated to them by the organization.

Lastly, 'participants' are persons who take part on both sides of the service exchange market. By the services they contribute (also after having passed thorugh a skilling process) they earn claims on a corresponding value from the organization's pool of services. Generally speaking the exchange of services between participant A and participant B is arranged via the organization (active 'matching'), though there is no objection to the two participants effecting the exchange on their own initiative.

The system becomes more complex and more interesting in social policy terms as well as more capable of expansion when it proves possible to interlink two or more local organizations, though only if the two participants concerned are not dependent on the same sponsor. If the networking between the individual sponsor organizations were highly developed, such an association would make it possible for them to give each other mutual cover in the event of service gaps and to perform overall the function of a 'deposit guarantee fund' in kind. Thus services that could not be obtained from one of the networks at the time and in the manner desired could be obtained without quibble from another network, just as airlines exchange passenger seat reservations.

Clearly, however, sponsor networking of this kind calls for a supervising authority not unlike a central bank. Such an authority would first ensure social and intertemporal confidence between participants in each of the individual organizations ('guarantee of deposits') and secondly would provide for the convertibility of services rendered to organization 1 into claims on organization 2. This case is represented in the diagram by participant E, who gives services to organization 1 and obtains in return vouchers (that is, claims on equivalent services) from organization 2. Conceivably the organizations involved might opt for a division of powers on an area basis or a functional division of labour. A further variant that can also be networked between the organizations is shown in the diagram as the relationship between participants F and G and organizations 1 and 2. This represents what might be called the 'micro-altruistic' relationship between participant F, who provides services to organization 2 and receives the appropriate vouchers, and then transfers the vouchers as a gift to her relative, participant G, thus providing G with purchasing power with which to obtain services from organization 1. Finally, the case of participant H might be envisaged, who donates part of her vouchers to the organization, thus occupying an intermediate position between the type of the normal 'participant' and that of the 'donor'. It is also possible to incorporate the facility of financing services by credit; in this case current services are paid for by a formal undertaking by the recipient – or by a third party, who then donates the credit – which can be called in by the sponsoring organization within a specified time, to provide equivalent services.

The prospect of a linkage between sponsoring organizations monitored by a supervising authority implies more than just the possibility of approaching the goal of 'nationwide' cover geographically; it also foreshadows a division of labour and qualitative diversification of the services that would then be available and disposable within the system as a whole. If different categories of services were networked it might for example be possible for vouchers received by a participant for performing personal social services to be spent on repairs or renovations. The range of choices, and hence the attractions of participation, would be increased by a further order of magnitude if, as Cahn fully envisages, the principle of the split currency, of prices being split in proportions to be determined, made it possible to include in the exchange mechanism processing services of which the prime costs, paid in normal currency, could be counted in as transitory items.

Implementing the scheme – some practical examples

As of 1988 local state laws had been passed and bills were under discussion for introducing SC programmes. At federal level, too, a bill was introduced in 1987 (S. 1189 dated 12 May 1987 and H.R.5690 dated 10 October 1986) designed to make federal funds available for periods of not less than five and not more than 15 years for trying out and promoting programmes of this type in individual states. As of 1988 this bill had not yet received approval.

These state laws and bills have many features in common:

• They are aimed exclusively at making caring services available for older people or at tackling the demographic, health, social and economic factors that have led to a dramatic intensification of supply problems in these fields that is likely to persist in the future.

- The laws require the competent authorities in the states concerned to set up an SC programme, but make available only very limited funds, and only for short periods, for implementing the programmes.

- Within the social, practical, financial and time constraints described above, the legislation, which has aroused lively and mainly approving interest in the press (see note 1), in practice permits only small to miniscule local pilot projects to be carried out.

In view of the contrast between the comparatively wide-ranging, long-term approval given by the executive to set up SC programmes and the relatively puny resources allocated to them, this would seem to be a classic example of 'symbolic politics'. In discussions about the legislation the financial tightfistedness was generally justified by saying that if ample resources were granted, large amounts of public money might be used as a 'deficiency guarantee' for honouring vouchers which, though they had been earned within the network, would not be exchangeable within it for the services required.

These peculiarities can be illustrated by the example of the Volunteer Service Credit Program (VSCP) of Florida State, set up under law F.S.410.201 in 1985. The law provides for the organizing of the exchange of non-professional care services through state guaranteed vouchers, but both on the demand and the supply side these are available only to persons over the age of 60 under the programme. The programme is intended to be implemented via a number of local sponsors, who are responsible for recruiting and training volunteers, matching suppliers and requesters, monitoring the quality of the services and checking the needs of the requesters. In the event that credits earned by individuals and the claims on services thereby engendered cannot be met by the service pool of the organizations taking part, the state social service takes over a service (deficiency) guarantee. On this basis five local pilot programmes were established between October 1985 and June 1986. The experiences and results of these programmes were analysed in a thorough evaluation study, also provided for in the law. This study (Barrios 1986) came to the following conclusion:

> The issue of greatest general concern is whether or not the VSCP has proved feasible and statewide implementation should be aggressively promoted. Unfortunately, pilot activity to date has not provided

adequate information for a definitive answer to this question . . . [The] 'test' of the program was simply not adequate to provide a basis for resolving the issue of statewide feasibility. (p. 46)

The laws passed in the state of Missouri and in Washington DC also suffered from the unduly small provision made for pilot schemes. Those in Missouri, passed in 1984, provided for a pilot phase of 17 months for which 75,000 dollars were allocated while in Washington DC the 'Service Credit Volunteer System' was enacted in November 1985 and provided with 100,000 dollars for a period of two years. None of these initiatives can be credited with a serious resolve to test the viability of the project and identify any weak spots, because the restrictions placed on them – reference to only one supply problem, completely inadequate funding and the limited social catchment area of the local organizations – made it impossible to arrive at a fully substantiated judgement one way or the other.

For all that, what was achieved by way of service provision on that pitiably small scale was not perhaps wholly negligible. In one typical case in Washington DC a local association named the Greater Southeast Community Center for the Aging came forward as a sponsoring organization. It had 31 'donors', 74 'recipients' and a core of 58 'participants'. Networking was also established with two other sponsoring organizations (a group of church parishes and an old people's home). The service programme was strictly confined to non-professional helpers and services. It is described as follows in the annual report on the project for 1987:

> The services provided through the program may seem insignificant to those who are physically hale. However, to the frail elderly, many of the tasks performed have made major differences to their personal comfort and feeling of self-worth. Examples of such services are: changing a ceiling light bulb in the bathroom of an arthritic person who is incapable of using a step ladder; defrosting the freezer of a blind person; providing transportation to health facilities, banks, supermarkets, etc., for a large number of program participants who are dependent on public trransportation services which they view as unpredictable and/or unsafe; doing yard work and thus preventing elderly individuals no longer able to cope with mowers and accumulation of leaves and litter from being stigmatized as 'bad neighbours'; and, perhaps most importantly, providing critically needed relief to primary care givers in households impacted by the victims of Alzheimer's disease.

It is worth describing here in greater detail a project that has been promoted since March 1987 by the Robert Wood Johnson

Foundation, the 'Volunteer Interchange Plan' (VIP) in San Francisco, in order to convey a lively impression of how SC works out in practice.[2] VIP is attached to a large centre for the aged belonging to the Pacific Presbyterian Medical Center. The programme, including all external functions such as the production and distribution of information material and relations with politicians, the administration and scientists, is run by two women, one a psychologist who works full-time, the other a social worker giving half of her time to the project. There is also some office help paid by the hour (in vouchers) and, of course, not highly skilled. The demands on the two managers appear to be non-specific and subprofessional, and yet very high in that they involve the performance of administrative and teaching tasks that demand, in addition to bilingual English/Spanish capability, human understanding, 'case consciousness' and the ability to deal with everyday problems and conflict situations. Despite receiving presumably very modest remuneration, the two manageresses have these qualifications to a very high degree. Their office equipment includes a telephone and a small computer, on which it was intended to run a matching programme; this, however, was not up and running at the time of our visit, and it appeared doubtful whether any serious attempt was being made to set it up.

VIP's services are available only to persons aged 60 or over. This restricted circle of recipients is offered only a small range of services, mainly consisting of 'accompanying and providing company', transportation, simple housework and translations (in descending order of frequency). Translation services are needed because 70 per cent of the recipients are Spanish-speaking and need to be helped out in English, especially in correspondence with public authorities. In addition, a small amount of 'heavy' work in the house and garden and in tidying up is organized; this is done by boy and girl students from a high school who 'donate' it without claiming credits. VIP has come to an arrangement with an expensive, well-to-do private high school that at any time two scholars can perform their 'community work', which forms part of the school curriculum, by giving services to old people.

Recruitment of participants – full participants, donors and clients – is an ongoing task of the programme, and it calls for greater efforts than were originally envisaged. There is a turnover of personnel when people move, become ill or die, not to mention as well the reluctance of some 'clients' to make themselves known and enquire about services, so that they have to be encouraged to do so. The project managers have also become aware of another trend, which they deplore; partners brought together by the programme 'drop out' after a time but then continue the exchange of services at the level of personal friendship and neighbourly help, without these transactions being 'credited' to the programme. One reason why this trend towards informality at the level of personal friendship and help is not welcomed is that it leads to a falling off in quality control and insurance protection. By the time the project had been running for ten months it had experienced many ups and downs both in membership and time allocated, and in January 1988 it mustered about 200 persons of all categories; at last count, 325 recorded hours had been 'converted'. A striking feature is that much emphasis is placed on pride, self-respect, public recognition and the like in canvassing for members and in public relations work. The acronym selected bears this out – VIP: very important person. A leaflet soliciting for members carried the sentence: 'We are implementing a new system of assisting each other. . . . WE ARE PART OF THE FUTURE.'

The introductory and training courses are not primarily geared to imparting technical skills, which are usually so simple that volunteers do not have to be taught them; the main emphasis is on creating relationships of cooperation, trust and responsibility.[3] The declared aim of the courses and events, held monthly, is 'to build a community' – to instil attitudes and develop routines that will make for smooth running of the programme. The women in charge of the programme appear to have in mind something akin to the creation of a professionally supervised and stimulated association culture. For the immediate future it is intended to enlist the services of a community college to run courses for SC programme volunteers within the ambit of its further education activities. Attendance at training classes totalling six hours is a required before participating in the programme as a volunteer. There are also further classes where attendance is rewarded with credit vouchers; their subject-matter includes some rather advanced social and gerontological curricular material.

The key task for the administrators in responding to inquiries and notifications of need is to provide services that are of adequate quality, timely and transaction cost effective (especially as regards journey time and cost), while avoiding friction, complaints, unpunctuality and so on. At present this is done by a process of 'spontaneous matching'. On the basis of personal experience and assessment, sometimes supplemented by handwritten notes and tabulated data, the managers rapidly reach a tentative solution (sometimes with a fallback arrangement as well), which they then speedily set up by telephone. The aim is to satisfy the requirement within 24 hours or less. An important aspect, which has always to be borne in mind in the specific case, is the language capabilities of the persons involved (English and/or Spanish). It is a striking fact that both the number of programme participants and the number of hours exchanged are still at a level at which this technique of 'spontaneous matching' does not appear to be reaching the limits of its capacity. But aside from that, it is questionable whether computerizing and formalizing the matching process would be feasible with a large volume, because the process plainly involves numerous experiential values and assessment skills which it would be difficult to formalize. This might be another reason why the development of the computer program (which the sponsor is promoting and calling for) is making such slow progress.

VIP's management is trying to introduce forms showing services requested and given (see document 3). The reason for this interest in having complete records of the actual turnover is the need to have information as to reliability, satisfaction, etc., for future matching. Another reason is that only recorded hours can generate credit claims, and hence complete accounting records are in the interest of the donors. But the administration, too, has a strong interest, for the success of the pilot project and the chances of its being continued and extended – providing continued employment for the organizers – are crucially dependent on whether the sponsoring organization and the hospital can be convinced that the 'turnover' justifies its continuance; and the evaluation criteria of the medical centre and the old people's home are – the managers complain – conservative and formal. Besides the interest in having a complete record of all services rendered, there remains the interest in quality control: VIP's managers believe that as a supplement to the central clerical work this function could be decentralized to a network of VIP participants who would provide a followthrough by advising, matching and supervising the service exchange.

Persons wishing to join the VIP programme as suppliers of services have to complete an entry form (rather demanding from a data protection point of view) and accept a number of obligations relating to confidentiality and automobile insurance. There is a group civil liability and accident insurance for both service providers and recipients. The managers consider this to be important, because it is the only way the marked privacy orientation of the clientele can be neutralized: nobody would allow an outsider into their own kitchen or go into somebody else's kitchen unless there were a guaranteed safety net against mistakes and accidents. Apart from its function of lowering inhibition thresholds, insurance is also important in promoting complete registration, because only if the provision of a service is notified in advance can an insurance claim be made if something goes wrong.

So far guarantee problems – relating to ability to pay – have not arisen. At present they are being partially circumvented by the element of compulsory work done by high school pupils which, as

VOLUNTEER INTERCHANGE PLAN
225 30TH STREET
SAN FRANCISCO, CALIFORNIA 94131
(415) 285-5615

RECIPIENT
NAME _____

REGISTRATION
NUMBER _____

SIGNATURE _____

VOLUNTEER
NAME _____

REGISTRATION
NUMBER _____

SIGNATURE _____

SERVICES (S) PROVIDED   DATE PROVIDED   NUMBER OF HOURS

RECORDED IN INDIVIDUAL ACCOUNT BY WHOM? _____
DATE _____

RECORDED IN AGGREGATE ACCOUNT BY WHOM ? _____
DATE _____

VOLUNTEER INTERCHANGE PLAN
225 30TH STREET
SAN FRANCISCO, CALIFORNIA 94131
(415) 285-5615

REQUEST FORM

Taken By: _____
Date: _____

Service Consumer: _____

Address: _____

X - Streets: _____

Telephone No.: _____   Bus Line: _____

Service Requested: _____

Special Instructions: _____

Service Provider: _____

Provider's Comments: _____

Consumer's Comments: _____

Number of Credits Awarded _____   Credits Recorded 1
To Provider _____
To VIP Bank _____
To Other , Name _____

Document 3. Credit voucher form of the Volunteer Interchange Plan in San Francisco (reduced)

mentioned above, represents a subsidy to the programme. The project managers are, however, giving thought to additional hedging measures. One problem as yet unsolved is that many participants put in claims for services even though not urgently in need of them, just because they have accumulated a certain amount of credits. This could be connected with doubts regarding the long-term viability of the project, an aversion to the risk of the currency becoming valueless. This sometimes leads to claims on services being submitted unexpectedly and in large blocks, entailing severe problems of matching. Two ways of overcoming or providing against such unwelcome spurts of business were under discussion. A limit of, say, two months could be placed on the validity period of the credits, making it difficult to accumulate large holdings; or else a limit both on the supply and demand side could be placed on usage per person per week. This would prevent service providers from becoming virtually full-time 'helpers out', and dissuade recipients from making sudden 'large purchases'.

Appraisal and conclusions

Up to the present, service networks of the SC type have been tried out in practice on such a small scale from every point of view that the experience garnered and assessed in the USA does not permit any well-grounded conclusions to be drawn. This is revealed by the fact that discussions about this system among American politicians and specialists are dominated by theoretical, normative and hypothetical views rather than by empirical findings about successes and failures. The following assessment is based on the unpublished record of a hearing in the US Senate on 12 November 1987 (US Senate 1987).

It appears that the American Red Cross is the foremost opponent of programmes of this type and of the extremely irresolute steps taken to give them a legislative framework. This organization has the support of 20,000 paid staff and no less than 1.5 million voluntary helpers in the USA. At the hearing of the US Senate Committee on Labour and Human Resources, Subcommittee on Aging, on the draft of a federal law to promote SC programmes in the federal states a woman representative of the American Red Cross advanced the following arguments against the SC model (cited in US Senate 1987). She said that the model contradicted the *philosophy and ethic of voluntary labour*. The spirit of voluntary work ('voluntarism') was 'a very American phenomenon and deeply embedded in the American character . . . and in our history since the earliest colonial days'. She expressed the fear that the widespread, intense interest in the organized exploitation and increased use of voluntary work could tend 'to dilute the original concept or inadvertently transform it beyond recognition'. The essence of voluntary work consisted in 'not receiving a *quid pro quo*'. Consequently the infiltration of a system of exchange into work done by volunteers must inevitably lead to the atrophy of its 'spirit', especially when, as in the SC system, the qualitative differences between individual services were levelled out and the balancing of supply with demand was achieved by a certain amount of administrative 'external arbitration'. This line of argument, which of course may have an unavowed background of 'organizational egoism' in associations dependent on 'traditional', that is unpaid voluntary work, and which is found in Germany in milder forms, constitutes a sizeable obstacle placed by 'social morality' in the way of the organized use of the potential of service exchange networks. Therefore any attempts to exploit this potential in the European context must face the question: can a 'stable mixture' (in place of antagonism and mutual sniping) be achieved between self-interested and altruistic motives for participating and providing services, and if so, how?

A second controversy of principle surrounding the SC system relates to the *valuations for tax purposes* and consequences of the system. A study of opinions and decisions in the matter made available to us in the US by the Finance Ministry and its subordinate regional authorities leaves us with the impression that it is their intention to leave the position as regards tax law completely unclarified until the volume and quality of the new interest in voluntary labour networked into an exchange system can be better forecast, while at the same time both the initiators and sponsors of such networks fear, and with reason, that inconsistent decisions by the tax authorities could destroy the system of non-monetary exchange. For if (to assume the worst case) taxes on income and holdings of vouchers had to be paid in ordinary currency, many potential participants would find participation completely unattractive to them. As Cahn says in an implementation study: 'A taxed service credit program . . . would deter many if not most individuals from earning service credits. Given a choice of volunteering and being taxed – and volunteering and not being taxed [for example with the Red Cross] or not volunteering at all, it is not hard to predict that no one will choose to be taxed for volunteering' (1987b:25).

Advocates of the SC system believe that there are two possible escape routes from this uncertain and potentially threatening situation: One of these exits is a *defensive* one. It involves claiming tax exemption on the ground that social services organized in exchange networks are charitable, non-profitmaking activities conducive to the public good. To do this it is necessary to demonstrate the difference between SC projects and those 'barter clubs' which under US tax law are incontestably subject to taxation. In the case of such barter exchanges the income derived from exchanges in kind is valued at 'shadow prices' in ordinary currency, and the recipients of this income have to pay the assessed tax *in dollars*. This defensive argument does, however, entail two problems. In the first place the endeavour to claim tax-exempting 'public benefit' excludes a possible and potentially desirable expansion of the networks beyond the narrow confines of simple social care services, because it introduces the ever-present risk that the tax authorities will then regard SC networks as barter clubs. Besides this, the sponsors of traditional voluntary work are using their sometimes considerable influence, spurred on perhaps by an understandable dislike of competition, to interpret the concept of the public weal so restrictively that even the social services undertaken by SC projects will no longer be covered by it.

Such risks of political semantics lead to the consideration of another escape route, going more on to the *offensive*. It involves accepting that holdings in Service Credits are taxable, but paying the taxes not in dollars but with voucher currency, since the income to be taxed was earned in that currency. The upshot would be that the taxmen themselves would have some holdings in the currency, which would at once give it legitimacy as a currency officially recognized as a medium of payment; there would also be the further and even stronger advantage that sums in this currency could not be used for anything other than subsidizing SC projects, such as remunerating administrative work needing to be done in such enterprises, which otherwise would in any event be paid for partially in voucher currency (see Cahn 1987a:10, 65).

A further dilemma that plays a part in the debate in America about the SC programme arises from the difficulty of discovering the optimum extent of regulation of SC projects by laws and authorities. On the one hand it is clear that too little assistance from and regulation by the authorities condemns the projects from the outset to the fate of a miniscule self-help undertaking without any significance from the standpoint of welfare policy, because it is impossible to see how the start-up and other transaction costs (such as confidence building between different networked organizations) could be provided other than by the use of public funding and helpful guidelines backed by the public authorities. But conversely the risk of over-regulation, in which SC projects would become fiefs of the administration, is viewed as equally perilous. Once legislators and public authorities were to incur the suspicion that their concern is not to tap *additional* sources of welfare but to subjugate potential for self-help in order to *replace* services hitherto provided from public funds, this would not only tarnish the 'political' credibility of the system; it would also offend the 'moral' preparedness of potential participants to take part. Treading the fine borderline between over- and under-regulation in the strategy of reform is a problem that certainly cannot be solved by general principles and guidelines, but only step by step in the light of experience. The balance of opinion in America on this question, reflected in the media commentaries quoted, favours proceeding with care in creating conditions in which the system may have a chance to develop, but not banking on its success. The instruments available to state intervention, namely money and laws, are obviously not the right ones for bringing an exchange system into life – since this is a system based not on money but on a currency of vouchers, not on formalized rights and duties but on freedom to participate. It follows that if setbacks are to be avoided the boundary between 'the system' and 'the outside world' cannot be crossed 'in one bound'; it can only be negotiated, if at all, by way of indirect encouragement, by providing helpful conditions without strings and by a 'supply policy' which rewards and supports promising initiatives after they have been proven rather than 'picking winners' in advance and taking them under the wing of authority (see Cahn 1987a:14ff.).

Finally, a fourth thread in the hard-fought debate about the SC system concerns the target group and the range of services to be offered. As we have seen, the laws enacted and under preparation in North American states on this matter are very closely geared to a single pressing social problem, that of care and assistance for old people in the community. This visible problem-relatedness may well have been the most important reason for the public acclaim and the *legislative success* scored by the system; but it may also have been one of the main reasons for the *failure in practice* that has to be acknowledged when the paucity of the results achieved so far is contrasted with the size of the problem. This apparent paradox is explained if we reflect that only a multifunctional exchange network operating in large population groups comprising a variety of age and social status will generate the incentive to participate, and that, for this reason, only a functionally 'diffuse' network can grow to the order of magnitude at which it can become self-supporting without the need for expensive government subsidies. But it is much harder to mobilize political pressure for such a functionally diffuse pro-gramme, that is, one not geared to specially needy target groups, than in favour of an obviously needy target group.

Critics of the legislative initiatives so far undertaken are therefore advocating that the starting point and sponsor should be a consortium of social associations (churches, trade unions, welfare organizations, etc.) rather than state policy itself. The first step would consist not in organizing a *specific* service programme for particular groups, but in developing an *alternative modus* of welfare enhancing activities and exchange relationships (cf. Coughlin and Meiners 1987). At least this approach would be more likely to result in the SC system's being no longer regarded as a limiting case of the 'single product economy', whereby the specific supply bottlenecks of specific social groups were to be bypassed, but rather as a supplementary system of production and exchange embodying a certain 'normative process benefit'.

8

The Netherlands: A Case Study of the Exchange Economy

The welfare state in the 1980s and the rediscovery of the exchange economy

The most important feature of the socioeconomic and political situation of the Netherlands in the 1980s was a high level of unemployment accompanied by a progressive dismantling of state welfare services. Many of the unemployed feel that it is useless to attempt to re-enter paid employment, and in consequence they are wholly dependent on help from the social services. Those who remain out of work for long fall to the lowest level of social assistance entitlement, a level at which they can only cater for the elementary needs of living. Furthermore the efforts of the state and of the public assistance services to effect savings on rent allowances, health services, public transport, etc., result in a worsening of the living standards of those sections of the population that are not economically active. Handicapped persons, young people, students, divorced women, foreign workers and the elderly lack adequate disposable incomes with which to buy themselves the goods and services they need in the formal economy. It is estimated that during the recession of the 1980s these lowest income groups lost 15 per cent of their purchasing power.[1] A minority of the unemployed is able to maintain a certain standard of living through informal economic activities, for example through occasional work on the 'black' or 'grey' market, on traditional and new forms of home working and so on. Yet many fear that by so doing they will lose their entitlement to state benefits. Moreover they frequently lack the qualifications, social contacts and other qualities that would enable them to participate in the informal economy.

These impoverished households contrive to improve their standard of living mainly through the so-called 'neighbourhood economy', that is through exchanging goods and services for only partial payment, or none, within their own households and within a network of connections among relatives, friends and neighbours. However, the decreasing size of households, the increasing distance from relatives and friends and the growing anonymity of neighbourly relations within cities inhibit the formation of such informal economic relations. These same social developments also bar the way to a return to lifestyles associated with large families and traditional neighbourly relationships. One possible modern alternative to traditional patterns of this kind would be a system whereby informal relations between households were organized under the aegis of an exchange network.

Since the mid-1980s there have existed in the Netherlands what are known as service exchanges, most of them formed on the initiative of the National Association of Centres for Voluntary Work (Landelijke Vereniging van Vrijwilligerscentrales). These are non-commercial projects for organizing the exchange of goods on a small scale, with the primary object of providing services to people who have low incomes but much free time, and of helping to raise their skill levels.

Lately, however, the exchange networks have attracted attention in the general political debate in the Netherlands about the 'crisis of the welfare state'. In this debate the Dutch government has stated that its reforms in the area of the social services will be governed by the principle of a 'caring society'. This pattern is to be used in an endeavour to mobilize spontaneous neighbourly assistance and care services through moral appeals, especially as a replacement for state services to older people.[2]

In the ensuing debate many voices were raised in favour of non-monetary exchange and assistance networks, which could help to mitigate the financial pressures on the welfare state and on individual households. Of the positions adopted in these scientific and political discussions about arrangements for the provision of social services two are of the 'informal' variety and two 'formal'. They are:

- the informal provision of services in the framework of the informal or neighbourhood economy;
- informal provision of services in an organized way, namely through involving organized voluntary labour and self-help groups;
- the supply of services by non-commercial welfare institutions, organized and assisted by the state; and
- the commercial supply of services through service enterprises operating in the market economy.

Latterly the debate has been concentrated mainly on the two first-named measures as potential substitutes for social services organized by the state, since the last-named measure (commercial supply) is generally held to be too expensive for most of the service consumers (see Zandstra 1987).

Questions

Our empirical survey of exchange networks in the Netherlands was geared to three research questions, as will also be the following account of our findings:

(1)   First we have to establish a *typology* of the various kinds of organized ownwork. On the basis of this typology the elements that are critical for the viability/non-viability and the specific effectiveness of these projects, initiatives and systems can then be pinpointed.

(2)   Secondly we examine the social, economic, cultural and ideological background and *context variables* of such initiatives, and of the social space they occupy. Who takes part in them, who initiates them, what specific goods and services are produced and exchanged, and how large are the substitution effects *vis-a-vis* the formal economy?

(3)   Lastly we inquire into the *future outlook* for moneyless networks of this kind. In order to assess their prospects of continued effectiveness we have to take account of their growth pattern, what causes them to stagnate or collapse, reported and observed difficulties and the solutions that are suggested or adopted.

The method adopted in this research was mainly that of sending written questionnaires to initiators of and participants in such projects.[3]

Types of moneyless exchange networks

At the beginning of our survey we identified 41 institutions, groups or persons that were currently organizing or had organized open exchange networks. These included 35 cases dedicated to the exchange of services, while in six cases the main activity was the exchange of goods. The networks concentrating on the exchange of goods included several that dealt in secondhand articles, one for the exchange of works of art and one apartment letting agency. However, in practice our survey was largely confined to service exchange initiatives, and we concentrated our written survey on projects for which we managed to discover the addresses. These initiatives can be distinguished according to (a) type of target group, (b) type of goods and services exchanged, (c) method of operation, and (d) the social milieu in which they work.

With regard to (a): In general the projects concern members of population groups who have both a large amount of uncommitted leisure time and small incomes. Many extremely large social groups come into this category – the unemployed, part-time workers, handicapped people, housewives and the elderly. Some of the projects are universal exchange networks in which anybody who subscribes to the current rules can take part; but some of the projects have decided to work with a narrowly circumscribed group, for example, to work with persons in receipt of social assistance, or to confine their coverage to women. There are also projects dealing almost exclusively with old people, as well as 'associations of young and old' (Jong en Oud Trust) or what are known as 'guild' projects, which have adopted the aim of organizing the exchange and transfer of the knowledge and skills of older people to other groups (see also Evers 1988:159f.).

With regard to (b): Depending on the range of goods and services they offer, the groups can be divided into those with an open, differentiated range and those that restrict themselves to particular services such as childcare, the communication of knowledge and skills, cooperation with hobbies and leisure activities.

With regard to (c): These initiatives can be further subdivided according to whether they operate wholly on a basis of moneyless exchange or whether they make partial use of the money medium in their activities. An example of the latter group is the Wisselwerk benevolent association in Alkmaar, which originally began as an effort on behalf of the unemployed and soon found that many of its clients were not in a position to 'pay for' the services they received with services of their own; these people were therefore permitted to pay the organization in money for the services they had received. In practice only a minority of participants now meet their obligations in kind. There is also a core group of full-time voluntary helpers, providing services to the most needy clients, such as households on the lowest scale of social welfare payments. In effect these helpers are working as an unpaid appendage to the municipal social services. So, in these cases, mutual help and the exchange of services are replaced by charitable work by volunteers, supported by gifts or public assistance. The reason for this is the internal division in the impoverished section of the population between a small 'active' part, which provides services, and a predominating 'passive' part, which participates only on the demand side. This initiative illustrates the transition from organized self-help and ownwork based on exchange equivalence to a form of charitable activity.

With regard to (d): As regards the areas covered by the operations in which exchange networks are active, there are as many cases where the activities are confined to a suburb or a residential area as there are cases looking to the whole town as a catchment area. One reason why projects limit their areas of operation is that they have been founded by bodies that are themselves rooted in a particular district; another reason may be one of homogeneity, because it has been decided that participants must to some extent be acquainted, have social backgrounds that are not too dissimilar and live near one another. Obviously these conditions are best fulfilled in a circumscribed neighbourhood. Conversely the larger projects taking the whole town for their catchment area are based on the expectation that a larger number of participants can be gained in this way.

Of more than 30 initiatives that actually operated a moneyless exchange system, only half survived the initial phase; the other half ceased operating after a shorter or longer period of activity. In March 1988 we encountered 17 active exchange networks with up to 1,250 registered members. Most of these were small groups working in a city district or a village; six out of the 17 networks stated that their operations covered a whole town.

Many of these projects had only recently begun to operate, most of them since 1985. From 1985 onwards the National Association of Centres for Voluntary Work was active in propagating the idea of exchange networks (cf. Landelijke Vereniging van Vrijwilligerscentrales 1987). It drew its inspiration from British and US examples (Tit for Tat, in Edinburgh, The Learning Exchange, in Chicago) and tried to transplant those patterns on to Dutch soil. In a project group dedicated to the 'new voluntarism', the various organizational and legal aspects of service exchange networks were investigated. On the basis of information material supplied by this project group the initiative was taken up by eight local centres, and local institutions such as women's groups, initiatives of the unemployed and children's shops took part in these projects. Where individuals took the initiative they were (unemployed) academics and social workers, and in some cases housewives. In general women, who after all are strongly represented in the official social services, are in the majority among the initiators of exchange networks of this kind.

The majority of the exchange networks we investigated had arisen in towns of differing sizes; only five of them were in villages or in the country. When these projects fail, this does not appear to be due primarily to space factors, since projects have collapsed in large, medium-sized and small towns and in villages. But all the networks that are working well are based in large towns (capitals of provinces) such as Amsterdam, Utrecht and Groningen, all of them also towns with an enlightened sociocultural climate.

Objectives and motives of the initiators

Among the social and economic problems cited most frequently by the initiators as motivating the founding of exchange networks are the following, in decreasing order of importance:

- the increasing isolation of households;
- the low incomes of the target group;
- the high and increasing price of the provision of services;
- Unemployment.

This indicates that the fight against the deleterious consequences of social isolation and marginalization is one of the most important aims of the projects. The object is to improve contacts between those affected by unemployment and other groups of the population who have to rely on their own powers and abilities, by the exchange of services and the activation of their own special skills – between single person households, recipients of social assistance, single women who are out of work, households with small children or old persons needing care. The objective is to promote exchange between persons in a similar social situation and to help them to begin cooperating, learning together and undertaking joint leisure activities.

Furthermore, exchange networks are also regarded as being an alternative to traditional forms of voluntary work. Whereas conventional voluntary work suffers from the disadvantage that the recipients always feel themselves to be in a dependent relationship and in the position of a supplicant, the aim of mutual help arrangements is to replace this one-sided dependence with reciprocity. But there are reasons for replacing the traditional forms with reciprocity even for the givers of voluntary help. In the first place there is the important problem that as the average age of the population increases there will be a correspondingly fewer people ready and able to perform voluntary social services. Moreover many people who are prepared to do voluntary work do not wish to do so under the aegis of an organization or a public authority; they prefer to help other people directly and without intermediaries. The mutual voluntary exchange of services in the form of exchange networks is viewed as a possible solution to the problem of satisfying the growing demand for unpaid services and making up for the diminishing appeal of such work and the declining number of people coming forward to do it (see van Loon 1987). It is noticeable that the organizers do not maintain that the establishment of such networks should be a substitute for social services provided by the welfare state. In practice, more modest, pragmatic and relatively apolitical considerations of benefit tend to play a larger part, centring on such concerns as how to organize mutual childcare, to create opportunities for the profitable use of uncommitted leisure time and to combat social isolation.

Working methods and patterns of organization

The principal hallmarks of the exchange networks are that they endeavour to organize the exchange of services and the mutual employment of skills (and in many cases produced goods as well) between persons who otherwise were not acquainted and who enter into transactions outside the normal market economy and without the intermediation of money. Those taking part in such networks can purchase services from one another without money if they are prepared to offer services in exchange. As was explained earlier, these counterpart services do not have to be offered to the person from whom the earlier service was received: in accordance with the principle of 'serial reciprocity' (cf. Boulding 1981:31f.) they can be performed for third persons. It should be realized that compensation by the serial reciprocity method takes place in three stages separated in time. In the first step, A procures a service from B and in return gives B a claim; in the second step A works off his debt by performing a service for C; the third step consists of C's performing a service for B, thus cancelling B's original claim on a counterconsideration. In this sense serial reciprocity can be regarded as a circulation or spiral of claim currencies. It would be very difficult to construct such a spiral of claims warrants without a suitable medium of transaction to act as a substitute for the 'money value' and without a mechanism for monitoring the issue of 'vouchers'. But if this moneyless method of settlement works well and a sufficiently wide range of goods and services is on offer within the system, geared to the demand, then it is in principle possible to exchange a large number of services and skilled tasks without making use of money as a medium.

Exchange is mainly based on the principle that 'one good turn deserves another', meaning that all services are treated as if they were equal, irrespective of how much trouble they require or the quality of the result. The non-monetary unit of settlement is based on this principle: with services it is usually the time taken, that can be measured in hours or by some other standard; in the case of goods, in some cases a points system has been developed. Because the service and the consideration are not exchanged directly and between the same people, bookkeeping becomes necessary to carry accounts showing the amount of the 'claims' and 'debts' of each participant. This may consist of written records, either through a central administration or through settlement notes completed by the participants themselves. Or it may be effected in a less formal, explicit manner, as is done in some of the smaller networks which leave it to their members to keep a mental count of services performed and 'owed', as is usual between friends and neighbours. Consequently we can distinguish two kinds of exchange networks, namely those in which the functions of bookkeeping and of bringing supply and demand together are performed centrally by a kind of 'service exchange'; and those in which only personal data on the participants and the type of their supply and demand are recorded centrally, and the central office does nothing more than send out to the participants lists of services offered and required.

We can now discuss to what extent organizational features, and in particular the extent of active 'brokering' by the central office, improve the operation of such networks. Of the 20 networks about which we have information on this point, 12 have active 'matching' from the centre while the other eight leave this function to the members. In total the 'active' networks have more participants than the others (883 against 185 for the other networks). Yet paradoxical as it may seem, it is clear that the networks that actively promote exchanges have a lower participation rate (based on the proportion of regularly active registered members) than those in which matching is left to the participants themselves.

The range of goods and services exchanged

Most of the services rendered in exchange networks consist of simple assistance, care and odd jobs; in addition, knowledge and skills are imparted either in private lessons or in classes organized for a whole group of persons. Only in a minority of exchange networks does the exchange of goods play a significant part. More than half of the projects also bring people together for hobbies and leisure activities. In most instances the exchange networks try to place the emphasis on organizing services that are difficult to obtain in the formal economy, either because they are very out of the ordinary or because (like technical repairs) they are very expensive.

Examples 1 and 2 show lists of the range of services offered by one of the smaller networks (in The Hague) and by a medium-sized one (in Utrecht). The list of services offered and requested in the Hague network clearly shows how the structure of the services exchanged is connected with the sex of the participants. Women generally ask for help with technical odd jobs or with simple, undemanding work about the house. Men offer technical services regarded as 'typically male' and in return ask for household and caring services. The offer and demand lists of the two networks also show how hard it is to harmonize supply and demand. It is in fact unlikely that all offers will be taken up and all notified needs met. Because of this mismatch, queues build up on both sides of the exchange structure and quite a number of participants find that their particular offers and needs cannot be traded even in the long term. Nevertheless, the more participants there are the greater the likelihood that the 'right' offer will meet the 'right' demand and vice versa. These matching problems go a long way towards explaining why small networks are not viable and why medium-sized and large ones tend to cease growing sooner or later.

Apart from the quantitative scale effect of large networks, they also exhibit a qualitative advantage. Because they have more members they have a larger pool of skills and capabilities to draw on. Consequently the exchange does not have to be confined to odd jobs; more complex services can also be placed on offer. For example, in the Amsterdam network not only housework, gardening and cooking are offered but also technically more demanding skills such as repairs to machinery and equipment, for example electric alarm clocks and washing machines, piano tuning, language and computer lessons, and even the services of architects and psychotherapists. Hence the scale effects of the larger networks provide an obvious explanation of the fact that large-scale networks with a whole town as their catchment area find it easier to overcome their difficult start-up problems than the smaller networks.

Features of the social structure of participants

More women than men take part in exchange networks in the Netherlands. Most participants are between the ages of 20 and 50; the average age of the Amsterdam network is nearly 42. By professional training a comparatively high proportion of members belong to the higher, better qualified groups (a large number of women in the medical and caring professions and men with higher technical or tertiary education, such as teachers, scientists and journalists). This

Example 1. Supply and demand list of a small network, Zeehelden-kwartier, The Hague, operating in 1986/87, 18–20 participants

Required (by)	*Offered (by)*
Ironing shirts, sewing (woman)	Ironing, washing, cooking, assistance with housework (woman)
Painting or priming kitchens, WCs and bathrooms (man)	Painting, woodwork, looking after pet animals (woman)
Wallpapering and painting (woman)	
Transporting and connecting up a washing machine (woman)	Painting, technical and repair service (man)
Simple household tasks, knitting a dress and other articles of clothing (woman)	Transport, simple technical and repair services, typing (woman)
Knitting socks for children (woman)	Practical household tasks (woman)
Repairing windows and roller blinds accompanying on weekend cycle tours (woman)	Sewing (woman)
Help with moving furniture (man)	Knitting and babysitting (woman)
Help with taking down a room ceiling (man)	Technical and repair services, changing lights, connecting water supply (man)
Furniture repairing (woman)	Simple household tasks (woman)
Cleaning gas-heating (woman)	Repairing toys, gardening, planting/replanting (woman)
Regular babysitting one evening a week, and sometimes at weekends as well (family)	Drawing and painting lessons, making earrings, teaching knitting, babysitting (woman)
Sharpening scissors (woman)	Housework, shopping (woman)
	Polishing silver, looking after animals, cooking, windowcleaning (woman)
	Taking dog out, shopping (man)
	English lessons, technical and repair services (family)

Example 2. Supply and demand list of a medium-sized network, Dit voor Dat, Utrecht, 1988, 77 participants

Suggestion list	Requested	Offered
Bicycle repairs	x	x
Winemaking	x	
Take meals together	x	x
Photocopying		
Learn garden planting		
Learn billiards		
Take up music	x	x
Play volleyball		
Transport services	x	x
Gardening	x	x
Learn to read music		x
Paint a door	x	x
Exchange holiday experiences		
Flower arranging		x
Feed cats	x	x
Go shopping together		x
Write poetry		
Learn to dance		
Painting/drawing	x	x
Mathematics lessons		
Clean out attics		x
Bake cakes		x
Make dolls		
Train a dog		
Develop films and photographs		x
Look after children		x
Type manuscripts		x
Haircutting	x	x
Teaching chess		x
Acting as a grandmother/grandfather		
Clothes washing	x	x
Giving a lift	x	
Partner at card games	x	x
Make surprise gifts		
Learn kite-flying		
Look after plants		
Do photoreportage		x
Exchange collections		
Do-it-Yourself advice		
Knit a sweater	x	x

Example 2. Continued

Suggestion list	Requested	Offered
Start a pop group		
Change the oil on a car		
Go for seaside walks	x	x
Model posing		
Organize a party		
Mend toys		
Teach word processing		
Run errands		x
Start reading circles		
Give piano lessons		x
City tour guide		
Make furniture		x

may have something to do with the present-day structure of the population in Amsterdam, where the traditional industrial working classes mostly live in suburbs while the skilled members of the new middle classes live in the city centre; it might also reflect the fact that initiatives of this kind have a particular attraction for people with something of an 'alternative' mentality. Be that as it may, the manual, technical and traditional craft occupations are very under-represented among the participants. This vocational cross section of the participants is something of an anomaly in view of the strong demand for technical and manual odd jobs, especially from women participants.

Other networks were unable to give us the vocational breakdown of their membership, but it is plain that a high proportion of participants is not looking for regular paid employment. In the Amsterdam exchange network this proportion is as high as 70 to 80 per cent, including those who are unemployed, and the composition of the groups in Alkmaar and Utrecht is similar. Most of the participants receive a comparatively low income from various state funds. It would therefore be true to say that the exchange projects recruit their members predominantly among groups of persons with low incomes and a comparatively large amount of free time. Yet all in all they have not yet succeeded in recruiting more than a minute proportion of the large number of persons falling into that category.

Arrangements for exchange

The services are accounted for between the participants mostly on the basis of working time accounts (the unit being hours or parts of a day). Only two of the networks surveyed have developed a points system whereby the differing value of the various services can be brought into account. Four more networks have entirely dispensed with an accounting medium: transactions consist mainly of bartering services. Furthermore in two of these cases no account whatever is taken of qualitative differences: all services are regarded as being equally 'valuable'.

In most of the projects the participants have to account for the services they give or receive by way of accounting forms or vouchers recording their 'debt' or 'credit'. The simple principle of this settlement method is illustrated by a babysitting circle in Groningen. On joining, each member receives ten blue cards with which parents can 'pay' a babysitter. People who wish to be permanent members of the circle have, of course, to 'earn' continued membership by giving services paid for with more blue cards.

With all the above settlement procedures the system is self-regulating, and the organizers' task is confined to gathering information about offers and requests and making it available. Circulation media such as vouchers are important as 'substitute money' in order to forestall the emergence of distrust in the value of the alternative currency. Too wide a divergence between the range of services offered and those sought will also cause the value of this alternative currency to fall, because the exchange process comes to a standstill and members will cease their activity, and then members still holding vouchers will be unable to use them.

As long as the organizations succeed in keeping the issue of vouchers under control and as long as none of the participants accumulates excessive 'debts' *vis-à-vis* other participants, the system can remain in equilibrium. Our examination of the Over & Weer network in Amsterdam showed that 70 per cent of the members were in balance as regards their services, that is they had performed and received about the same number of services. Only a minority of 10 per cent ordered more services than they themselves performed, and they are counterbalanced by a group of 20 per cent who provided more services than they themselves called for. Since most networks are small enough to be transparent it is impossible for some to cheat and enrich themselves at the expense of others; and in view of the attitude of solidarity that prevails among the participants, the risk of misuse is not a problem. Indeed, there is some disposition to 'underconsume', since many participants are more inclined to offer services than to make use of them. Therefore new members are given a 'starter credit' of a certain number of vouchers, to encourage them to begin by putting in requests.

It would in theory be quite possible for confidence in the currency to be undermined by participants getting unduly 'into debt'. But in systems that have a central bookkeeping function this risk is precluded by setting a drawing limit of 20 to 25 hours, above which no further 'debts' may be contracted. The voucher currency as a whole is guaranteed by the potential of its active members to provide services. Misuse leading to loss of confidence can also be prevented by introducing accounting 'strip cards' (see document 4). Services received are entered on the front of these cards, together with the hours involved. And the arrangement is that the 'bank' will issue a new card only when the old one is full up on *both* sides of the account, so that participants are compelled to arrive at a balance, at least from time to time. Moreover under this arrangement the service provider can see whether the recipient is a 'conscientious' participant or not, and this too may well have a sobering effect, making for confidence building. It also provides the 'bank' with valuable information regarding quality and quantity, time and place and those taking part in the transactions.

Main problems in the initial phase

One has only to consider the large number of such initiatives that have come to grief, and the equally large number that are not working at all well, to see that it is no simple matter to get an exchange network of this kind up and running. Organizers we have canvassed say that the two most difficult tasks in the early stages are to obtain financial backing and to recruit participants; by contrast, no difficulties were experienced arising from the regulations of regional or municipal authorities. By and large, local authorities were in favour of such initiatives, even if their support was usually decidedly lukewarm. Usually, too, the labour offices charged with preventing illicit work, distortion of competition and displacement of labour accepted the exchange activities as constituting 'volunteers at work'. Seldom, however, did local authorities pay subsidies that were sufficient to employ the necessary staff.

All the projects were organized by people working in an honorary capacity, who were often able to have assistance on a half-day basis from professional social workers. Initiatives covering a whole town area need something like 7,000 guilders worth of non-monetary

STRIPPENKAART

'WISSELWERK'

nijkcentrum Dukenburg, Heijhorst 70–39, tel. 452221.
Geopend: dinsdagmiddag: 15.30–11.00 uur.
vrijdagavond: 19.00–21.00 uur.

aangeboden diensten			ontvangen diensten		
PER UUR 1 STRIP	DATUM	PARAAF	PER UUR 1 STRIP	DATUM	PARAAF
SOORT WERK BIJ NO:			1 SOORT WERK DOOR NO:		
SOORT WERK BIJ NO:			2 SOORT WERK DOOR NO:		
SOORT WERK BIJ NO:			3 SOORT WERK DOOR NO:		
SOORT WERK BIJ NO:			4 SOORT WERK DOOR NO:		
SOORT WERK BIJ NO:			5 SOORT WERK DOOR NO:		
SOORT WERK BIJ NO:			6 SOORT WERK DOOR NO:		
SOORT WERK BIJ NO:			7 SOORT WERK DOOR NO:		
SOORT WERK BIJ NO:			8 SOORT WERK DOOR NO:		
SOORT WERK BIJ NO:			9 SOORT WERK DOOR NO:		
SOORT WERK BIJ NO:			10 SOORT WERK DOOR NO:		
SOORT WERK BIJ NO:			11 SOORT WERK DOOR NO:		
SOORT WERK BIJ NO:			12 SOORT WERK DOOR NO:		
SOORT WERK BIJ NO:			13 SOORT WERK DOOR NO:		
SOORT WERK BIJ NO:			14 SOORT WERK DOOR NO:		
SOORT WERK BIJ NO:			15 SOORT WERK DOOR NO:		
SOORT WERK BIJ NO:			16 SOORT WERK DOOR NO:		
SOORT WERK BIJ NO:			17 SOORT WERK DOOR NO:		
SOORT WERK BIJ NO:			18 SOORT WERK DOOR NO:		
SOORT WERK BIJ NO:			19 SOORT WERK DOOR NO:		
SOORT WERK BIJ NO:			20 SOORT WERK DOOR NO:		

Name: _____ DATES:_____

Adres: _____

Telefono: _____

STRIKT PERSOONLIJK

Document 4. Accounting 'strip card' of the Dukenburg 'Wisselwerk' exchange network in Nijmegen resources annually, so that the subsidies granted were sufficient for only one or two years. Since most of these networks do not charge membership fees, and the others only miniscule ones, they have no other source of income. To become self-supporting they would need to charge a membership fee of at least 40 guilders a year, which would naturally make it even more difficult to recruit members. Networks operating in a restricted area can work more cheaply, and their running costs for office and administrative work are often taken over by a local welfare organization.

When asked what were the major difficulties encountered in running an exchange network, 40 per cent of the respondents replied that they had problems in contacting their target group and recruiting participants from it. In their responses 25 per cent said they were not satisfied with the activity rate of participants, and 40 per cent mentioned difficulties in connection with the 'active' matching of supply and demand. But in most cases the difficulties are attributed not to the exchange network arrangement itself but to the behaviour of participants.

Participant behaviour and the problem of matching

We gained the impression from our enquiries among members of the Amsterdam exchange network that on the whole they were satisfied with the way their network was working. In fact the Over & Weer group constituted a very 'active' exchange network. Despite this (or because of it?) the rate of participation by members was rather low. In 1987, the first year of the network's existence, membership grew from 50 to 160 participants. Even if not all the activities were logged statistically, the annual report of this network indicated that only some 120 of the members took part, and these with an average turnover of five hours per head per year. Our own enquiries pointed to a similarly moderate level of activity by the members. More than one in four of the members replied that so far they had not provided any services under the network, and nearly half of them stated that they had done so four times or fewer. Only a quarter of the members had provided services more than five times. According to the Over & Weer annual report, male members took part more frequently than women. Both in Amsterdam and in Utrecht, those members who performed any service at all did only 1.4 hours a month. This is far less than the number of hours spent on average per head in doing ownwork in the family home in the Netherlands. For example Baartmans et al. (1987:67) discovered that householders among the 576 persons they questioned spent 11.8 hours a month on maintaining their homes, furniture and fittings, and even tenants spent 6.7 hours a month. A large time budget study carried out in Holland revealed that adults in Holland spend on average eight hours a month on voluntary work (Knulst and Schoonderwoerd 1983:63).

Despite the limited comparability of the population groups surveyed, comparative figures of this kind show first that these self-organized forms of ownwork were comparatively marginal 'supplements' both to occupation in the formal sector and to household work proper. Secondly exchange networks up till then were still far from functioning as a way of activating the unused working time of people outside the formal economy and offering them a relevant way of obtaining services. In the third place it would seem that exchange networks based on mutual self-interest in doing voluntary work have a smaller motivating effect than traditional forms of voluntary work – a finding that contradicts the conclusions drawn by van Loon in 1987 and by Coughlin and Meiners in 1987.

This brings us back to the question of how to explain the comparatively weak intensity of participation in even the large networks. As was mentioned earlier, in the large exchange networks two factors play a part. On the one hand these networks do have more difficulty in putting specific offers and requirements into contact with each other compared with the smaller ones. But on the other hand it must be presumed that such difficulties are lessened by the greater variety of skills and capabilities available in the large networks, so that they should find it easier to satisfy a variety of demands. The question of the relationship between these two factors and how it can be used to explain the low rate of participation was investigated with the aid of the demand and offer lists of the Over & Weer network organizing exchange between 250 members in July 1988. The question posed was how many of the services asked for in ten categories of services could actually have been matched with a suitable offer. The object was to establish to what extent the non-participation of members could be explained by the difficulties to be overcome in finding the right supplier for one's demand, and vice versa. In other words, we were trying to discover the potential success rate for transactions within a large network.

Table 1 shows in summary form a quantitative picture of the possible exchange transactions within Over & Weer, that is of the transactions that could have taken place on the basis of the manifest offer and manifest demand. As we shall see later, there is a further possible discrepancy, that between the total of 'suitable' supply–demand relationships and the total of transactions that were actually consummated.

We can see from table 1 that there is a hypothetical area of overlap,

Table 1. Structure of offer and demand, 'turnover corridor' and 'degree of clearance' in a large network: 'Over & Weer', Amsterdam, July 1988, 250 participants

Category of service	(1) No. of demands posted	(2) No. of offers	(3) 'Turnover corridor'[a]		(4) No. of demands actually fulfillable[b]		(5) No. of unfulfillable demands[c]	(6) No. of unused offers[d]		(7) Total of unfulfillable demands and unused offers[e]
			as prop. of demands	as prop. of offers		as prop. of demands			as prop. of offers	
Admin. services	7	22	100%	32%	7	100%	0	15	68%	15
Language lessons	22	34	100%	65%	15	68%	6–8	19	56%	25–7
Cultural and creative activities	39	53	100%	74%	18	46%	20	32	60%	52–3
Technical and repair services	24	17	65%	100%	13	50%	13	5–8	38%	18–21
Occasional manual jobs	54	37	69%	100%	50	92%	4	8	22%	12
Personal social services	32	42	100%	76%	22–7	75%	5–10	12	28%	17–22
Simple housework	53	112	100%	47%	46–8	90%	3–4	18–71	63%	21–75
Leisure activities	3	9	100%	33%	2	66%	1	7	78%	8
Recreation	1	19	100%	5%	0–1	0–100%	0–1	18–19	97%	19–20
Services while on leave and absent	8	28	100%	29%	4	50%	4	23	82%	27
Total	245	373	89%	59%	177–86	74%	56–65	157–214	42–57%	214–89 (35–45%)

[a]Potential for transactions based on the relationship between cols 1 and 2. [b]Degree of clearance. [c]Col. 1 minus col. 4. [d]Col. 2 minus col. 4. [e]Col. 5 plus col. 6.

defined by the offers for which there could have been a suitable demand, and vice versa. This area of intersection marks the 100 per cent level of the possible transactions in the system (column 3). However, as column 4 shows, for a number of reasons this 100 per cent level cannot be fully utilized. One of these reasons is the pressure embodied in the 'rules of the game' for at least a periodical settlement of accounts. In practice this means that although a 'suitable' demander for a given service may very well be discoverable, the enquirer may already be so much 'in debt' that he cannot satisfy that requirement by accepting the offer that is available. Another obstacle to transactions is the fact that the list given in table 1 only gives comparatively rough descriptions of categories of services, within which the specific demand may differ from the service actually offered (for example, in the 'language teaching' category a participant wishing to brush up his French will obviously not be helped by a teacher of Spanish). The table shows that something like half the offers made by participants cannot be implemented, either because they are too specific or because on the contrary they are so elementary that anyone could offer them (and in this respect a 'supply overhang' develops), or else – as in the category of simple household tasks – anybody can perform them for himself or herself, and this gives rise to a 'demand gap'. In other words, on average only half the participants can 'place' their offers of service, while only a quarter of the potential customers articulates a demand 'out of line with what is on offer'.

Thus there is a comparatively substantial area of overlap between the totality of what is on offer and the totality of what is demanded, which might be thought of as a *corridor of potential turnover*. A further problem surrounds the question what proportion of the total potential turnover is actually achieved. As was hinted earlier, the total size of the network has a bearing on both problems – of *size* and of the *degree of exploitation* of the 'turnover corridor'. As regards the problem of the 'turnover corridor', there must be a strong presumption that as the number of participants increases, so likewise does the range of offers and demands, until finally there is 'something for everyone' there. However, the growing size may reduce the degree to which the turnover corridor is cleared, because the search activities needed to bring the 'right' offer together with the 'appropriate' demand (and vice versa) increase exponentially. But irrespective of this possible trade-off between size and degree of clearance of the turnover corridor the initial assumption, that as the size of the network grows the 'average quantity' of matching groups of offers and requirements will also grow, is open to doubt. This would occur only if the qualitative scope of both supply and demand were to increase in a random way, that is to say that the mismatch would

Table 2. Structure of offer and demand, 'turnover corridor' and 'degree of clearance' in a medium-sized network: Dit voor Dat, Utrecht, July 1988

	(1)	(2)	(3)		(4)		(5)	(6)		(7)
			'Turnover corridor'[a]		No. of demands actually fulfillable[b]			No. of unused offers[d]		Total of unfulfillable demands and unused offers[e]
Category of service	No. of demands posted	No. of offers	as prop. of demands	as prop. of offers		as prop. of demands	No. of unfulfillable demands[c]		as prop. of offers	
Admin. services	3	6	100%	50%	2	66%	1	4	66%	5
Language lessons	2	20	100%	25%	4	80%	1	16	80%	17

Cultural and creative activities	9	13	9	100%	69%	2	22%	7	11	84%	18
Technical and repair services	4	2	2	50%	100%	1	25%	3	1	50%	4
Manual odd jobs	32	17	17	53%	100%	13	40%	19	4	23%	23
Personal social services	4	6	4	100%	67%	2	50%	2	4	66%	6
Simple housework	22	37	22	100%	59%	10	45%	12	27	73%	39
Science lessons	1	1	1	100%	100%	–	0%	1	1	100%	2
Leisure contact	18	27	18	100%	67%	13	72%	5	14	52%	19
Looking after children/animals	7	20	7	100%	35%	7	100%	–	13	65%	13
Transport	4	2	2	50%	100%	2	50%	2	–	0%	2
Total:	109	151	90	83%	60%	56	51%	53	95	63%	148 (57%)

Refer to table 1 above for notes on column categories.

not persist because the sum of services offered and the sum of services demanded was subject to systematic distortions.[4] And yet an examination of a smaller, only 'medium-sized' network shows that such distortions are to be expected and that hence the scale effect of large networks in increasing turnover does not have the relevance attributed to it (see table 2).[5]

Table 2 again shows a supply overhang that cannot be cleared, though in this case it is somewhat higher (63 per cent compared with about 50 per cent). This in fact warrants the conclusion that as the size of the networks decreases the proportion of the services on offer that fails to find a taker increases. It follows that the larger networks are likely to be more able to cope with discrepancies between the structure of supply and the structure of demand. They make it possible to lower the proportion of unfulfillable demands and unsaleable offers, even if not drastically. For, as table 1 shows, even so large a network as Over & Weer in Amsterdam shows a large overhang of unused offers that have as it were the status of 'alternative unemployment'. This must be presumed to affect the motivation of members and participants, for if members have unfortunate experiences with, or little confidence in, the 'saleability' of their own services, they become inactive and others who might join do not do so, and this in turn worsens the percentage size of the 'turnover corridor'. It would seem that these processes give rise to a kind of self-inhibition of the exchange, leading to stagnation of the exchange network.

With regard to the second of the two problems mentioned above, the degree of clearance of the 'turnover corridor', it should be remembered that (a) not all of the possible combinations of suitable offers and suitable demands are actually discovered and negotiated, either by the originators or the central agency, and that (b) not all the links that are found and negotiated are actually implemented. In the case of the Amsterdam network a detailed tally revealed that only about one-third of the contacts facilitated by the central office were implemented; this may have something to do with the distances and times involved, as well as incompatibilities between what was offered and what was required. In that respect, clearly even the most active matching centre, such as that of Over & Weer, cannot do more by way of increasing the clearance factor than provide the information, since nobody can be compelled to provide a proffered service or to take up an offer. Consequently, a great deal depends on the mental and cultural dispositions of the potential partners to the exchange, to take the trouble to make suitable mutual arrangements and to overcome the many hazards and uncertainties of a transaction that is not regulated by price. This leads us to a consideration of the motives and experiences of the participants.

Motives and experiences of participants in moneyless exchange

People who take part in exchange networks are motivated primarily by considerations of a social nature. To accept services and also to provide them, in both cases making and strengthening social contacts, is a source of some satisfaction. Over and above this, considerations of economic advantage play a varying part in the process. Many participants are attracted to such schemes because by taking part they can pursue several objectives simultaneously; they procure themselves various services and assistance for which they do not have to pay; very often they obtain help and advice on aspects not covered by the bureaucratic, formal service organizations. Then there are participants who are too isolated in their immediate social surroundings to find anybody to do occasional jobs, or else they simply want to make contact with different people. Such motivations clearly have more weight on the demand side than on the offer side. The latter is motivated both by the desire to use personal skills and accomplishments and by the traditional motive of performing voluntary work without an eye to personal advantage. All in all there is a mixture of pragmatic, social and economic motives.

Nevertheless, participants make very little use of the system. About half the respondents state that they have ordered services from the network between one and four times in a year, and half said that participation had not made any noticeable difference to their monetary expenditures. On the other hand two-fifths said they were able to save at least 'something', for example on making and repairing clothes, the repair of electrical equipment, piano tuning, haircuts, laying down floor covering, gardening, etc. Savings were also made on private music or language lessons received from other participants without payment. Sometimes the object is not to save money on services for which one would otherwise pay, but to obtain services that could not otherwise be afforded. Only a small number of participants state that they have saved a lot of money – meaning 100 to 200 guilders. In view of the high hourly charges of professional hairdressers, electricians, joiners or gardeners, amounts of that order point to only a modest use of the network's informal resources. Therefore even the most active participants could not really maintain that their membership has had appreciable financial effects; it must be assumed that there is no direct financial incentive to take part in these activities.

A majority of participants is satisfied with the quality of the services and help they have received; only one in five state that they have on occasion been dissatisfied. As regards the possible waiting time between notifying a requirement and having it met, nearly three in five said that they had received the services offered at the right time and that the time taken was reasonable. One in five stated that they had had to wait 'some time' and another fifth that they had had to wait 'a long time'. In most cases such waiting periods were said to be due to difficulties in finding an offer to suit the enquirer's requirement. Participants have neither a financial nor any other kind of incentive to provide their services really quickly. Enquirers have no way of holding service providers to a quick 'delivery', with the result that in general there can be no guarantee that the help will indeed be provided within the desired time limit. However, since the network we examined had only a modest turnover, most of the respondents saw no reason to complain about delays and lateness.

In the case we investigated, the speed with which offer and demand could be brought together depends mainly on the organizational work done by the central office. The favourable comments received indicate that most members are satisfied with the way this office performs, both in its role as an active matchmaker and with the chosen form of settlement of transactions, the 'strip cards'. Despite the fact that 'financial savings', allegedly the second most frequently cited reason for taking part, are in reality effected only by a small active minority of participants, most of the members of this exchange network are very satisfied with the system. This provides further confirmation of the fact that participation in networks of this type confers still other advantages.

Intangible benefits of service exchanges

What is this 'process benefit' – the sum of the intangible benefits of belonging? And to what extent is the need for social contacts, which is an important reason for joining, actually met?

During our survey we asked participants in the Amsterdam project what they had found especially attractive and satisfying about belonging to the network. Some of the answers we received were consonant with the above analysis, while others referred to the actual experience of the exchange process. A small proportion of the respondents said that they experienced satisfaction in both being productive and thereby helping others. But a very few participants either openly admitted their self-interested reasons or implicitly assumed that self-interest was what motivated all participants in their transactions.

Making fresh contacts is also seen as an additional advantage, but in practice only a small number of participants regards contacts as important. They are 'often very nice' and have a certain 'element of surprise, because one never knows whom one is going to meet'.

We also asked respondents whether they had ever pursued their acquaintance with other network members or whether they had effected exchange transactions with people outside the exchange network (an affirmative answer to this question could indicate that members prefer to make exchange transactions with people they know and trust). Four-fifths replied that they had not gone in for relationships of this kind. Some participants stated expressly that they had no interest in personal contacts, while many said it was burdensome to have to make contact with other network members whom they did not know.

One of the most important reasons why members became inactive or gave up membership appears to be disappointment over the fact that the requirements they notify cannot be met quickly enough, or at all, because the services on offer are insufficient in quantity or quality; another reason is lack of time for exchange activities. When asked whether, in the light of their experiences hitherto, they wished to remain members or to resign, nearly 90 per cent of respondents said that they wished to continue their membership. Unlike other projects of this nature, Over & Weer was experiencing a membership increase amounting to some 70 persons every six months. Notwithstanding the problems that have arisen in attaining the goals they have set for themselves, our case study has shown this to be one of the most successful projects of its kind in the Netherlands.

Findings and conclusions

Our aim in undertaking this case study in the Netherlands was to discover whether, and if so to what extent, the organization of informal exchange networks can offer a solution to the problems that increasingly confront private households in today's world. These problems include solitariness and isolation, falling real incomes and declining ability for self-help. The findings of our investigation show that the provision and exchange of unpaid services in organized form entails a number of problems. These problems relate to:

- the formation of exchange networks;
- the recruitment of activists and organizers who could make themselves responsible for the necessary preparatory and administrative work without payment;
- the recruitment of members;
- the matching of offer and demand;
- the low motivation of members to participate;

- the comparatively unskilled and discontinuous nature of the services offered; and
- the limited economic and social advantages participants can draw from cooperating in exchange networks.

Of the 30-odd most recent attempts to set up moneyless exchange networks only a small number of projects appears to be viable. Success, where it occurs, can be attributed to the skilful organization of the servicebroking; this in turn is due to the sustained commitment of highly motivated honorary staff, and equally to a sufficiency of potential among the members themselves, which alone makes the exchange possible. Exchange networks covering entire urban areas have been able to overcome their initial difficulties because they succeeded in enrolling a sufficiently large number of members. Initiatives geared to a limited target group and special categories of potential members relied on the assumption that they could benefit from the similarity of their members and their familiarity with one another; yet these do not exhibit a greater readiness to participate. They have a good chance of survival only where there is a strong and regularly recurring need for mutual help.

All the other small, unspecialized exchange networks appear to be working unsatisfactorily because they have too few members and consequently the offer of services, and their turnover, are too limited. Large networks have succeeded in overcoming this 'disadvantage of small scale', but their problem is how to organize the matching of supply and demand for special services between members. It is likely that such difficulties go far to explain the fact that even in large networks a considerable proportion of the members take no or very little part in the proceedings. Other obstacles in the way of more intensive participation are:

On the supply side

- the absence of financial and material incentives;
- the absence of adequate qualifications or skills and discouragement arising from the fear that one's own contribution may not be attractive;
- the distances between members;
- the mental stress caused by moneyless exchange between persons unacquainted with one another;
- the fact that many members are short of time;

On the demand side

- the small income-substitution effect of the system;

- a certain tendency to 'underconsume' arising from the fact that many members find it easier to give than to receive;
- the predominantly unskilled nature and uncertain quality of the services offered;
- the naturally limited need for odd jobs to be done in one's own home;
- inhibitions about contacting 'strangers';
- the fact that many people prefer to enter into informal exchange transactions with people they know, and the availability of such exchange relationships within their circle of acquaintances;
- the absence of a financial or material incentive to 'take' unpaid services, where sufficient funds are available to procure such services in the formal economy.

All in all our findings tend to raise doubt as to the practicability of moneyless exchange systems, at least when they come into being more or less spontaneously, remain confined to particular village or urban subcultures and do not have the necessary variety of supply, so that they soon enter a phase of stagnation as regards the numerical strength of their membership as well. It appears that the alleged advantages (the utilization of disposable working time by the introduction of an alternative medium of circulation) accrue in reality only to a small minority of very active participants. Moreover exchange networks of this kind exclude in principle all those who are not (or no longer) in a position to make contributions of their own, while those who can make their own contributions are unable to find 'takers' for these services and on account of this mismatch become, as it were, the 'alternative' unemployed.

Up to the present it is not clear whether and how initiatives of this kind can succeed in attracting a larger amount of public funding and effective support. The fact is that so far they are attracting only a tiny proportion of the population groups who might be helped by the system in dealing with the problems that typically face them. Some large groups among those who might be thought likely to benefit from such a system appear to have little inclination to join; they include young people, students and the long-term unemployed from the traditional industrial labour force. Since younger people usually have their sights on a position in the formal economy, they tend to view with suspicion all forms of work outside the formal economy that are not remunerated directly in cash (see Knapen and Heerdink 1986:50; ter Huurne 1985). Students might be thought to have the 'alternative mentality' that might dispose them, in view of their slender financial resources, to join such exchange networks. But they do not join because nowadays they, too, are under greater pressure of time. And for the long-term unemployed from the traditional industrial workforce the system cannot seriously be regarded as a practical solution to the strain on their finances caused by being out of work. Thus the only remaining social groups who may be presumed to have an interest in the exchange of services between households on a non-monetary basis are those permanently excluded from the formal economy – the handicapped, older women without a job, single person households of the middle-aged middle class, people who have taken early retirement and 'the young elderly'. If members of these groups take part, they do so primarily not for financial but for social reasons.

Arguments from normative politics can also be adduced for the scepticism expressed here. For example in the 1980s a Dutch pressure group called Women in Social Work accused the woman manager of a local exchange network of 'in the last resort simply accepting the modern form of poverty and in effect going along with the division of society into an underclass and an upper class'. In the eyes of Women in Social Work the exchange networks are engaged in building up a 'poor people's economy' from which there would be no escape. They criticize the founders of a used clothing exchange network by saying that unemployed women should claim the right and the income to buy new clothing for money just like other people. They condemn exchange initiatives as being directed against economic emancipation.

However, before getting involved with 'radical' objections of this kind with their obvious anti-reform overtones, it would be well to take account of a number of socioeconomic developments that create a situation in which there is a great and real need for an effective system of personal services in society. In the Netherlands governmental economic and social policies have created the conditions for a 'poverty economy' for more and more people. Very recently the lowest social assistance payments for young people below the age of 27 were lowered by 25 per cent; housing supplement was reduced, part payment by patients for medicines and medical aid was introduced, students' bursaries were reduced, and the budgets of the caring services were cut; and these are only some examples of the economy measures taken by the government which seriously depress the incomes of those already living in difficult economic circumstances. At the same time the efforts in the sphere of economic policy to combat long-term unemployment have been confined to lowering the price at which labour power is offered, while the minimum wage is being abolished, first for young work-seekers but also, for example, for some entrants to the academic professions. As conditions of employment have become more flexible, a situation has developed in which many employees, especially women, can only obtain part-time work, and their earnings are little if any higher than the lowest social security payments, or even, in extreme cases, below them (see Vlek 1986:189f.). In this socioeconomic situation the informal economy, whether in its 'spontaneous' form of unorganized help among family members, friends and neighbours, or in the organized form of exchange networks, used goods sales, etc., is an important and indispensable supplementary system of securing a living alongside the considerably reduced system of state-organized social security.

9

The Search for New Ways of Organizing Social Commitment in the Federal Republic of Germany

There appear to have been no interhousehold moneyless exchange systems in the Federal Republic of Germany similar to the highly developed Service Credits scheme in the USA or the LETS system in Canada. One reason for this dearth of experience with moneyless exchange systems, in the past as well as the present, is the fact that comparatively early on a social security system was introduced which, notwithstanding some setbacks in recent years, has developed into a wide range of relatively high-grade social assistance provisions for dealing with a great variety of problem situations in society. In a nutshell, the welfare state rendered the search for self-organized forms of social assistance (apparently) superfluous. Only since the mid-1970s, when both the material limits of this security system and the counterproductive effects of bureaucratic provision of services became apparent, has the search been on for reform strategies and alternatives. Another reason is that there is in Germany a strong tradition of voluntary service, the roots of which go back to the nineteenth century. Unpaid activities, irrespective of whether they were organized by government departments or unofficial welfare institutions, have for many years occupied the space between the family and professional systems of welfare. However, in the era of the 'colonization of the lifeworld' (Habermas) this traditional way of providing services is under increasing threat, so that (in our view not yet sufficient) thought is being given to a rearrangement of the pillars in the overall system of social assistance.

In the first section of the present chapter we intend briefly to consider these structural changes and 'fissures' in the traditional 'honorary' pattern. In the second section we wish to describe in more detail 'Ownwork House', a project that of all the projects in the

Federal Republic seeking to discover new ways of organizing mutual help activities[1] is the one most likely to date to provide points of contact for a practical trial of the system to be proposed in this book (see part IV).

Voluntary unpaid work

Elsewhere in this report (see pages 63–4) we have already referred briefly to characteristic features of the way in which 'honorary' service has traditionally been organized. We pointed out that when inquiring into the potential of honorary helpers, what motivates them and what are the limits of their usefulness, it is useful to distinguish between unpaid activities performed in organizations (in this case primarily welfare associations) and those that tend to occur in an unorganized fashion. In the present section we should like to amplify these thoughts by going into greater details about the problems arising from the structural changes in the sphere of voluntary unpaid work, for in our opinion these changes make it necessary to look for new institutional methods of meeting people's needs. However, we do not intend to discuss all the literature on voluntary unpaid work; we would simply like to draw attention to some seminal observations about trends and proposed solutions that are to be found in the most recent literature, and to put forward the results of interviews we ourselves had during the summer of 1988 with representatives of charitable organizations, including the local Caritas organization in Dortmund and the East Westphalia District Association of the Workers' Welfare organization (Arbeiterwohlfahrt – AWO) all of whom are familiar with the specifics of organizing voluntary work at local level.

During the last few years political discussion on voluntary work and the social services has reached unprecedented heights in the context of the rediscovery of self-help and 'new subsidiarity' (cf. for instance the contributions in R. G. Heinze 1986 and Müller and Rauschenbach 1988). In particular the former Berlin senator Ulf Fink has attracted attention by making practical proposals for governmental promotion of unpaid voluntary commitment and has taken the first steps towards implementing them in what is known as the 'Berlin model' (see for example Fink 1986). One of the principal reasons for this resurgence of the voluntary principle is that it is expected to lighten the financial load on government social assistance budgets. But it is questionable whether a political 'rationalization strategy' of this kind can succeed, since not only is the potential in terms of abilities to help shrinking; even where it exists it is not very easy to harness. It is true that surveys and other empirical studies concerned with voluntary social commitment report a good degree of *readiness* to engage in such activities, but the practical response is much smaller. It would therefore be unwise to overestimate the potential for unpaid voluntary work, especially if it is (a) called on by formally organized institutions and associations, and is (b) utilized in comparative anonymity.

The discrepancy between subjective willingness to serve and the actual potential in honorary helpers is emphasized by the welfare organizations themselves; they are encountering increasing problems in finding recruits. Although the total number of honorary helpers in the six leading associations is somewhat roughly estimated at 1.5 million in the statistics on non-governmental welfare institutions (see Federal Study Group 1985) sample surveys show that willingness to do voluntary work has been receding markedly for some considerable time. Data from the Allensbach Social Survey Institute indicates that in 1962 it was still 49 per cent, but had fallen to 37 per cent by 1979; during the same period refusal to do unpaid social work rose from 49 to 59 per cent (see Olk 1987:86f.). Then the regard in which the welfare organizations are held – which also plays an important role in the recruitment of voluntary workers – has been further eroded by the discovery of some abuses and financial scandals in non-governmental welfare organizations. The well-publicized improprieties in some establishments hit the welfare organizations at a time when they were in any event declining in importance because in recent years self-organized groups had been posing an increasing challenge to the monopoly of traditional welfare activites. This growing problem of acceptance is also referred to in the study by the Prognos organization on the 'development of non-governmental welfare services up to 2000' (Prognos AG 1984; see on this whole debate Bauer/Diessenbacher 1984; Gernert et al. 1986; Boll and Olk 1987).

Even though accurate and reliable data on this subject are only available in rudimentary form, all the surveys and statistics indicate that the traditional way of helping others, that of the 'good sort', is dying out. Voluntary work in social services has been predominantly a sphere for women of middle-class origin in the age range 40 to 60 years, and the average age is steadily increasing. Over two-thirds of all voluntary workers are women (see Federal Study Group 1985; Olk 1987; Braun and Röhrig 1987 and Schöpp–Schilling 1988). In the Caritas association in Dortmund which we investigated, about 90 per cent of the helpers are women; most of these women are without formal employment, in their mid-forties and upwards, closely linked to their church; most of them continue with their voluntary work until prevented by age or other reasons. Even though in this particular case the priest, who contacts potential voluntary helpers in his parish directly and tries to persuade them to become involved, does not expect to encounter significant shortages, there is no doubt that the circle of potential helpers is shrinking, not least because more and more young women are taking employment in the formal economy. This is under discussion throughout the Caritas association, and consideration is being given to financial incentives, perhaps in the form of hourly pay, to supplement the usual practice in the association, which is only to reimburse out-of-pocket expenses, on request.

Whereas the traditional pattern of honorary work survives in strength in the Caritas branch we examined closely, in the Workers' Welfare (AWO) in Bielefeld there are opposed trends of 'old' and 'new' attitudes to voluntary work, the former working in the context of the association and the latter being less organized. AWO does indeed still have a permanent core of helpers doing unpaid work for the association; they number some 5 per cent of the 1000-odd members in the East Westphalia district. But even here there are already signs of a change in motivation. Those holding to the traditional concept of honorary work are for the most part women and men (from social democratic and trade union circles) who can use their experience of life and their vocational knowhow in the work. But an increasing number of younger women in the district, though signing on, are not willing to perform the traditional services; instead they are forming groups of a self-help or similar nature, consonant with their needs and range of interests. Our interviewee thought that this development was traceable both to the waning effectiveness of family-based support systems, despite the fact that these were still seen as playing an important part in the overall system of help and support activities, and also to the growing importance of self-help groups as an indicator of lacunae in both voluntary and public welfare provision. Self-help groups arise particularly where there are 'niches' that have either not been filled at all or else only partially by the traditional activities of the associations. Examples of such niches in Bielefeld include help for drug addicts and delinquents and work among foreign workers. There is also, as our interviewees expressed it, a clear discrepancy between paid work and honorary work; it is claimed that in recent years the full-time workers have exploited and discouraged the voluntary workers and to a degree kept them subservient. While this trend is apparently making it increasingly difficult to mobilize and motivate women and men as voluntary helpers, there was said to be a growing need for people to take responsibility for organising self-help for themselves and others in a like situation. Experiences like this from practical work 'at the sharp end' are being reflected in the AWO's basic programme (see AWO 1988), which speaks of a structural change in honorary commitment and says that the voluntary work 'of the past' is more and more acquiring a self-help character.

When one considers the wide variety of motives leading people to devote themselves to voluntary work it becomes evident that pleasure in being active and the desire to help others are basic elements in such motivation. But whereas with Caritas it is church-based and religious motives, acting in accordance with Christ's command to love one's neighbour, that plays a major part, with the AWO it is consciousness of togetherness, the common commitment to a sociopolitical ideal and the feeling of belonging together in the association that are in the foreground. Some members also take part for more personal reasons, from 'vanity', from wanting to be there ('to get away from housework'), self-affirmation and so on (the 'helper reflex'). Financial considerations, such as boosting the household finances through reimbursement of expenses, not only the out-of-pocket ones but also for the time spent, do not apparently come into it, at least up to the present. Traditional voluntary workers (and their associations) hold that the reward for the commitment must arise directly from the activity itself, and this means that incidental expenses, for travel and so forth, must also be met from one's own pocket, not constantly claimed from the association.

The impressions regarding unpaid work which we gained in the Caritas and AWO areas we examined, and the way it is regarded by representatives of these associations, correspond with the statements that appear in the literature, and which are supported by empirical investigations, about the service potential of unpaid work (see among others Glatzer 1984; Braun and Röhrig 1987; Olk 1987). There is indeed both residual and new potential for self-help groups, but the gradual erosion of traditional motives for helping and the growing volume of female employment discourage any exaggerated hopes that informal networks of this kind will grow in importance without additional incentives from the state or the market. Contemplating immediate on-the-spot experience as it relates to the global relationships in society, one is bound seriously to doubt the suitability of the traditional unpaid pattern for closing the 'services gap':

> All in all it must be said that honorary social work based as it is on unpaid, untrained, unorganized, voluntary work for others is losing its power to survive. Traditional honorary work is being eroded both by the changed demands on honorary social work as a part of the system whereby needs are met and by the change in the expectation of reimbursement for the energy invested in unpaid work. (Rauschenbach et al. 1988:236f.)

In the light of such obvious defects and functional limitations affecting honorary activities – limitations that cannot be counteracted by the spread of the self-help movement – the optimism with which many politicians are now proposing to exploit this allegedly 'fallow' potential appears surprising (see Fink 1987 and several contributions in Fink 1988). It would seem more realistic to assume that the traditional forms of association are fading away and that as yet no new forms of organization ('intermediary structures' – see Berger and Neuhaus 1977) have taken their place to mobilize the shrinking 'old' and the limited 'new' potential for unpaid service. This judgement is borne out by the results of the social policy strategies that have been adopted in the past few years to attract and retain men and women to staff the unpaid social services. Despite a number of advertising and public relations campaigns and despite financial incentives for more voluntary work and self-help it has not proved possible to activate large sections of the allegedly fallow potential for helpful activities and to channel it (see for more detail R. G. Heinze et al. 1988:171ff.).

Nor is it surprising, in view of this rather sobering state of affairs, that the subject of 'compulsory service', perhaps in the form of an obligatory year of social service, is again coming up for discussion in political circles. Although such compulsory service, which needs a good deal of monitoring, is not markedly efficient, the proposal is being put forward not only by advocates of a 'strong' state (rather like the proposal to make recipients of social assistance work for their money) but of late also by the green-alternative camp. Opielka (1988) argues for the introduction of a 'social service' on the pattern of today's civilian (alternative military) service or service with the fire brigade, lasting from three to four years and obligatory for all men and women. But whether, as Opielka assumes, 'many ambitions in social fields' would really be awakened by such service is doubtful in view of the lack of motivation revealed by empirical enquiry and of the quality problems inherent in compulsory service. The search is therefore still on for new institutional arrangements for meeting real needs, neither based on compulsion nor too much oriented to the traditional structures of voluntary work as hitherto practised by charitable organizations (see also Evers 1988).

'Ownwork House'

We should now like to describe in detail a West German project explicitly designed to offer a solution to the problem of the 'modernization trap' in which, as described earlier, the private household has become imprisoned: the Ownwork House (Haus der Eigenarbeit) in Munich.[2] This house provides the infrastructure needed to expand household production. It provides rooms, equipment, material, specialist advice, skill training and communications facilities – resources lacking in modern, small format households wishing to become more self-supporting. Moreover reliance is not placed on those traditional (altruistic) motivation structures in which, as already outlined, there has been a gradual erosion in the context of commitment to unpaid work.

Ownwork House was opened in October 1987 in Heidhausen, an inner residential quarter of Munich with good communications and a predominantly artisan population with plenty of initiative. The two-storey building, situated in an inner courtyard, contains professionally equipped leisure workshops for woodworking, metalworking and weaving as well as multipurpose rooms for social activities. In the entrance area a 'junk caff' has been set up to an original design made from old materials. There is a small stage that can be used for theatre try-outs and other cultural activities, besides serving as an exhibition area. All members may use the premises on any day except Sundays; they can rent the workplaces in the workshops or the multipurpose rooms, make use of the specialist advice that is available in the evenings or take part in courses, projects and events. Reasonable fees are charged for participation in any of the above facilities. One hour's use of the workshop including expert advice costs for example, 7.50 DM, a ten-hour card 60 DM. The charge for two hours of the children's workshop on Wednesday mornings is 3 DM.

The House is run by a non-profitmaking association, which at present draws all its financial resources from the 'AN Foundation', a 'research company for the promotion of initiative, mutual help and joint action'. It has the legal status of a private registered association. Since its foundation in 1982 the AN Foundation has been promoting socially innovative projects and/or academic support for such projects. In 1988 Ownwork House was the largest of the foundation's projects and was reckoned to cost about 400,000 DM to run;[3] these costs, less receipts from the fees collected for courses, use of workshops, etc. (about 70,000 DM) were borne by the AN foundation. However, this generous support was looked on only as start-up financing designed to give this 'social experiment' a good send-off. The project was meant to be virtually self-supporting after three years; this was to be achieved through fees for courses, the loan and use of facilities and through innovative financing arrangements (such as workshop rental against specialist advice) so that municipal authorities might be induced to take an interest in supporting follow-on projects.

The aim of Ownwork House is to encourage and equip people living in large cities to do ownwork. One of the concept papers defines 'ownwork' as follows (Horz 1986:1): 'making and doing things for oneself socially and in practical handiwork and creative artistry.' A wide variety of objectives is subsumed under the general heading of the 'promotion of ownwork', and their relationship to one another does not seem to be very clear. The House aims at providing opportunities for meaningful use of leisure time and initiating mutual help, but also at helping to build up partial economic and social self-sufficiency structures. Rather in the style of a pointer to infinity it is stated that:

> Ownwork House seeks to strengthen people's self-reliance and self-sufficiency and to diminish alienation. Ownwork is seen as an act of self-affirmation and self-development. In this sense OH might be seen as an island of freedom and self-affirmation in an alienated world. Furthermore OH wishes to help to fashion the culture of this district by establishing consciously contrapuntal motifs to prevailing trends, whether it be the throwaway mentality or the craving for luxury, the isolation of single parents or the use of pesticides in food production. (Redler 1988:55).

Such a utopian declaration may serve as an inspirational idea or a stimulus to thought, and certainly good arguments can be advanced in favour of the criticism of the market society and the consumer mentality which it contains. But as a theoretical underpinning for an experimental system the concept of ownwork appears somewhat simplistic. Is there really a latent need for self-sufficiency at work, as is assumed in the concept papers, and if so, who experiences such a need? For which problem situations can OH offer a solution and which needs can be met? And is the provision of a suitable infrastructure in itself a sufficient prerequisite for its intensive utilization?

However, these obvious weaknesses in the theoretical conception are counterbalanced by three factors when it is tested in practice, so that the chances of success for the project are by no means as slim as the foregoing remarks might seem to indicate. For one thing, the men and women working in the project are extremely motivated and committed. They identify strongly with the utopian aims of the project – or, in their own words, 'with the philosophy of the House' – and reflect critically on their own work. The future of the House will depend crucially on their commitment, their skills in dealing with visitors and their readiness to learn from mistakes and 'blind alleys'. Secondly, stress should be laid on the accompanying research which is planned to run for a period of three years. The woman political scientist entrusted with this task is following the progress of the project as a 'semi-detached' person with 'critical goodwill'. As she sees it, her task is to 'hold up a mirror to the OH project and its initiators, to ask questions and to address contradictions' (Redler 1988:6), and to examine closely the way the project is being tackled with reference to its practicability and reproducibility. Thirdly and lastly, the objective of becoming self-financing has been adopted as an aim of the project, and this will compel its initiators to pay attention to needs that actually exist. Moreover in view of the massive start-up financing that has been granted, the initiators and the project team feel a very heavy burden of responsibility to ensure that the project does not end in failure.

The first practical results relate to the start-up phase of the project during the first nine months, and therefore too much weight should not be attached to them; but they do seem to confirm the impression gained from a reading of the concept papers, namely that expensive equipment and the reforming zeal of the project team will not of themselves suffice to make the project a success. Furthermore the starting point of the project – to provide the infrastructure for ownwork in a centrally situated *building* open to everybody – creates conditions that imply a long acceptance phase and cannot be suitable for everybody's needs. Locating the ownwork distant in time and space from other household duties does indeed help to counteract privatization and isolation and create opportunities for social contacts and communication; but on the other hand some people might be deterred from entering by fear of being expected to display their own rudimentary practical skills (under the gaze of a professional adviser), and (potential) users may encounter organizational problems in fitting a visit to the House into their daily routine.

The numbers of people visiting during the 'open hours for work' in the workshops fluctuate considerably, from none to ten; there are no more than five users on any evening in the individual workshops while skilled advisers are available. A number of courses and initiatives have been formed or have chosen the House as their meeting places; they include students' pottery groups, kindergarten projects, two theatre groups, two vegetable cooperatives and courses for relaxation exercises. So far no exchange relationships between users have come into being. The idea was to do *ad hoc* matching of offers and requirements using a blackboard. It is difficult to obtain figures as to the total number of users, the difficulty being to define what is meant by a user. If everybody taking part in any courses or groups or appearing frequently in the workshop is counted as a user, in the first nine months some 250 people made use of Ownwork House.

But by and large only a core group of about 20 regular visitors has emerged, the majority being men in the 25–40 age group with training in some manual skill.

Users of Ownwork House appear to be motivated individually by some permutation of the following factors:

- price (money saved by ownwork);
- quality (high quality products or services produced by individuals);
- individuality (individually tailored, non-standard, unusual items);
- training/advanced training/skills acquisition;
- 'working differently'/social contacts/communication.

Notwithstanding all the candour and adaptability of the team of helpers the problem seems to be emerging that what the House offers, in obedience to the claim of its initiators – a call to self-chosen work and to 'education' – only partially coincides with the interests of potential users. It is as yet uncertain whether a 'middle way' can be found between what the House offers and demands and what the users need and are interested in.

On legal grounds alone the House cannot be used for commercial purposes, as this would jeopardize its charitable status. The initiators in any event strongly emphasize the conceptual distinction between ownwork and commercial utilization. The staffers put forward the 'ethos of ownwork' and rebut the charge of illegal working, sometimes raised in discussions, by claiming that it is 'working differently'. However, the unemployment exchange did not accept this interpretation and refused to let the project managers have Ministry of Labour premises on the grounds that if the idea were followed through logically it would destroy jobs. So far there have not been any difficulties with the many artisan workshops in the district (there are more than 40 joiners and cabinetmakers). The initiators of OH went to the firms on their own initiative and offered to cooperate with them, but there was no reaction. Only with one alternative joinery does good cooperation exist. The professionals are to use their skills, while routine work can be done by untrained persons themselves; this gives rise to an additional requirement, that could not be financed otherwise.

It was originally planned to engage as technical advisers craftsmen who had ceased working, but this has not yet proved possible, and so an arrangement was made with two professional cabinetmakers to give technical advice free of charge, in return for which they were to be allowed the use of the workshop for their own purposes when few users were about. The managers of the project regarded this as simply a 'temporary solution' which, although it would bring some life into the workshop, embodies a considerable deterrent risk. The search for suitable technical advisers is a particularly crucial problem because, as the initial experiences show, the teaching abilities of the adviser concerned have a great deal of influence on how the offered technical advice is received. Advisers who unwittingly make it obvious how much cleverer they are than the pupils and 'take over' the instruction awaken a traditional 'teacher–scholar relationship' and discourage especially those who had ventured into the workshops without any previous training in manual skills. 'Advice at home' might well prove to be an important additional card to play, and there are plans to introduce it. A technical adviser can be 'hired' for an hour or two, so that any initial contretemps can take place in the privacy of the home.

To cover itself against claims for liability, the OH has taken out a very economical global liability insurance policy, on which so far no claims have had to be made. People wishing to use some of the woodworking machines have to produce a certificate of competence, or else the services of the specialist adviser are used – and paid for.

A great variety of publicity work is done, virtually on a permanent basis, for the only way to attract the numbers of users the organizers hope to enlist is to make the project very well known. There was an opening ceremony and a 'taster week'; posters and leaflets are distributed; a planned programme of events takes place in the House; articles frequently appear in the press, and there are often reports on the radio and television; there were plans to advertise on underground trains in the autumn of 1988. The media are very interested, and it has never really been difficult to get articles into the newspapers. The abbreviation of Ownwork House (the Haus der Eigenarbeit – HEi) has become established as a powerful advertising symbol.

All in all, practical experience reflects the initial difficulties encountered by a project that came along with high innovative demands, even under the very favourable conditions attending the birth of Ownwork House. We assume that one possible reason for the fact that provision of a suitable infrastructure will not lead to any increase worth mentioning in the ability of private households to meet their own needs is that under the prevailing conditions, especially the persistence of a small 'operational size' of private households, there will not be sufficient incentives to undertake more ownwork. Networking of households and the generation of exchange relationships are hardly likely to occur of themselves. The experience garnered so far by OH confirms that such relationships need an institutional structure which is well thought out and a suitable medium of exchange. Ownwork House might conceivably lend itself to being an ideal basis for a solution of this kind, which we have called a 'cooperation circle', since exchange relationships would create sufficient incentives to use its facilities, time certificates could mobilize the resource 'time', and conversely the infrastructure of Ownwork House could offer the material and skill preconditions for an increase in self-supply. The future of Ownwork House will depend on whether the objects of the project, which hitherto have been somewhat starry eyed, can be redeveloped under the pressure of practical necessities into a realistic concept for promoting the ability of households to meet their own needs, so that these promising beginnings do not get bogged down into a 'run of the mill' inner city centre or an alternative community centre offering just one more adult education curriculum.

10

Functional Weaknesses of Moneyless Exchange Networks

This section is not intended to provide a conclusive comparative assessment of the ways in which exchange can be organized informally, without the use of money as a medium, with the examples described from the past and present, in Germany and elsewhere; here we shall simply try to set out in order the most important criticisms.

These criticisms relate to those characteristics of the networks described which must be held responsible for the fact that all the projects have proved to be shortlived or non-viable or exceptional solutions for extreme situations, or to have had only marginal effects on the satisfaction of material and social needs. The reasonable and attractive basic concept of the 'reskilling of time', of egalitarian exchange, free from exploitative relationships, and the market-like and hence voluntary socialization by means of multilateral exchange has repeatedly led to experiments and fresh endeavours in this field, spurred on at some times by the pressure of material need and at others by visions of social reform, and often by a mixture of the two. Yet during the century and a half of such endeavours no pattern has appeared sufficiently effective and transmissible to be able to serve unequivocally as a blueprint for introduction into the social conditions prevailing in the closing years of the twentieth century. In part III we shall offer some theoretical considerations, and in part IV some practical and constructive ideas, as to how these defects might be overcome, but first we briefly list them as they have come to light in the description and analysis of the networks we have examined. They are the following:

1 *Problems of size* It is obvious that the initial spontaneous growth impulses of moneyless exchange networks do not suffice to catapult them to an order of size at which they can be self-perpetuating. In their initial phases such networks are nourished by the surge of

confidence and the 'solidarity capital' possessed by people who belong to more or less tightly knit social groups (families, relations, colleagues at work, members of organizations and associations, neighbourhoods, the populations of small islands or of districts affected by economic depression, socially homogeneous wards or suburbs, ethnic and religious minorities, refugees from the same country of origin and so on). But once the limits of the particular social frame of reference have been reached, the very factor that was such a potent help at the beginning turns into a barrier to further growth.

2 *Problems of diversifying the range of goods and services offered-* These problems are closely connected with problems of size: the smaller the numbers participating and the more homogeneous the structure of the participants, the narrower the span of the services they both offer *and* require, the smaller is the advantage to be gained by joining and the slower any further growth. This vicious circle will become apparent especially quickly if the homogeneity of the participants leads to their all having a great need for category A services (say babysitting), while there is an excess of offers in category B (say help in submitting applications to authorities) which cannot be 'sold' within the network because there is little or no call for them. So the antinomy of management is that while the mutual trust needed for transactions does exist in homogeneous groups, there is not a sufficient overlap between offers and needs, and vice versa, in which transactions could take place.

3 *The problems of 'privatism'* Many signs and experiences from the projects and experiments described indicate that in modern social structures the threshold of the private and intimate sphere in individual households is fortified by strong cultural and emotional values. The consequence is that in the trade-off between material advantages and an unconditional preservation of the sphere of the private household an equilibrium of values prevails in which *very high* and *very certain* material advantages (or the avoidance of corresponding disadvantages) are needed in order to counterbalance *marginal* sacrifices of the privacy, tranquillity and social inviolability of this sphere. The only practical conclusion to be drawn is that this attitude can be overcome, if at all, only by a step-by-step, cautious approach, giving time and opportunity for a reassessment of these preferences in the light of experience, and trusting that (if all goes well) 'the appetite will grow with eating'. It might assist such reassessment if people who have taken part in exchange networks regularly were to make known the 'process benefits' of participation.

4 *The problem of matching* This refers to the problem that is

particularly serious with services, but is also acute with goods: what is the appropriate social mechanism for bringing together a posted requirement with a suitable offer – suitable in all the four relevant dimensions of quality, quantity, place and time. Disregarding for the moment compromise solutions, this problem can be solved either in a hierarchical, administrative way or in an egalitarian, voluntary coordination of offer and demand. There is no doubt that, especially if appropriate information technology is employed, turnover grows, increasing the contribution of the network to making supply and demand compatible among its members; but on the other hand there is a loss of the voluntary and spontaneous nature of the transactions, in that the suppliers (and furthermore possibly the customers as well) have orders allocated to them and requirements specified for them. It has to be expected that the curtailment of freedom and of discretion inherent in such a system will make an unfavourable impression on the circle of participants and inhibit its further growth. Conversely, voluntary coordination is likely to stimulate interest, for it preserves a quasi-market freedom in coordinating supply and demand; yet the number of 'bulls eyes' is likely to fall in proportion and the costs and risks of search in the coordination process are likely to rise. Together these two effects lead to the same result as in the former case: there is a slackening of enthusiasm for taking part and contributing services, only now it is not because the participant feels 'preempted' but on the contrary feels 'neglected'. Obviously there are difficult problems of optimization here, for what is needed is a solution that avoids *both* the above alternatives.

5 *Problems of confidence*   When exchange transactions take place between strangers using certificates as a medium, problems of confidence arise that are the mirror image of those arising between buyers and sellers in markets where money is the medium. Whereas in markets the greater risk lies with the party who hands out abstract liquidity and receives in exchange concrete goods or services (which might fail to provide the hoped-for use value), in voucher markets the one who carries the greater risk is the one who gives away a 'simple' service that can be easily assessed by the recipient, and receives in return a 'consideration' whose legally guaranteed and bankable value is not immediately distinguishable from any other piece of printed paper. The voucher gains its 'value' only through the double confidence invested in it, that (a) in the more or less distant future there will be somebody who *acknowledges* this value, and (b) that this (as yet unknown) future party to a transaction will then have *something to offer* which is subjectively at least equivalent to that service which was the consideration for the preceding trans-

action. This dual (and doubly risky) trust is especially liable to be disappointed and a dubious long-term speculation unless it is *either* confined to the family members of the donor or the donor's community (in which case the disadvantages mentioned under (a) and (b) earlier will follow), *or else* is underpinned and covered by guarantees of the voucher currency itself and of the proffered supplies.

6 *Problems of distribution* Informal exchange networks suffer from a characteristic that is both well documented and bewailed as a paradox: those sections of the population who can most easily overcome the problems cited here are least likely to have urgent need of the welfare enhancements provided by the system, and vice versa. This paradox reigns not only in respect of income and assets distribution in society, but also in respect of the age profile: old people most in need of help are least able to provide 'consideration' of their own. The consequence is that exchange networks of the kind examined here can be relevant and attractive only if a 'mixed structure' materially, socially and in age is achieved. Specifically this means that the transactions must bridge both the social divide between people who have 'a lot of time and little money' and those for whom the reverse holds true, and also the divide between the potential suppliers and takers of different categories of services, as well as spanning the temporal divide between different age groups. This too brings with it difficult problems of construction which, even if they were solved, would only show up yet another paradox: that attractive solutions to particular problems of social policy can be looked for only from strategies that are not specialized and *confined* to solving the said problems, as for example poverty and social assistance.

PART III

Towards a Theory of Moneyless Exchange

11

Strategic Advantages of Money as a Medium of Exchange

In order to understand the problems of moneyless exchange we must briefly recapitulate the specific virtues of money as a medium of exchange; then we can discuss the handicaps attaching, by contrast, to money substitutes such as vouchers and parallel currencies, handicaps that have to be overcome.

A feature of ordinary money as a 'legal' medium of payment is its extremely small transaction costs. Transaction costs are the totality of the valued inputs of resources and risks arising in the transfer of services between agents in a contractual relationship. Two kinds of transaction costs should be distinguished. They refer to 'whether' (that is, the accomplishment of a transaction) and 'how' (that is, its qualitative harmony with the contractual requirements and other expectations of the person receiving the services, including their timing and other conditions).

First, as regards the 'whether' of the payment, bourgeois law on contracts, debt and the punishment of financial misdemeanours, and the jurisprudence implementing its rules, provide very refined and effective instruments that ensure, with a high degree of reliability and as a rule with small transaction cost contributions falling on the creditor, that any existing payment demands can be successfully pursued. The transaction costs that arise are, as it were, subsidized by the general jurisprudence.

Secondly as regards the 'how', there are remarkably few problems involved in settling transactions with money. Both for domestic and international transactions, states through their central banks standardize a currency that enjoys a monopoly position in the settlement of payment claims, which are always expressed in certain currencies. Consequently the debtor is always *able to use* the specified currency to pay (instead of being obliged to use supplementary or different kinds of payment, the type and quantity of which can easily give rise to arguments); and conversely the creditor always *has to* accept payments in this currency in satisfaction of his claims (and, thanks to the monopoly position of the money medium, maximizes his range of choice in respect of any further purchases in which he engages). In this way (and because of the inherent 'absence of quality' in money, in that every banknote is worth as much as any other of the same denomination and its exchangeability is entirely unaffected by whether it is old or new) conflicts between buyer and seller as to whether a given claim has been settled with the 'correct' consideration are to a large extent eliminated.

Any imponderables relate only to the intertemporal and the international exchange relationships of current domestic to future domestic or to foreign money, and to the real value of the latter; but these questions never apply only to *single* parties to a contract; they are settled through the credit, currency and stability policies of the central bank as the general framework for *all* buyers and sellers. The only conflict that can arise between specific parties to a contract relates to the time of payment; but after the lapse of a certain 'period of grace' the creditor can treat the 'how' question in this matter as a 'whether' question, as we have described it above, and can make use of the legal processes provided for the purposes.

We can sum up this brief excursus into the characteristics and advantages of a social money economy sanctioned by the state by saying that *sellers* of goods and services (creditors with monetary claims) always enjoy extreme transaction cost efficiency. They can be relatively certain of receiving what is properly due to them, without even having to pay for this privilege. In other words, there is always less resistance to accepting payment than to accepting any other kind of economic action; the person who offers money will always encounter less hesitation in the other party than one who tries to place goods or services with others. Buying is not only 'easier', it is also 'more risky' than selling.

Every monetary transaction can be divided into two sequential sections of time: (a) the section *before* buyer and seller conclude the agreement, and (b) the section *after* the agreement is concluded. The saying quoted above that 'buying is easier than selling' refers to advantages that the buyer enjoys during the former of these two sections. Because the money that the buyer is prepared to pay represents a value that *everybody* desires to possess, because it is standardized by the state, every individual buyer has less trouble than every individual seller in 'closing the sale' – simply because money will appeal to practically anybody whereas in comparison any particular good or service has a much smaller group of potential takers.

But once the sale has been concluded and a contract signed, during the *second* phase of the exchange process, the relations between buyer and seller are reversed, and not only because once payment has been made the seller is now in a position to appear as a buyer with the money he has pocketed. It changes even before then, because the seller always has less trouble in performing the contract under contract law (that is, in the sense explained above: smaller transaction costs) than the buyer. It is seldom a serious problem to the *seller* whether he or she will receive what he or she hopes for and has agreed with the buyer, namely the purchase price that is fixed as to quantity and time of payment; he or she no longer has to fear 'unwelcome surprises' as soon as he or she enters the phase *after* concluding the contract, in which the agreement he or she has made only needs to be implemented. In this phase it is the buyer who bears comparatively the greater risk: he may well fear (though in very differing degrees according to the goods involved) that the goods or services he has bought do not have the characteristics that the seller promised or that the buyer expected. And in any event more transaction costs will be involved in dealing with disappointments (perhaps by making claims under warranty or guarantee or by claiming faulty workmanship) than a seller may incur when he or she has to make a neglectful buyer pay the agreed price.

The reference to this advantageous (because virtually risk-free) situation of the creditor is only intended as a backcloth to highlight the special transaction cost problems of non-monetary arrangements for settling transactions. If we combine the two distinctions between the formal and the informal economy on the one hand and between the transaction risks of sellers and buyers on the other hand into a single matrix, a clear and as a rule quite dramatic advantage gradient between the two positions in this matrix appears (see figure 3). Sellers in the formal economy are in the best position, because the advantages of legal tender referred to earlier give them a high degree of assurance that their requirement will actually be met. Buyers in the formal economy take second place on our scale of transaction risks, for although they cannot be nearly as certain as the sellers whether they will obtain all the characteristics they expected regarding quantity and quality, place and time, nevertheless there is a plethora of standards and procedures in commerical and contract law, as well as those provided by trade associations, which in all these areas provide relative protection against unpleasant surprises in the form of 'dud packages'. Indeed, such protection is to a certain extent in the interests of the manufacturer and the seller, who are both competing for customer confidence where branded goods are concerned and for this reason, in their own interest as a matter of market strategy, take care

Agents Structures	Sellers	Buyers
Money economy	e.g. central bank, civil courts 1	e.g. craft regulations, licensing regulations 2
Informal economy	? ("confidence")	Inspection and judgement from experience 3

Figure 3. Transaction cost situation of buyers and sellers in the formal and the informal economy (the diagram boxes contain *examples* of the respective guarantors and guarantee mechanisms and the numbers indicate the ranking of decreasing security and/or increasing transaction risks)

to relieve the buyer of some of his or her transaction costs by such measures as quality control, general terms of business, quality guarantees and 'money back' offers, even if these result in some addition to the price. In the case of both artisan goods and services and of personal and social professional services, all the developed industrial countries, and especially Germany, have an abundance of officially monitored standards affecting vocational qualifications (in the form of licences, permits, job descriptions, certificates, state examinations, professional codes of conduct and so on), which offer the buyers or customers of such services a certain guarantee of quality and competence. Despite all this, however, the buyer is worse off than the seller once the contract has been signed, because he or she is open to disappointment in the purchased goods with respect to quality (or with a feeling of regret that the buyer misjudged his or her real preferences as subsequently revealed). This risk of disappointment generates transaction costs for the buyer.

In the case of informal exchange transactions which do not involve the use of money – for example where work is done in exchange for vouchers – the parties suffer a further worsening of the transaction cost situation. But in this case the balance of advantage between buyer and seller is reversed. We are thinking here about the standard case of 'simple' services such as arise routinely in the area of the household and its immediate surroundings. By definition these services are such that the impressions, experience and skills of an ('average') buyer are quite sufficient to enable her (or him) to judge whether 'she got what she wanted' (and if she 'really wanted what she got'). Of course the seller has no 'certificate of competence' to flourish, and if the buyer is deceived (or self-deceived) as to the quality of the service to be expected this will not as a rule lead to a suit for damages in the civil courts; nor should it if, say, a hedge is not quite properly cut. Inspection and common sense, combined with the expectation that the present transaction will not be the last and that the prospect of the parties' meeting again will exert something of a disciplinary effect on the 'seller', add up to an informal quality assurance and bring the 'customer's' risk down to an acceptable level.

On the other hand, the situation of the seller in informal markets looks to be less favourable, for what he or she takes in exchange for his or her service is not 'money' but a voucher – a claim on services of a type as yet unknown, to be cashed in on a date not yet certain against another participant in the network, perhaps unknown at present to the seller. If the seller is to agree to accept payment of this kind in return for his or her services, he or she must have a reason for crossing the 'confidence threshold'. In the first place he or she must be confident that the worth of the currency extends through time and across the social space, and in the second place he or she must believe that the network services on offer in the future will include some that are of interest to him or her.

After these considerations as to the graduated transaction risks existing between sellers and buyers in the formal and the informal economies it is not surprising that types of service exchange using a non-monetary medium only arise spontaneously in exceptional circumstances and even so remain sporadic and highly susceptible to breakdown, even after they have passed a certain threshold of economic size and of continuity, despite the possible and often very concrete advantages they embody. Contrary to what Adam Smith and the classical writers on national economies thought when they posited 'A certain propensity in human nature . . . to truck, barter and exchange one thing for another' (Smith 1977: 117). this so-called 'natural' propensity seems to develop only within the framework of particular institutions, that is to say under the institutional umbrella of the money economy and of private law, and these are needed to open up an area in which it can develop and flourish.

Outside the sphere of the money economy an exchange of services only occurs either if the exchangers themselves do not intend to be exchangers of if the exchangers themselves do not intend it to be an exchange of services. The former case describes the situation in which the reciprocal giving and receiving of economic advantages occurs in *command*-organized social organizations, as for instance in firms or bureaucracies, but in such a way that the contribution made, for example by the development department of an industrial enterprise to the resources of the manufacturing department (and vice versa), is made not on the basis of mutual voluntary arrangements but on the basis of directives and controls on the part of a company management, to which both departments are subordinate. Thus in this case an at least formally voluntary exchange is replaced by a vertical coordination, which makes the exchange appear as an objective result of working together but certainly not as an intention to cooperate. Therefore such cases can be described as *a hierarchical solution to the transaction problem.*

The converse case of an exchange taking place objectively but not by intention is one in which, although the participants act consciously and voluntarily, they do not regard and intend their transaction as an exchange. The relevant example here is provided by families (and other forms of association whose members are bound to each other by the medium of *binding social standards*). Whereas in the case of firms and administrations the transaction cost risk is 'regulated away' through built-in lines of command, within the latter societies it happens because of the obligating effect of social standards. Intrafamilial relationships between spouses or between parents and children may very well partake of the nature of individual exchange transactions when viewed from outside. Yet the positively explosive power of conflict that would be released as soon as this exchange were effected *as* an exchange – if it were to be consciously and calculatingly seen by those concerned from the viewpoint of competition and equivalence – would inevitably disrupt the integrity of the family association in an instant.

Consequently, this problem of excessive transaction risks is overcome in relationships within the family between the generations (or the marriage partners) paradoxically by taking relations of love, sympathy, goodwill and mutual care for granted as being the rule, which enables the participants to undertake within more or less wide limits and long periods not to ask whether they are in fact receiving what others 'owe' them. This exchange calculation is replaced by the standard that one should 'selflessly' regard the advantages of the other as being one's own advantages. The paradox with this *solution to the problem of transaction costs through fellowship* is the fact that the source of conflicts is inhibited by making its non-observance into a rule. This encourages a preference for accepting advantages for others and sacrifice for oneself, in contrast to what outside the context of the family would rank as advantage to oneself in an equivalent exchange. Such a paradoxical arrangement can of course only exist if it remains strictly confined to the interior of the family or other association and is prevented from spilling over into the surrounding society.

12

Examples of Moneyless Transactions outside the Informal Economy

There can be no doubt that the dominant form of exchange in modern societies is the one in which *money* is used as the medium. There is a widespread impression that the opposite to this, the pure exchange of goods (barter), is an insignificant peripheral phenomenon in modern society, confined to a few cases of sporadic transactions between the owners of similar goods (for instance, the exchange of houses or apartments, of foreign stamps between philatelists, of garden produce between neighbours or holiday homes between family friends – see Dalton 1982). Between these two extremes, of exchange via the money medium and the exchange of goods, there are quasi-exchange transactions making use of money *substitutes* or of a 'special money' or a 'parallel currency' for particular markets. Many examples can be adduced to show that both barter and, in particular, the utilization of 'special currencies' can provide certain participants with certain benefits in certain markets, and this has led to a considerable reactivation of these forms of transaction so that they are only supposedly 'antiquated'. We shall now briefly describe some of these examples and the transaction cost advantages they possess in comparison with ordinary money.

(1) The American detergents group Proctor and Gamble makes available free of charge to private television transmitters throughout the world a series of entertainment films together with broadcasting rights in them. In consideration of these attractive programmes, which cost the TV companies nothing, the companies make advertising time for the firm's products available without charge or at greatly reduced prices. The advantage for the manufacturer of the detergents (and of the TV series) conferred by this moneyless barter between

programme and advertising time is that, through the scale effects of worldwide distribution in the context of a strongly expanding market of private TV broadcasters, the real costs per broadcasting hour of creating entertainment programmes are driven down far below the figure that the various transmitter stations (many of them small, local ones) would have had to shoulder for their own productions of comparable quality. An additional advantage for the TV company is that it can pay for this attractive raw material from the media industry in a 'currency' that it can, so to say, *manufacture itself* (almost like an illegal money printing press), namely with the transmitting time and the programme positions that are a by-product of the transmission. Unquestionably, both parties are advantaged: the detergent manufacturer buys advertising time far more cheaply than if it were commissioned in the usual way, and the series effect offers a certain guarantee that this advantage will last for some time; on the other side, the TV broadcaster gets the programme hours more cheaply than if they had to be produced inhouse or bought in. As long as this barter transaction can be concealed from the public, the broadcaster need fear no backlash in the form of doubts as to commerical independence, etc., and as long as it is concealed from the tax authorities both sides can perhaps expect additional tax-saving advantages (*Der Spiegel* 1988: 149f.).

(2)   A regional engineering industry association in West Germany goes in for opening up distribution channels for tomatoes. This line of activity, surprising at first sight for such an organization, makes commercial sense because these are Bulgarian tomatoes, and German suppliers of machinery to Bulgarian factories can be paid for their deliveries with the proceeds of their sale. Scarcity of foreign currency in the customer's country compels the latter to have recourse to bartering tomatoes for machines, and the association is providing a service which is at the same time an incentive to become a member, by making it possible to change the receipts from this barter transaction back into normal legal tender. So this in effect is a special currency organized by the association, which enables both sides to engage in transactions that would not otherwise take place; and because of the tomato marketing organization that has been built up, that currency is backed by the normal currency. Barter transactions of this kind are a regular feature of international trading, especially between developing or state trading countries and Western industrialized ones: they are known as 'countertrade'. Some estimates place the volume of this trade at 20 to 30 per cent of the total of international trade (Rotstein 1985:73).

(3)   In domestic trading as well there are some impressive examples of the efficiency advantages of barter trading relationships, though

the question who brings buyer and seller together and who guarantees the value of the credit notes made out in the units of account that do duty as a parallel currency has always to be settled. This problem can in fact be solved perfectly well on its own by a profit-oriented firm and not only, as in the foregoing examples, by way of contracts, associations and similar organizations. One example in the Federal Republic of Germany of a commercial solution to this problem is provided by the Barter Clearing and Information Company (BCI) which has offices in Vienna and Munich. The service sold by this firm consists in matching barter transactions between offerers and potential purchasers of used capital goods. The transaction is carried out with a giro transfer as follows: the seller of a capital good is not paid the amount of an invoice, but receives a non-interestbearing credit with which he can make his own purchases (and will do so promptly to avoid losing interest). In the same way the buyer receives an interest-free credit for up to nine months, after which time, however, he must pay it in good money. Clearly those taking part enjoy the considerable advantage in respect of transaction costs that as sellers they save on advertising and sales promotion costs and as customers are spared the costs of search they would otherwise incur. These transaction costs are covered by BCI by computer-assisted data research, for which an annual membership fee of between 1,000 and 10,000 DM (graded according to the turnover of the companies taking part) is charged. In West Germany this company now has more than 22 provincial offices and 400 district branches, and a membership of 4,500 companies. Reports from the USA for 1987 estimate that turnover from settlement accounts of this kind amounted to 350 billion dollars (*Frankfurter Rundschau* 1988).

(4)   Money substitutes and parallel currencies are also used in dealings between firms offering goods and services and private households. A far from complete listing of transaction media used in business and barter deals includes the following: credit cards, food tickets, vouchers, multijourney cards for public transport, coupons, credit notes, discount stamps, advertising premiums (for instance, for new subscribers to journals and periodicals), sample packs, advertising gifts, etc., etc. This colourful variety of marketing tools and strategies, some of which are employed not only by companies but also by state service organizations, are being researched by a special section of business management studies, marketing studies, and worked up into sales promotion strategies (see Kotler 1984).

(5)   Voluntary work also offers some examples of a certain neutralization of the money medium. This obviously occurs wherever services are performed for reasons of solidarity, charity or altruism for specific persons who need them. But if the services needed are of a kind that

have to be bought, a gift of money is not the only conceivable way to make such a purchase possible. The way a school in America manages its finances illustrates an original circuit whereby gifts in kind can be transformed into normal purchasing power without the interposition of an employer/employee relationship or a market transaction. As the school's personnel budget is not sufficient to pay for the additional teacher required, and as furthermore the parents were not in a position to make the needed funds directly available, they have had recourse to the following successful mixed strategy between gifts in kind, gifts in money and purchasing. First the parents were asked to offer precisely described gifts in kind (such as gardening, transport and purchasing services, 'party service', drawing up a will, and so on); next these service offers were auctioned at a full parents' meeting and the proceeds of the auction credited to the purpose in view. A feature of this arrangement at both stages was that it was not concerned with the extent to which those taking part were motivated by gain (for example, the motive of 'purchasing their freedom' from making monetary gifts by substituting gifts in kind, or the motive of buying a service cheaply at auction) or wishful to further the common good by making gifts in money or kind.

In this connection it is pertinent to refer to innovations in social policy, some already implemented and others being widely discussed, whereby 'useful activities' could be rewarded with claims on income, even though such activities were not necessarily of a commercial nature. Well-known examples are the crediting of time spent on education in assessing claims to social security payments, and the proposal to use 'social insurance credit vouchers' in payment for caring and other social services performed informally. The same principle is sometimes applied in the rent laws, where a tenant who has carried out maintenance or improvements to rented premises is repaid by a rent reduction.

(6) A pure exchange of services, without even an indirect usage of the money medium, occurs not only within family and neighbourhood networks but also within professional groups, especially artists and scientists. Painters and draughtsmen use part of their production (which in any event is sometimes hard to sell) by trading it for products of their fellow artists, and in this way acquiring sizeable collections. There is often an intensive exchange between groups of musicians, which includes counselling, friendly criticism, the loan or gift of musical arrangements, mutual recruiting for engagements and helping out with musicians, instruments and other tools of the trade. All this can result in substantial monetary savings. It is usual for the smaller scientific and literary periodicals to exchange advertisements

and free subscriptions, and for scholars to exchange publications and special reprints on a reciprocal basis.

(7) Yet another 'hybrid' amalgam of monetary and goods exchange occurs, again in the USA, in commercially run goods exchange networks. The principle of such networks, which bear such names as Pattern Research Exchange for Open Network (in Denver, Colorado) or The Learning Exchange (in Evanston, Illinois), is that in return for a membership fee individuals and organizations can be put in touch with sources of information and learning, some of them highly specialized, offered by other network members or with organizations, which members can use free of charge. This is a case of the commercial production of quasi-collegial relationships of help, advice, exchange and instruction, the financial advantage being the avoidance of the costs of search for people in need of specialized information. Of course networks of this kind can exist and function efficiently only because of the advanced state and wide diffusion of information and communications technologies.

There are two interesting common features possessed by every one of these instruments. First, by switching from money to a different medium the seller reaps the advantage of being able to exert a smaller or greater measure of control and influence over the buyer and/or of potentially saving some of the costs which would otherwise be incurred in marketing goods and services. In some cases, as with the use of universal credit cards, there is also the advantage that the buyer can save on costs and risks (for example the costs of always having the right amount of cash available at the right time, with its concomitant risks of loss and theft), for which buyers are willing to pay a price to the credit card companies. Some examples of the seller's advantages and gains in control can be seen in food vouchers – with food 'tickets' the quantity of individual consumption is rationed but vouchers (especially in social assistance, in the USA the important 'food stamps') confer control of the quality range of the goods consumed; in public transport multijourney cards that can save on ticket offices and clerks; in advertising, gifts and promotional prizes ('gifts are like hooks') which obligate the customer to the seller and improve the latter's chances of increasing customer and brand loyalty, and so on. For the customer too there are often considerable advantages, especially the receipt of price concessions in return for accepting the limitations on freedom of choice. To the customer who goes over to the use of non-monetary transaction instruments this 'farewell to money', which usually takes place voluntarily, appears as an exchange whereby he or she gives up a part of the range of choice and in return can exercise the remaining choices more economically. 'I may be giving the public transport organization interest-free credit when I buy the next ten journeys in advance, but I save money on each journey and do not need to go to the ticket office,' and so on.

If we think of the manifold examples of non-monetary transaction procedures encountered even in quite modern economies, indeed breaking new ground in those economies, and of their obvious advantages to both parties to the transaction, the idea that these advantages could be available not only in transactions between investors or between manufacturers and households, but also in exchanges *between private households* no longer seems at all eccentric. As has been shown, avoiding the use of money can make the transaction costs between the partners to the exchange firm and calculable; it may do away with search costs and the risk of disappointment on both sides. And above all in this way resources (such as free time) that would otherwise have remained 'valueless' because they were not susceptible of being converted into ordinary money can be brought into exchange relationships. It looks as though, for the lack of suitable institutional provisions and aids and for lack of organizing capabilities of their own, households in modern societies are largely prevented from enjoying the advantages that nearly all the other economic agents draw from non-monetary transaction media.

13

Transactions in Exchange Networks: The Problems Reviewed

In part I, we tried to produce evidence to show that in principle moneyless exchange networks between households could be an effective and innovative instrument with the aid of which problem situations of a sort common in modern households could be overcome in a welfare enhancing manner. The issues relate to the way households with much spare time exist side by side with those with little spare time; and to the diseconomies of scale of the small 'unit size', comparatively low incomes and instability of monetary income flows. And yet when we reviewed past and present examples of the application of networks of this kind the general conclusion emerged that among the great variety of patterns and types of organization none of the solutions was unequivocally suitable for large-scale imitation either quantitatively as regards turnover volume and the number of members, or qualitatively as regards long-term viability and growth potential. We shall now try to set out systematically the weak points of such networks; this classification will also form a guideline to be used in chapter 14 for making constructive proposals for developing a pattern that could turn out to be workable.

Figure 4 shows in diagrammatic form the relevant variables and problems of construction. The horizontal axis shows the relationship between offer and demand, the total volume of demand (OLCD) being defined as the product of q participants demanding p hours of services, and in r_n (c,e,f,i,j,m) categories of qualitative performance. Over against this demand is an offer (ABMN) defined by the same three dimensions. For the relationship between demand and supply it is first assumed that the number of persons and the amount of time is the same on both sides: OD = AN = q and AB = DC = p. In other words, the rules and obligations of membership do not allow of any 'free loaders' such as would appear if OD>AN, nor are there any 'honorary' helpers, who would appear if AN>OD OR

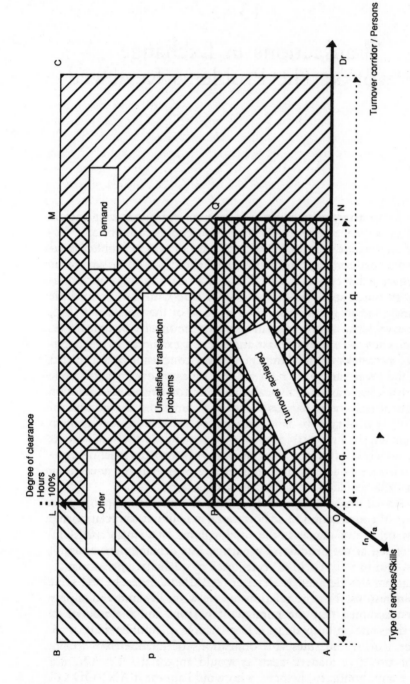

Figure 4. Structural problems and control variables of exchange networks (personal, time and quality parameters of offer and demand; turnover as the product of the turnover corridor and the degree of clearance)

AB>DC. On the other hand a mismatch in the third dimension, that of quality, is to be expected, as it concerns the nature of the services that are offered and demanded: r_a (a,c,e,f,h,k) r_n. This means that the composition of the *types* of service differs in quality between the offer and the demand side. The differences ABLO = NMCD are explained only by the difference between r_a and r_n, that is, the qualitative mismatch between supply and demand.

This qualitative discrepancy will occur even where there is only a small diversity between supply and demand. It is expressed in our diagram by the fact that the part of the demand defined as NMCD is of such a nature that the qualitative requirements that arise there cannot be met from the available offers, while conversely there is no demand for the ABLO portion of the offer. Only the area of overlap OLMN, which we will call the *turnover corridor*, indicates the volume of transactions that would actually be *possible* in a given system.

That concludes the discussion of the *production* problem illustrated in the horizontal dimension of our figure 4. Now the question is: on what does the size of the area of overlap between the two blocks of offer and demand depend? A first answer would be that it depends on the size of the network – the number of persons in OD = AN. But this answer is open to two objections. The first refers to the circularity involved in the fact that the size of the number of participants will be not only a cause but also a consequence of the *relative* size of the turnover corridor ON:AD. For, from the dynamic viewpoint, new participants will join the network only if attracted by a sufficient degree of probability that they will find in the network offers for their special requirements and takers for the services they offer – in other words, that on joining they will not land in fields ABLO or NMCD. Thus a membership that is 'too small' can be explained by an insufficiently large turnover corridor, and this in turn by too few members: it is the vicious circle again.

The second objection is as follows. As the number of participants increases the quotient ON:AD will grow only if there is a high positive correlation between the growth rates of q and r_a and/or r_n, which means that the *quantitative* growth of the number of participants must be accompanied by a *qualitative* diversification of the types of offer and demand. That will not occur if the age and social structure of the (newly joining) members is very homogeneous. For then the situation might arise for example that a lot of objects of the semiprofessional handicraft type not saleable in commercial markets are piling up on the supply side, while their makers are seeking predominantly repairs and household services, which are not on offer within the network. Only if growth in the number of participants is accompanied by a qualitative diversification 'in all directions' will the turnover corridor grow both absolutely and relatively. This relationship naturally holds true in the reverse direction; if supply is diversified and readily finds takers, new members will be attracted to the network.

Both these theoretical considerations and the experiences discernible in the projects and patterns that have been described prompt the suggestion that the relationship between the number of participants and the turnover corridor is shaped like a U-curve. Very small networks with a limited range of services (to take the extreme case, two-person single-good economies) exhibit a large turnover corridor. The trend is for all the services offered to be used and all requirements satisfied – as when two neighbours each take in one newspaper and they exchange them after reading. But if the number of participants grows, it is likely to do so in a way that is not sufficiently diversified socially and qualitatively, so that the relative size of the turnover corridor shrinks, discouraging new members from joining and leading to stagnation. Only beyond a comparatively high threshold, characterized by 'large' memberships and 'diversified' structures of offer and demand, does the system reach equilibrium and the possibility of self-sustaining growth. Thus in terms of this hypothesis the problem consists of finding ways in which this dangerous plateau of medium size and medium diversification can be traversed and conquered so that the circular relationship between the turnover corridor and the number of participants assumes the form of an ascending spiral.

And in fact the patterns and projects described contain within themselves a number of rules and provisions that can definitely be interpreted as means of encouraging such an impulse. For instance, if close communication links exist or can be created between offerers and demanders, this would cause the proportionate size of the turnover corridor to grow. At its simplest, this could be done by appealing to motives of neighbourly helpfulness and communal solidarity, and bringing them into play. If this were successful, then in the context of a more or less broad spectrum of undemanding activities there would always be on offer 'just what was needed' and the potential suppliers could have timely information of the need through appropriate neighbourhood communication networks. Conversely, people with requirements would be encouraged by the existence of this 'customer-friendly', flexible offer of services to welcome published offers and to take the opportunity of satisfying requirements which previously they might not even have known about.

Still, adaptation arrangements of this sort are rather primitive, unreliable means of harmonizing supply and demand, more suited to relationships between relatives, associates and friends than to exchange networks between strangers. These call for more formalized channels of communication, usually taking the form of lists of offers and demands that are distributed to participating households in the hope that offerers will respond to posted demands, and that demanders will actually make use of the services that are offered. But even lists of this kind are a relatively inefficient instrument when the problem is to harmonize the qualitative structure of offer and demand. The usual outcome will be that most of the participants 'can't do business' with most of the offers, and vice versa, for lack of the necessary knowledge, skills or equipment, or may even feel themselves to be disqualified for lack of the necessary self-assurance and social skills to go after the requirements that have been notified.

In view of these problems, which arise both in informal communication and in the more formalized kind involving lists, there is a further effective step that is actually taken in most of the SC projects in the USA, involving a more or less structured *hierarchical* coordination of offer and demand. Where this is done it results in the social structure of a voluntary fire brigade: when the need arises a hierarchical structure is activated and calls members to the scene of activity at the right time. This way of organizing the coordination of supply and demand certainly has the great advantage of being able to widen the turnover corridor reliably, but it also has the serious disadvantage of requiring participants to hold themselves in readiness for any 'orders' that may come through, irrespective of time, place or nature. A certain preparedness of this sort can be assumed only if people are compelled by law to exhibit it (as in the case of social or civilian service), or in the context of voluntary work for charitable or similar organizations, where 'instructions' can bring into play a kind of authority based on personal obligation. And while in such cases what we have called the turnover corridor is maximized, the number of participants (not to say the range of activities) becomes limited, because preparedness to be 'drafted' outside the social bounds of vocational and business links must be presumed to be very limited, and also because only a minority of requirements lend themselves to being met by 'drafted' and hierarchically controlled agents.

A fourth way of dealing with the problem represented on the horizontal axis of figure 4 consists in linking up exchange networks both with the charitable welfare services sector and with the normal market sector for coordinating offer and demand. This way appears both promising and innovative. A dual linkage of this kind, sketched out in the programmatical work of E. Cahn (1986, 1987a) and incorporated into the workings of SC projects, results in the following structure. Part of the unmet demand NMCD is covered by a 'deficiency guarantee' underwritten by welfare organizations, charitable associations, church congregations, etc. But these services are not (or not exclusively) provided from charitable and philanthropic motives; members of the exchange network have a prior *claim* on them. The basis of this claim is that previously a part of the offer overhang (ABLO) not at the time covered by current demand, was used on behalf of the needs of these welfare institutions and paid for with the necessary vouchers. In this way a collective external exchange relationship arises between the members of the network as a whole and the welfare agency, resulting in a relative enlargement of the turnover corridor within the network. In the same way as a bank accepts payments and issues credits, the welfare agency would take up parts of the overhangs of offers in which it was interested and in return would be in a position to close gaps in demand. This is further proof that such exchange networks by no means inevitably lead to a stunting of 'altruistic' motives; as has been shown, they can gain considerably from activating them via the mechanism of a 'bank'.

The second of these links consists in creating a bridge between the internal economy of the exchange network and the market economy outside. In the most trivial case this linkage might take the form, say, of a piano tuner who finds himself with his offer in field ABLO, withdraws this unused offer, places it instead on the ordinary market and uses the income so earned to satisfy his demand, which is not covered by offers from within the network, in the area NMCD. However, if in addition the possibility that must be postulated always and for everybody were to exist, that is if a high demand for labour went hand in hand with high incomes and service offers of acceptable quality and reasonable price, the problem that concerns us here would to a large extent disappear. Nevertheless it must be expected that if such favourable conditions existed the *relative* size of the turnover corridor would increase, simply because the two fields of offer and demand overhang would decrease. The much less trivial case of a link between the exchange network and the ordinary market economy occurs if – as in the example of the LETS system in Canada – a way is found of exchanging within the network itself not only 'complete' services produced internally but also value creating and value adding services leading to composite services which might include a large proportion of externally procured 'preproducts'. This would facilitate a strong upsurge of types of service suitable for turnover within the network, always provided that – as in the case of LETS – there were dual currencies and the principle of the 'dual price tag' which provides a flexible link between production within and outside the network.

In addition to the production problems dealt with so far, the solution of which determines the size of the overlap between offer and demand (the turnover corridor), *transaction* problems constitute a second class of problems coming up for solution in exchange networks. These transaction problems include all the costs (and assessable risks) preceding, accompanying or following acts of exchange. They include the costs of search involved in putting offerers and potential customers into contact, and the costs and risks involved in giving both of them a reasonable assurance that they will receive, or have received, the 'right' answer to their requirements, expectations and needs. The conditions of membership and other 'rules of the game' of the exchange network in question determine how much exchanges within the network cost and what risks they embody, and hence in the last resort whether, for whom and under what conditions it is 'worth' joining the network in view of these costs and risks. To speak more accurately, the rules of the game determine the extent to which the 'really' possible turnover corridor, defined as the overlap between services offered and services demanded, will in practice be cleared (OPQN). In other words, the magnitude that has to be maximized is neither the absolute nor the relative size of the turnover corridor; the efficiency of the system is measured by the 'greatest possible' clearance of the 'largest possible' turnover corridor.

The *degree of clearance* dimension of the problem is represented by the vertical axis of our diagram. We should make it clear that the distinction between 'turnover corridor' and 'degree of clearance' is an analytical one, and a real link is to be assumed at least in the sense that an extremely low degree of clearance will make it unattractive for new members to join, and this in turn will diminish at least the absolute size of the turnover corridor, and probably its relative size as well. It must also be assumed that an (absolutely) 'larger' turnover corridor will cause the search costs and perhaps the risks of disappointment (in the case of exchanges between strangers) to rise as well. Consequently the turnover corridor would, unfortunately, be a positive function of the degree of clearance, but at the same time the degree of clearance would be a negative function of the turnover corridor (and vice versa). The result of this inverse relationship would be that (depending on the available 'transaction technology') there is an optimum absolute turnover corridor defined (a) by the fact that it must not continue to grow if the search costs and disappointment risks are not to become so large that participants begin to withdraw, and (b) that it must not shrink so much that (potential) participants have no incentive to join in.

The 'ideal solution' to the problem of clearance would be achieved if three expectations, based on experience, were to prevail:

1   that if what one requires is actually on offer in the network, it can be *easily found*; and conversely
2   that if what one wishes to offer is actually needed by another participant, it can be '*sold*' without the expenditure of a lot of time/money/effort; and
3   that neither on the demand nor on the offer side is there serious reason to fear that one will later have cause for regret at entering into the transaction.

The further away an exchange network is from this ideal state, which is identical with a clearance factor of 100 per cent, the larger is field PLMQ. Thus the size of this field represents the extent of unsolved transaction problems.

The projects described incorporate many rules and precautions designed to bring the way in which the network actually functions closer to this ideal state, thus realizing its potential efficiency to the highest degree achievable. To attain this, efforts are made to bring existing offerers and demanders together as rapidly, smoothly and appropriately as possible, and to provide quality assurance for recipients and confidence for sellers.

BRINGING OFFER AND DEMAND TOGETHER (MATCHING)

In discussing the cases in the Netherlands we made a distinction between predominantly 'active' and predominantly 'passive' approaches to this problem. Active variants, as found in the majority of SC projects in America, provide for the persons offering to be brought together with those having requirements via the sponsoring organization or the 'bank', whereas in passive systems it is left to participants themselves to make contact (by telephone). It cannot be said with certainty which of these two alternatives (and the many conceivable mixtures and variants of them) is likely to bring about the greater degree of clearing. Active systems place the initiative on the demand side, and have the advantage that matching can take place quickly and accurately through a computer program and on the basis of all the data held in the files (for example as to the time, location and quality characteristics of the offerer concerned). Their disadvantage is that offerers tend to be 'sent out' and instructed to do the job; a directive relationship with hierarchical overtones comes into existence, some way removed from the conditions of a 'free' market transaction and easily capable of stifling the motivation of potential suppliers to offer their services and participate.

The predominantly passive form of 'brokering' has its corresponding advantages and disadvantages. Typically the headquarters simply makes available condensed information about the types of service on offer and the telephone numbers of the offerers, leaving it to participants to initiate contact. In such cases a lot depends on how frequently these information lists are updated and distributed. Another important criterion for the success of this system of matching are the 'inhibition thresholds' that always have to be negotiated when making contact with strangers, and how widespread are social and cultural routines and skills that can help in this situation. Another important issue is reaching agreement on mutually convenient timing and location for the transaction. Undoubtedly the passive system of matching has the advantage that the specific conditions of the transaction can be directly negotiated between the parties without the intervention of the central office, which could easily be swamped by such tasks if it were not of an authoritarian cast. The services required must be described accurately, so that the offerer can check them for feasibility; agreement must be reached as to when (times, days of the week, commencing dates) and how long (agreed duration of the job, especially when this is to be made the basis for payment by means of vouchers, etc.). Moreover when offerer and demander live some way apart there arise questions of travel time and cost and how these are to be paid for. All this is administratively difficult to settle, and inevitably has side effects damaging to motivation; so a passive form of institutionalization might be preferable, especially one that succeeds in providing suitable encouragements and aids to induce members to cross the 'inhibition thresholds'. Social events of various kinds can often help in this process.

QUALITY ASSURANCE

SC projects in the United States in particular are concerned to ensure, by a variety of arrangements, that the recipients of services are satisfied with what is offered and that it really meets their actual requirements. To this end they run training courses for the providers of simple social services; they issue detailed rules of behaviour and carry out random checks, customer surveys and so on. Generally speaking the problem of quality assurance has two aspects: making sure that 'the job is done properly', for example that a garage wall is painted in the right way; making sure, too, that 'nothing wrong is done', for example that shrub borders alongside the wall are not damaged. Only when it is reasonably certain that both these conditions will be met can the necessary routines of the exchange be brought into play.

An important result of our investigations in this area – one, more-over, that is relevant to any practical trial of such exchange networks – can be summed up by saying that these networks only have a very limited ability to solve the transaction problem inherent in quality assurance from their own resources and finances, that is to say without external support. Where there is a satisfactory way of doing this, they often rely on cultural 'prepayments' in the form of relations of confidence and social control relationships specific to their location and milieu. But they pay for this advantage by being unable to expand beyond the boundaries of the milieu in question. Or else they exercise a certain administrative control over their members in general and those offering services in particular, which they are able to do only because, as in most of the SC projects, they operate in practice as subordinate appendages of social and health authorities and similar institutions and hence can afford to impose fairly strict controls on their members; but even so this control gain has the result of virtually confining the clientele to social groups whose members, because of their disadvantaged socioeconomic position, can be expected to accept them.

A possible alternative to these somewhat limited expedients might be to approach the problem of quality control, and therefore confidence assurance, by 'transaction cost subsidies' coming from outside. For in practice all that exchange networks can do of their own accord to forestall disappointments on the part of service recipients is to screen out 'risky' offers in the area of professional services (for instance, health-related ones) and always to remember that although the recipients can expect 'usable' services that meet reasonable expectations, they should not expect them to be of the same quality as the leading goods and services available on the market. All that can be expected beyond 'precautionary measures' of this kind is that if and when the volume of turnover rises sufficiently this will inevitably give rise to effects of specialization and practice that will tend to drive out really inexpert, faulty and hence unsatisfactory performance of the services offered. Further than that, solutions to the problem of quality assurance must always depend on assistance from *outside*. Such assistance might take the form of making available equipment and personnel, consultancy services, training and skilling programmes and the acceptance of liability.

Confidence-building by suppliers

For a currency to be acceptable as a transaction medium, sellers of services (that is recipients of payments) must have sufficient reason for believing that they will be able to use the payments they have received to make their own purchases, the place, time and nature of which are as yet unknown. Whereas for a normal currency this guarantee is given by the central bank and cognate institutions, no corresponding guarantee function exists for vouchers and other parallel currencies. The fact that the official currency enjoys quasi-monopolistic privileges over against other possible transaction media has even led some commentators holding unconventional opinions on constitutional law to claim that this is an infringement of the principle of equality in the welfare state and that similar guarantees should be available for other media as well (see for example Suhr 1988a:74ff.). We cannot go into detail here regarding such far-reaching opinions, although they could lead to interesting results and defensible proposals for rules to deal with these problems.

It is even truer of the problem of confidence building by suppliers than of that of quality assurance for recipients that it cannot be solved *only* by the totality of the participants, but that help is needed from an external source of supervision and guarantee. One extreme – and certainly exaggerated – form of confidence protection would subsist if an outside body were to declare its readiness to convert holdings of vouchers at any time or under defined conditions, fully or partially, at a fixed or variable rate of exchange into the official currency, or else to come in with an 'indemnity bond' to provide the service that was desired but not obtainable from offers currently available within the exchange network. A weaker form of confidence building would subsist if the guarantee on the supply side of exchange networks made provision for the 'collateral security' to be given by an external source, such as a charitable organization. In each of these cases the apparently paradoxical effect would certainly appear that a very 'strong' confidence assurance is also one that remains purely nominal. If every participant knows that he can call on the collateral at any time and thus make his exit unscathed, offers will be forthcoming in such variety and profusion that nobody will have occasion actually to call on the indemnity.

The problem of confidence building on the supply side is complicated by the question as to how long vouchers should remain valid. This problem is defused if very short validity periods are agreed, or are encouraged by suitable arrangements such as vouchers being non-interestbearing or gradually decreasing in value; for then every participant has good reason for trying to get rid of the vouchers again as soon as possible, like the Bear in the card game of Pit. This will speed up the circulation of vouchers, thus stimulating and stabilizing the whole operation. Yet on the other hand there are good arguments in favour of having, perhaps even encouraging, vouchers with a long 'shelf life'. For one thing, it would enable much larger 'purchases' to be made with vouchers, such as building, conversion or renovation projects worth hundreds or even thousands of working hours. Another argument for preferring 'long life' vouchers is that (as was shown in chapter 2) the volume of institutionally uncommitted time, which by definition is the only kind that can be made available for the exchange network, varies considerably throughout the life cycle. Thus there may be good reasons for accumulating a credit balance of claims during periods when free time is plentiful, to be used during periods when time is much more committed. This recalls the idea of a 'social insurance system on a time basis' that is discussed from time to time. Under such a scheme time spent, for example by mothers on family and educational work, would be calculated as a credit, that might be spent later on not only as a money claim (as for a pension) but alternatively to purchase services measured on a *time* basis. Such a 'time account' could be saved up for a long period and utilized later, palliating both the 'retirement shock' of the 'young elderly' with their sudden, forced retirement from business life, and the equally vexed problem of the increased dependence of the very old on social services. These few hints must suffice to indicate that consideration should at least be given to designing the parallel currency of service vouchers in such a way that they could have a long-term use as well. But, as with the official currency, this will not happen unless there is an authority that will safeguard the real value of the parallel currency and the amounts of credit accumulated in it to ensure that the risks associated with its use are not so great as to constitute a deterrent.

PART IV

The Cooperation Circle System

14

Proposals on the Practical Design of the Cooperation Circle System

In this chapter we should like to set out in more detail specific, practicable *suggestions* for the design of a sociopolitical experiment which we call the 'cooperation circle system', and which we have already outlined in chapter 3. We have deliberately refrained from going into excessive detail about rules and regulations, for fear of producing something that was too comprehensive, confusing and generally offputting. Moreover, a great many individual questions can be resolved only in the context of local political priorities and circumstances. What is presented here therefore is an outline of the essential pattern with its scope for variations, which can only be filled in step by step in the context of a particular embodiment of the system. Only the test of practical experience will show what the system can do.

Furthermore we must stress from the outset the supplementary, compensatory role of a *'parallel economy'* the system is designed to play in the sphere of the domestic environment, to avoid loading it with unrealistic expectations and consequent disappointments. The objective is not to achieve near self-sufficiency of supply, but to strengthen the structure of self-help capability, in the full realization that the vast majority of goods and services will continue to be provided by and from the formal economy with its medium of money. It must also be realized that 'cooperation circle' type supply systems will not prove to be practicable nationwide in all kinds of social space and for all groups and classes of the population, and that their continuance over time can only be promoted with incentives, never really guaranteed by political and administrative means.

The services that can be offered

The cooperation circle concept is designed to involve as many actual and potential members of such an exchange system as possible in making their own productive contribution as frequently as possible to as wide a range of activities as possible, while creating opportunities for the satisfaction of needs at reasonable cost and with acceptable quality. The better this quantitative goal of wider participation can be achieved, the more probable does it become that suitable offers will be forthcoming in response to requirements, and vice versa. On the other hand there are reasons for thinking that it would be more prudent initially – at least during the experimental practical trial – to place the emphasis on 'everyday activities' and for 'risky' services calling for high and specific qualifications (for example those concerned with health or safety) to be included only with caution and as exceptions. Too great a difference in the 'value' of the services exchanged would undermine the plausibility of the time standard on which the vouchers would be based, and serious problems of liability and guarantee might arise.

We give below a list of the kinds of services we have in mind, which may be assumed to be within the capabilities of most people to perform without prior qualifications or advanced training or capital equipment; in other words, the requisite tangible and intangible household capital can be assumed to be available. We distinguish between (a) object-centred and (b) person-centred services:

Object-centred services in the household environment

- Building, maintenance, cleaning and servicing of dwellings, including small modernization projects (e.g. thermal insulation) and installations;
- Repair and maintenance of fittings and equipment;
- Laying out and tending kitchen and ornamental gardens, and possibly small-scale agricultural activities including the care of domestic animals;
- Maintenance of and minor repairs to automobiles and other vehicles;
- Room clearance and possibly taking over parts of the house refuse removal;
- Purchasing, storage and preparation of food;
- Making, providing, altering, repairing and caring for textiles;
- Other improvements.

Person-centred tasks in the domestic environment

- Simple personal services to children, sick, handicapped and aged people, including non-specific services such as 'visits', 'providing company', reading, etc., relieving professional assistants and carers ('respite care');
- Shopping, procurement and transport services;
- 'Party service' and catering;
- Assistance in contacts with authorities and the courts (for example, filling out tax declarations) and with manufacturers of retail goods (e.g. making claims under guarantees, advice on purchases, etc.);
- Advice and assistance with setting up, operating and using technical equipment such as cameras, entertainment electronics and computers;
- Teaching and instruction such as help with schoolwork, language teaching, music lessons, cookery courses.

Without doubt this list of suitable service offers could be extended, and participants themselves might well open up new fields for exchange transactions facilitated by vouchers. These might include the purchase or sale of used goods, especially consumer durables, against vouchers, or hiring out equipment and even furniture. At all events, experience in North America points in this direction.

Even though initially the 'less skilled' activities are expected to preponderate in cooperation circles, this does not necessarily mean that no professional or quasi-professional services could be offered. Nevertheless since, as mentioned above, the price formation mechanism has been restricted by linking the (indivisible) credits to the standard of actual time spent, thus excluding considerations of quality or skill, an automatic limitation on the offer of 'demanding' activities is built into the design of cooperation circles. Anybody who can expect to earn high fees in the free market or the 'grey economy' for his or her services will hesitate to join a cooperation circle – at least if he or she is guided by considerations of economic cost–benefit. If such a person nevertheless becomes active in a cooperation circle, that person will be motivated by other than purely economic considerations, and this could also be an important motivational resource in lessening potential disputes about the differing valuation of activities.

The list of suitable goods-centred services includes a number of improvement activities. This refers to activities designed to supplement, improve and convert (pre)products that can be purchased in conventional goods markets or produced individually in the household by ownwork. For a flexible linkage between internal and external production to exist, there would have to be a split currency and the principle of a 'dual price tag' (see chapter 6). For example, the supplier of a total service would have to show the (money) price of the raw material or the pre-product as well as the (voucher) price of the additional value created separately. This applies to all cases in which a total service incorporating externally procured pre-products is offered (but only to such cases). Experience from Canada indicates that the incorporation of value adding and improvement work of this kind can add considerably to the activities possible within a cooperation circle.

Legal structure of an association

Under the legal system prevailing in the Federal Republic of Germany the organizational form of a 'registered society' appears to be an appropriate legal form for a cooperation circle to adopt. To a large extent this relieves its founders and administrators of liability claims, and it does not face intending members with such strong commitments as to deter them from joining. A further advantage is that such an association can be started with only a small number of members, and that even considerable changes in the size of the membership do not influence the stability of the external, legal form. Moreover, a registered society can engage employees, and can receive and administer contributions and tangible assets from third parties. Both these powers are important if the state, municipalities or foundations make help available in the form of personnel or material support.

An alternative to forming a new society would be to build up a cooperation circle through an already existing assocation or even by cooperation between several bodies, associations, trade unions, cooperatives or church parishes. If this were done it would be important to ensure that anybody living within the catchment area of the cooperation circle could take part and that the exchange activities did not remain confined to the previous members of the sponsor concerned or of the founding societies and associations. Which of these alternatives – forming a new society, grafting it on to an existing one or bringing together several societies and associations – is the most appropriate depends on the individual circumstances of the particular case. In particular it is useful to bear in mind that more complex structures become possible when cooperation circles are linked to charitable organizations by means of a voucher system, as described earlier in chapters 7 and 13.

It would be possible in a cooperation circle for the *board of directors* of the society to assume the management functions, as is the practice in most such societies and is facilitated by the legal form. The board would be responsible for the following tasks:

1 Public relations in general (advertising and information for potential members);
2 Circulating information about offers and requirements to participants (perhaps by lists with 'small ads' updated monthly or more frequently). Consideration might also be given to 'brokerage' activities by the board, putting it on to an 'active' basis. This would be done both on request and also whenever contact-making appeared to be taking too long;
3 Maintaining a list of members and collecting a once-only entrance subscription;
4 Supervising the voucher bank.

Contrary to the practice in many small associations, the managers of a cooperation circle need not be expected to give their services without remuneration; one possible alternative might be to pay them in vouchers.

The legal structure of an association involves the question of the rights and duties of *members*. All individuals in a certain catchment area could be eligible for membership; they would simply have to pay a single membership fee and agree to the rights and duties of membership. The fees would have to be used to cover running expenses such as paper, printing, postage, the procurement and maintenance of a showcase, etc. But they need not be so high as to deter potential members; it would also be useful in certain cases to accept payment of the entrance fee in time worked (for the cooperation circle), for example in the maintenance of equipment. Members should be able to leave a cooperation circle at any time, though if at the time of leaving there were unpaid debts in vouchers these would have to be settled on leaving, in ordinary money if need be.

The bank and credit creation

In order to control the issue and circulation of the vouchers that form the basis of the exchange network a bank will be required, operating under the supervision of the board of the association. All that is necessary is that someone elected by the members and responsible to the board should perform the following functions according to a few simple rules (that person can be remunerated, partly at least, in vouchers).

1 Every member on joining shall pay an entrance fee and if necessary an annual fee, these to be paid in ordinary currency.

2   On payment of the entrance fee each member shall receive a certain number of vouchers (for example, two).

3   Every member is entitled to draw credits from the bank in vouchers, the limit perhaps increasing with length of membership. As regards an upper limit for drawings, something like 50 vouchers might be appropriate. The bank will keep accounts about the issue of these vouchers and their repayment. No interest would be paid on drawings.

4   When credits are issued the recipient would undertake to repay them within a certain time (say no later than one year) or failing that to pay a prescribed sum per voucher in lieu. In order to speed up circulation and turnover it is advisable to incorporate automatic devaluation. If this is done, the bank will have at least two further things to do:

5   To speed up transactions, i.e. the circulation velocity of the internal currency, every two years there could be a complete devaluation of the vouchers then in circulation. The bank would then issue new vouchers, which might be of a different colour. All members whose accounts were in balance would be able to exchange their old vouchers for new ones;

6   A slightly more complicated but probably more manageable and effective solution would be for the seller (i.e. the recipient of the voucher) to write on the back of the voucher after each transaction the date and perhaps the membership number of the other party and to authenticate it by signing. This would provide a basis for implementing the rule that vouchers that had not been in circulation for say three months would lose their value as an internal medium of payment. This would have the side effect that after circulating for a certain period vouchers would be filled up and would have to be exchanged at the bank for new ones, thus enabling the 'used' vouchers to serve as information slips concerning the people participating and the volume of the network's turnover. It would also be important if outsiders contemplating some form of assistance wished to be reliably informed about the number of participants and the turnover.

7   To prevent these measures from destroying the possibility of saving large amounts of vouchers for large projects or as a nest-egg for old age, there should also be 'voucher savings books', that is to say long-dated certificates, available at the banks. These should, however, be subject to a notice period of perhaps a year for withdrawal, to enable the bank to accumulate the reserves needed to encash the holdings.

Time as a unit of account

In conformity with previous models and practical trials with inter-household exchange systems, time should be the unit on which vouchers for a service, expressed in the internal currency, would actually be based, thus creating entitlement to other services requiring the same amount of time. This ruling deliberately ignores two factors:

1   it ignores the fact that even for one and the same job *assignment* the result of one hour's work may differ markedly according to the performer's degree of skill, effort and experience; and
2   it also ignores the fact that, even with the same amount of working *effort*, the value of the job on the ordinary market, measured in units of money, is subject to wide variations. This price and value gradient (depending on conditions of skill and scarcity) between different kinds of work affects the sphere of informal work inasmuch as the savings effect if 'more expensive' work is commissioned is naturally much greater than that achieved if 'run of the mill' work is commissioned.

However, there appear to be good grounds in both cases for overlooking such differences on the basis of the time standard. With regard to (1), the recipient of the service, who might conceivably not be satisfied with the efficiency and vigour of the supplier, has the opportunity of compelling the supplier to do work of satisfactory quality and amount by direct communication, as by negotiating, complaining, warning and so forth (the 'voice' principle) and finally, if such means fail, of breaking off the transaction with this supplier and accepting a competitor's offer (the 'exit' principle). This amalgam of social communication and market mechanisms should help to set limits to the 'scatter' of the qualities of individual performances and to promote some sort of standardization as to what can be expected as a 'normal' and 'acceptable' standard of performance.

As to (2), the levelling out of the market difference between different types and levels of skill in services, there is much to be said for refraining from grading services according to their 'value' and having instead a unified standard of the hours spent for *all* services performed. First, it does away with the decisional, administrative expense that would be involved in grading different kinds of activities. Second, this solution accords with a demand for egalitarian standards and thus enlarges the circle of people who can summon up the confidence to make their own successful and profitable contribution to a cooperation circle by offering their own services; for even if they themselves have but 'little to offer' – perhaps doing shopping or providing company for others – they obtain in return entitlement to skilled, desirable services from others, without fear of being exploited. In the third place the limiting effect that this egalitarian arrangement would exercise on the offer of really high-value services in thoroughly desirable. For it would diminish the attractiveness of bringing demanding professional or skilled services (for example those of tax consultants or electricians) into the informal network to any considerable extent, just because their exchange value would be no greater there than that of any other service; and in this way it would protect the legitimate professional and vocational interests of those who could offer such services in minimizing 'black' competition. Indeed, in some cases the virtual exclusion of professional services from informal networks might be objectively in the interest of the recipient of such services, in relation to liability, guarantee and quality assurance. A final clinching argument for this proposed rule of 'unified valuation' is that there would still be some incentive to bring demanding and skilled services into the network, since it can be assumed that these services (such as supplementary lessons, language and music teaching) would be specially in demand owing to their increased saving effect, and would therefore create favourable opportunities for those offering them to earn vouchers without incurring any great transaction costs such as waiting periods or search costs.

In any event, time will lose its preeminence as an exclusive unit of account in moneyless exchange systems of the cooperation circle type if secondhand goods are also included. While generally speaking there is no difficulty in exchanging comparable periods of time, in this case the internal currency would facilitate normal price formation mechanisms.

Exclusion of pricing

The proposed unified time standard for all services (with the exception of trade in secondhand goods) signifies that the price formation mechanism usual in markets where money is the medium of exchange would be put out of action. This involves the conscious acceptance of the risk that the imbalances that may be expected to arise between offer and demand will not be able to be smoothed out by lowering the price of 'excess' supply and raising that of services in short supply relative to demand. Were price formation of this kind to be permitted it would be foreseeable that sooner or later the price differentials for different kinds of services that exist in ordinary markets for labour and services would arise within the system of the organized exchange network, with the inevitable result that people offering unskilled services would be faced with such unfavourable exchange ratios for the 'run of the mill' services they offered that they would no longer have much reason for belonging. In other words, if the principles of the market economy are to be expected to engender an exchange ratio of 'ten lawn mowings for one change of wheel bearings', the exchange system can only be expected to collapse because it has ceased to be of economic interest and has become discouraging and positively degrading, with a consequent loss of participant motivation on both sides of the exchange.

On the other hand it is no simple matter to prevent a price mechanism from coming into existence. One measure, useful but not of itself sufficient, consists of dividing up the time-based voucher currency into units representing whole hours (and perhaps multiples of hours); that would at least make it more difficult to introduce discounts or supplements to take account of scarcity situations. However, this 'technical' measure does not overcome the 'moral' problem that obviously faces us here. This problem can be subdivided into two parts: the 'black market' problem and the 'queuing' problem.

1 *'Problems of the black market'*   The attitude taken by neoclassical economic orthodoxy to this problem can be summed up in the contention that wherever free price formation is made difficult or impossible an escape mechanism in the form of black or grey markets will come into existence, reflecting the real relationships of scarcity. In the present context this would lead to the expectation that the normal money economy would come into action as the 'black market' if there were no other way to take account of scarcity relationships. This can be illustrated by two mirror-image cases. First, assume that the members of a cooperation circle have a large number of vouchers earned by services, but that the current mix of goods and services on offer does not coincide with demand. So the participants find it unattractive to spend the vouchers they have accumulated. Instead, the natural and logical thing for them to do in such circumstances, according to the economists' forecast, is to try to dump their superfluous vouchers on the ordinary market (which for our purposes is the 'black' market) in exchange for money. Second there is the converse case, in which the services on offer are greatly in demand and scarce, raising the question of whom among the many potential customers shall be served first, if at all. In market economy terms the answer is obvious: the one who makes the highest bid. But since prices are fixed and tied to the hour standard, this avenue is closed. Economic prediction would suggest that this standard should be bypassed, with bidders acquiring the goods or services by making

additional payment, or 'greasing palms' in ordinary money.

These illustrations show that it is by no means easy to insulate the parallel economy based on vouchers from the prevailing money economy. At all events, this cannot be done either by *technical* means or by administrative controls; even authoritarian political regimes, with their policing arrangements, have difficulty in combating black markets in their own goods and services. Therefore the only viable solution is the *moral* commitment of the participants in a cooperation circle; *they* must determine that if imbalances between supply and demand arise, they will resist the temptation to digress into the money market. The rule that a purchase of services (or the sale of vouchers) for money is an offence against the common basis of business practice and mutual confidence can prevail only if it is accepted voluntarily; it cannot be enforced by the threat of penalties and the like. This makes it all the more important that every member of the network should be aware from the outset of the insidious nature of such temptations and the vulnerability of the network to them.

2   *The queuing problem*   This second problem does not become apparent until the first one has been solved. The question is: if the quality imbalance between supply and demand cannot be solved through price formation and the rationing effect thereby introduced, how is the balance to be effected? There is need to distinguish between two variants in the queuing problem as well. In the first, potential *suppliers* of services are waiting for takers to pay for their services with vouchers. It occurs when what is on offer is not what is required, and this engenders a need to alter the composition of the proffered supplies without using the mechanism of price signals. This is possible because the exchange network described is essentially an economy of 'run of the mill' services, and therefore one in which the suppliers are not limited by skills and an institutionalized division of labour to offering only one particular service. Another feature favouring flexibility in adapting to what is required is that all the potential suppliers can easily ascertain – through their own experience, empathy and observation, through informal conversations and enquiries, with the aid of some discreet broking by the headquarters staff – which services are required, when, by whom and in what volume. It may be assumed that the interest of potential suppliers in earning vouchers with which they in turn can purchase services will provide some incentive to make use of such job-search aids. Thus a comparatively dense communication network is a prerequisite as a substitute for the price mechanism, to provide signals as to the services in demand at any given time.

Conversely, a queue may be forming on the *demand* side. It consists of people who urgently need something they are ready to pay for with vouchers, but which is not to be had at the right time in the type and quantity demanded. In this case, too, the disparity must overcome without recourse to the price mechanism through personal communication, perhaps by postponing some of the excess demand with honeyed words so that the insufficient supply is eked out over time. One advantage of this might be that supply is effected in accordance with neither the priority criterion of the ability to pay more (as in the market) nor that of the queue (as with public services, 'first come, first served') but – as with professional services – on the objectively just criterion of the urgency of the need. At all events it may be assumed that, once certain routines, acquaintanceships, situational understandings and confidence relationships have been built up, both the quantitative equilibrium between supply and demand and the distribution of a temporarily scarce supply will be regulated, even without the price mechanism, in such a way that these problems will not inevitably place the existence and extension of exchange networks in jeopardy.

To the extent that this market equilibration through communication is achieved, the 'pessimistic' assumptions of the analysis of the economic model predicting a breakdown of such exchange systems might very well be falsified by human capacities for communicating, agreement and evaluation of social relationships. Conversely, experience shows that the introduction of exchange and quasi-market arrangements for satisfying demand by no means inevitably leads to the sudden extinction of benevolent care for fellow human beings and for solidarity, or changes all relationships into those of 'payment devoid of feeling' and an egoistic maximization of personal advantage. Far from cutting the ground from beneath these virtues, an exchange arrangement like the one sketched out here actually creates more opportunities for them to flourish and be put into practice.

Internal channels of communication

We have referred repeatedly in the preceding sections to the importance of a dense communication network between the partners to the transactions. The informal level, such as the contacts that arise 'spontaneously' between people living in a given physical catchment area of a cooperation circle, are of special importance in this connection. If additional opportunities of communication were established in the context of an 'active association life' with an emphasis on social events, this could lead to greater frequency of interaction, thus facilitating the balance between supply and demand in the cooperation circle.

Yet both practice and theory counsel considerable reservations as to a strategy aimed at altering an open 'exchange network' into a 'closed' association system. Therefore the problem of optimization revolving around the question whether the organizers of a cooperation circle would be better advised to mount active, intensive efforts at 'brokering', or whether a more passive, waiting posture is to be preferred calls for very careful consideration, and the solution should be approached with caution. The experience gained in other countries and reported in part II suggests that an intermediate course may be the wisest one. In the USA (Service Credits) very 'active' institutions made a pressurizing, preemptive and hence counterproductive impression, while in the Netherlands a relaxed attitude proved unsuccessful. A middle way might be one where in principle everybody was responsible for marketing his or her own offers and for tailoring them to the demand, but that a few additional means of communication could be created, such as supporting publicity, an information sheet, consulting hours at the bank, etc.

Liability and guarantee

As with all transactions, so with services exchanged under the auspices of a cooperation circle, conflicts may sometimes occur about the type, quantity, quality and timing of delivery of services. The question therefore arises, how should such conflicts be dealt with? Fortunately the quality of service problem is to some extent defused by the fact that most of the services are simple activities in which 'not much can go wrong' and the likelihood of complaints is correspondingly reduced. Furthermore everybody who commissions such services knows that in most cases they will not be performed by skilled specialists. There is also the learning curve; once a supplier had given unsatisfactory service, the same supplier would not be chosen again. Even so, that is no justification for minimizing the problem of quality and of the conflicts to which it may give rise. For the services performed in houses and the domestic environment are particularly susceptible to causing breakdowns, damage and injuries in the personal sphere of the recipient of the services and they may give rise to conflicts, and in serious cases to liability claims. Even the thought of such possible consequences can inhibit decisions on membership and participation. There are several ways in which such conflicts can be warded off and settled:

(a)   The most 'economical' but probably ineffective solution would be expressly to exclude liability in the constitution of the association and for members to sign a waiver relinquishing the right to pursue possible cases of civil liability against other members – though this might not be valid in law.

(b)   The statutes of the association could profitably incorporate a code of ethics, which could if necessary be very detailed and comprehensive (see chapter 7); such a code would lay down rules about acts and omissions, thus giving members some assurance that they need have no fear of malpractice in their dealings with other members. Such standards, which in any event would mostly do no more than lay down in writing the rules of normal civilized behaviour in society, could be supplemented by an internal complaints mechanism and perhaps an arbitration procedure within the association.

(c)   Yet another alternative is to insure against civil liability cases. A variant would be for the association to recommend members to conclude a private liability insurance, or even to make it obligatory; another one would be for members to have a group liability insurance, as does Ownwork House as described in chapter 9. Finally, insurance services might be a form of subsidy to be given by outside agencies (such as the municipal council) to exchange networks to promote their longevity; in that event the council would be making a contribution towards transaction costs at a very reasonable rate.

Another problem might become acute if a person with a requirement, who had already earned vouchers, could find no suitable offers in the system. This would present the problem not of a guarantee of the quality of individual services but of the guarantee of the *purchasing power of the currency*. A solution to the problem of the guarantee, with reference to these variants, was discussed earlier in chapter 13. It consists of a default guarantee to be provided by an entity outside the exchange network. This might be for example a charitable organization whose standard services could be paid for with the vouchers of the cooperation circle, if a member in possession of vouchers could find no satisfactory offers within the system. In consideration of this service, the outside organization would have a claim on services from the cooperation circle, and it might well be advantageous to grant corporate membership to institutions willing to provide 'default bonds'.

Ways of providing incentives and promoting long-term stability

There can be no doubt that, for the reasons given, it is very important to the ability of cooperation circles to function in the way here described that they should receive moral, institutional and some material support from the state and other public bodies, especially the labour exchanges and the tax authorities. There is the danger that labour exchanges might adopt the rule that unemployed people who were active in cooperation circles were no longer 'available for work' on their books, and hence would lose their entitlement to unemployment pay and/or supplementary assistance. A similar problem arises in connection with decisions on entitlement to income support. In the same way the tax authorities might insist, as in the American example, on treating such turnover as 'income' for tax purposes. Unclarified legal positions of this kind regarding the field of activity of these authorities, and the resulting uncertainties as to the legal position with regard to transactions can trigger a strong disincentive effect.

It is critically important to the viability and effectiveness of a cooperation circle that it should have a sufficient number of members and that these members should use the circle with with sufficient intensity. Because such transactions are, or should be, voluntary (and in this respect quasi-market ones) they cannot be directly promoted from public resources. The most that can be expected are indirect instruments for providing incentives for many people to participate, and participate intensively. The logic of the argument so far would seem to suggest two principal ways of attempting this: (a) to increase the velocity of circulation, and (b) to promote specialization and scale effects.

With regard to (a): if the volume of turnover is to be maintained, care must be taken to see that vouchers, once earned, are *rapidly* converted into demands for services. This is the only way to avoid 'everybody waiting for everybody else' – in other words to ensure that vouchers are not hoarded until their possessors see an opportunity of exchanging them for something that is in short supply and would cost a lot on the ordinary market. The less hoarding there is, the greater the likelihood of a strong demand for everyday, not specially demanding services as well. Apart from the automatic depreciation under association rules already referred to, external incentives to maintaining and increasing turnover can be provided if public promotional funds are promised in the event that certain turnover targets are reached or exceeded in a given period. For this purpose a reliable record of turnover within the cooperation circle would have to be forthcoming, and this could be done discreetly and efficiently if the vouchers were dated and signed, as was suggested above.

With regard to (b): the provision of benefits in kind and of human capital from outside sources might be another way to promote specialization and scale effects in cooperation circles, thereby enhancing their attractiveness. Typical benefits in kind might be renting a workshop or lending powerful tools of better quality than those of DIY standard. By support through human capital we mean making personnel available for specialist advice on how to carry out certain tasks. The availability of such aids would make for increased efficiency and a higher standard of workmanship, which in turn would evoke stronger interest in joining and taking part.

The attractive effect of assistance from outside could probably be reinforced if contributions in kind were promised in the event that a certain volume of turnover were to be exceeded within a given time. In practice this might mean that if a cooperation circle exceeded a given number of transactions within a stipulated period – say an average of 50 hour-units per member per year – it would be awarded half a salary from public funds as a 'growth prize'. The incumbent might manage the banking and 'job-broking' activities of the board, or perhaps be responsible for counselling and skilling offerers of services in manual, domestic or social work subjects: or maybe do both these jobs.

Such assistance need not come only from state or local government sources. Donors could also be private foundations, housebuilding cooperatives, church parishes, welfare agencies, local trade union organizations and even commercial firms.

Possible links with other institutional sectors

By virtue of the characteristics described here, the cooperation circle concept occupies an intermediate position between the market, the state, the household and other systems for producing and distributing goods and services conducive to welfare, including those of voluntary associations. This inevitably raises the question of coexistence and potential overlaps among these varying types of institution.

1 The very fact that vouchers can be *gifted* gives the cooperation circle an entry point into the traditional network of family and relations. For donors this has the advantage that in helping those near and dear to them they can confine themselves to activities which can fit into the needs, the location and the age and living conditions

of the recipient. When the vouchers of a cooperation circle are used as a gift voucher, the recipient is to a degree offered a choice as to which services he or she will 'buy' with them, and from whom. This constitutes an excellent argument for linking up family connections with non-monetary exchange systems.

2   Where a number of cooperation circles are working fairly successfully in adjacent areas, horizontal networking between them can be considered. A 'federal' structure of this kind could lead to a considerable broadening of their range of services for the cooperation circles taking part. Of course such an extension is possible only if all those taking part can be sure that when exchanges are effected with neighbouring cooperation circles they will receive services comparable with those of their own cooperation circle. In the long term this calls for an external body to exercise appropriate supervision of the quality of the participating cooperation circles and thus ensure that their vouchers are truly convertible.

3   Welfare organizations could play an important role as guarantors. A practical way of setting up such a link, in terms of the concept outlined above, would be for members of a cooperation circle to be in a position to provide a welfare organization with services, in return for which the agency would make its own services available to members of the circle. It would be particularly advantageous if welfare organizations would undertake to provide an outlet for 'excess' offers and conversely to make available a given service in short supply within the circle, in return for vouchers. This would foster the growth of trust between the members of a cooperation circle, since it would increase the likelihood of the 'right' offer being available in response to a given requirement.

4   It would even be possible to forge links with private commercial undertakings. Ownwork plays an important part in housebuilding and modernization. Yet it often happens that 'ownworkers' wishing to contribute a 'muscle bank' cannot do so because they cannot provide enough time or muscle power or because they lack the necessary skills. If however they were able by commitment within a cooperation circle to build up a store of vouchers, they could invest this at the appropriate moment to 'purchase' the extra services when required from other members of the cooperation circle interested in building and repair work and possessing the necessary skills. Not only the members themselves, but also building and handicraft firms might prove to be interested in a 'muscle bank' of this kind, topped up by vouchers, for by the organized contribution of assistance 'unpaid' in money they could open up fresh opportunities of turnover. Food retailers might also be presumed to have a similar interest; with suitable organizational preparations they could help to make it easier for bulk purchases to be made on behalf of several households, with the purchasing itself being paid for in vouchers.

15

Cooperation Circles and Social Reform

In the last chapter we described the forms of organization and the rules of procedure under which a moneyless market between private households could function. Such a blueprint is of course subject to variation and has to be adapted to the local political conditions and legal framework. It is the starting point for experiments in organization rather than the result of an inflexible logical construction. All we would wish to do here is to show that it is possible to implement the idea of a synthesis between the market and society organizationally.

Another question concerns the extent to which a cooperative exchange network can become a supplier of services and goods to citizens. To what extent can moneyless transactions become a substitute for normal markets operating with the money medium? Is it realistic to expect that cooperative exchange networks will ever be in a position to neutralize the specific transaction costs and choices offered by the money economy and thus to establish a more logical and more egalitarian system of harmonizing supply with demand?

There is a modest answer to these questions; there is also one with far greater pretensions. The modest answer is that by their very nature cooperation circles can only be marginal gap-fillers. For that reason they should not encourage hopes of far-reaching social reform, because the realistic prospect is that only a comparatively small number of services in comparatively low-level categories can be exchanged by households through such networks, and hence exchange networks can perform only a restricted range of operations, because their typical members do not have the political clout needed for an expansionist strategy. On this view exchange networks are a supplementary microstrategy rather than offering the prospect of widespread reform of society.

It cannot be denied that this modest, 'realistic' view may prove to be the correct one. Yet one is tempted to explore briefly here the alternative, 'bolder' answer to the question as to the potential for reform possessed by cooperative systems of non-monetary exchange, and this for two reasons. In the first place it is a well-tried rule of social and political praxis that what is objectively possible cannot be achieved unless the sights are set *higher than* what is objectively possible. In this way the 'utopian added value' of reform plans can become a productive strength of realistic efforts towards reform. What is realistic cannot be known until what is actually unrealistic has been discovered in practice.

The other reason for pursuing the 'immodest' answer to our question a little further is somewhat arcane. It is related to lateral connections and complementarities that obviously exist between the cooperative exchange pattern and other movements looking towards social and economic reform that are finding defenders and champions in several countries in Western Europe at the present time. We are referring on the one hand to the demand made by many trade unions and most of the social-democratic and green parties for a *shortening of working hours*, and on the other hand to the equally topical proposals and demands for the introduction of a *basic income*, though this admittedly is advanced vigorously only by a variegated minority consisting of liberals, greens and a sprinkling of communists. Between these two sociopolitical movements and the project for cooperative, moneyless exchange there is a close relationship and a process of mutual reinforcement. It is therefore conceivable that a broad coalition of these reform projects and of the political activists behind them might come into being, providing an answer to our question that is both 'bold' and 'realistic'.

The central problem with which all these projects of reform are concerned is the present situation of high unemployment and the precarious future of 'employment'. There is an expectation widely shared by social scientists, economists and politicians that neither in the present nor in the foreseeable future for society and the economy will the labour market be able to absorb the productive energies and potential for activity of all the people who are seeking employment. The corollary is that the labour market will not be able to provide the incomes and necessities of life that these people require. This will result in increasing fragmentation and partial impoverishment of labour, arising from widespread unemployment and the spread of badly paid, insecure jobs on the fringes of the labour market. Increasing numbers of people all becoming ever further distanced in their experienced and expected pattern of living from the ideal of industrialized society – that of full-time, steady, skilled and adequately paid employment. What is more, this pattern of a 'normal working life' is not only objectively unrealistic; for some sections of the community it is losing its attraction, with the result that values and lifestyles no longer centred on paid employment appear to be on the increase.

The obsolescence of the full employment capitalism of the welfare state and its economic, political and cultural mechanisms of social integration is nowadays the common theme of all the politicians and their projects. The New Right is reacting to this challenge with nationalistic, racist and sexist demands aimed at reserving the opportunities of gain, suddenly in short supply, for the 'white man'. Neo-liberals advocate bringing back full employment through lower wages, deregulation and more 'flexibility'. Traditional trade unionists and social democrats place their hopes in a new edition (this time supranational) of Keynesianism. We shall not spend more time here on these solutions, which have little that is new to offer.

There is, however, novelty in the demand for a curtailment of working hours, which since the beginning of the 1980s has been bound up with the goal of equal distribution of the opportunities of employment and earning a living among the population, an aim which is 'good for society' (and not only with the aim, which is 'good for the individual', of creating more freedom for the individual manual or brainworker). Another innovation is the call for a basic income, to which all citizens should be legally entitled, irrespective of whether they are employed or are willing to take up employment. This demand is based on the argument, first, that the labour market is not in a position to absorb the whole of the labour force existing in society, and that, second, the industrial and 'postindustrial' societies are indisputably 'rich' societies even without utilizing their labour potential to the full – in other words, that they can both afford for economic reasons and are obligated on moral grounds to provide those sections of the population which have no part in the labour market with the necessary means of subsistence, modest though they be, without setting any conditions or making further demands.

Both these proposals are new, elegant and radical – but they suffer from the critical drawback that it is not clear how the political motives and incentives needed for their implementation are to be created. The distinguishing mark of a good reform proposal is that it is not only advantageous 'to everybody' in its results, but also desirable and attractive 'to each and every one' in course of realization. For only when this happens is there a sufficient probability that the advantage to the group will actually come to pass.

This drawback becomes visible in connection with the shortening of working hours in the following sequence. By definition, shortening of working hours is of *immediate* benefit only to persons already in work. Yet they have to pay for their increased leisure by accepting a cut in wages (or wage increases that would accrue if working hours were not shortened). This negative effect must be expected to increase in proportion to the increase in available time, for when a person already has plenty of free time the negative marginal gain of the lost wages exceeds the positive marginal gain of the extra free time. Let us assume, however, that the employees affected by the curtailment of working hours are not thinking only of their own interests, but have a fellow feeling for their colleagues who are out of work, and who will benefit *indirectly* from the curtailment of working hours. But even on this assumption, individuals will have no logically com-pelling motive for supporting the strategy of shorter working hours that is good for the workers as a whole. For how can they be certain, in view of possible reactions by the employers, that their sacrifice will actually pay off? The employers might, after all, respond to the reduction in working hours either by speeding up the introduction of labour-saving technology or by quickening the tempo of work or by making the location and duration of work flexible – and in all three cases it is unlikely to have a beneficial effect on the level of employment. So it is impossible to be sure that the indirect, 'com-radely' effect intended will actually occur. In the light of this uncer-tainty people will tend to give precedence to their own individual advantage, and at this point employers will be able to make employees 'offers they can't refuse', and so influence them to opt for more wages instead of fewer working hours. In this way the strategy of curtailment of working hours, which we have assumed here to be of general benefit, will fail, because in the existing structure of motiv-ation and incentives individuals would not be motivated to carry it through.

Neither would voters become imbued with this motive, even though they could in theory compel a government to pass laws bringing in shorter working hours, thus generating more employ-ment. But a majority will not so decide, because the unemployed and their families are a minority and because the majority who are employed will expect gross national product to decrease if the macroeconomic input in working hours is lessened. In short, the demand for shorter working hours suffers from a 'motivation gap'; although it might be best for everybody if it could happen, it is by no means in the perceived interest of the individual to demand it, or to support those who are demanding it.

It is conceivable that this critical motivation gap, that has clearly been responsible for the failure of the strategy in many countries in Europe, might be largely closed if properly working arrangements for moneyless exchange on a large scale were already in place, because then the extra leisure time gained by the individual employee would be 'more valuable' to him or her. They would then have the opportunity of using that part of the extra time not needed for recreation, family, hobbies and so on in cooperation circles. This would make the loss of income bound up with the shorter hours easier to bear and accept, as it would now be possible to satisfy some of the needs that had previously been met by money purchases by way of moneyless exchange. And for the macro-economy shorter working hours would have the rational motive that the working hours 'lost' from gainful employment would no longer have to be considered as 'wasted' or 'fallow' working potential; instead they could be welcomed as a resource gained, with which useful work could be done outside the money economy. Thus there is a case for linking the campaign for shorter working hours not only with the conventional objective of full employment, but also with that of building up networks of informal exchange. Such a linkage might be expected to provide both of these reform projects with a stronger motivational impetus than is likely to be generated if they are pursued in isolation.

A similar effect of synergy is likely to accrue if the system of moneyless exchange in cooperation circles is combined with the call for a guaranteed basic income. For while this reform project too is regarded by many politicians and academics as being a solution to social and political problems that is both good for the country and also just, considerable doubt persists as to whether individual citizens have sufficient reason and motives for campaigning for the introduction of a basic income or for tolerating the working of such an arrangement. These doubts too can be illustrated in a simple 'game'. Assuming that a basic income at an adequate level and financed from taxes has already been introduced, a sharp demarcation line would emerge between category A (the majority of employed persons, who as taxpayers are 'net payers' into the system) and class B (those making use of their entitlement to a basic income). Class A would constantly look down on the mebers of class B for shunning honest work. Members of class B would feel discriminated against because, even though their income was adequate, they were condemned to inactivity and excluded from taking part in 'normal' working life, and the social recognition and respect that go with it. Furthermore members of class A would endeavour, either (if they were honourable) to transfer *individually* into class B, that is to give up their heavily taxed paid employment and to live on the basic income, or else to force through *jointly* political decisions that would drive down the basic income to poverty level or below (which indeed would happen as a consequence of the first alternative, too, as ever more claims were made on the finite funds available to pay for the basic income). Conversely it would be attractive for members of class B to improve their modest basic income by illegal or semi-illegal work, and this too would be bound to undermine both the tax base and the political and moral basis of the arrangement.

But if the introduction of a basic income were under political discussion in a society, this pessimistic prognosis as to the probable behaviour of all the other participants would militate against a decision in favour, since everybody would necessarily assume that *after* such an arrangement had been introduced this spiral of suspicion and conflicting strategies would be set in motion. Many left-wing commentators on social policy maintain that some day in the distant future a well founded and monitored basic income system may prove to be a desirable arrangement, but that in the meantime it is bedevilled by so many uncertainties, conflicts and possible snags that it is better not to take that road for the present.

Here again we encounter the tension between the logic of events (or the social effects flowing from them) and the logic of processes that lead to those events and are made up of many small steps that have to be taken by individuals. We believe that even if a guaranteed basic income were to be introduced, the effects of cooperative exchange arrangements consummated outside the money economy would tend to mitigate this tension between process and result. If cooperative exchange arrangements were already in place, this would weaken the case for class A citizens looking down on class B citizens. After all, persons drawing the basic income might very well be those who were spending a great deal of time and energy on undertaking informal activity not remunerated with a money income. For a transitional period and in order to smooth the way for the process of reform it would be perfectly possible to make the drawing of basic income conditional not on preparedness to take up paid employment (as in the case of unemployment pay) but on preparedness to take part in cooperation circles and similar cooperative exchange systems. This would also remove the justification for reducing the amount of the basic income to the poverty level by amending legislation. In the same way, class B citizens would no longer have reason to complain about discrimination and marginalization, because they would be pursuing an activity that was socially accepted and valued, though not in the paid employment sector; furthermore, part of the attraction of participating in paid employment illegally would cease to exist. In this way an established system of cooperative, moneyless exchange might come to exert a catalysing effect on the implementation of other projects of social reform, such as the curtailment of working hous and the guaranteed basic income.

In conclusion, we should like briefly to show that there is also a catalytic effect of this nature working in the reverse direction. In the two examples discussed above we made the assumption that large cooperative exchange systems were already in place and that *for that reason* there would be fewer obstacles to the implementation of the other two reform projects than if such systems did not yet exist. If this is correct, it becomes even more urgent to discover how we can speed up the process whereby such cooperative exchange systems may be established. There is good reason to believe that this could be achieved by successes in bringing in shorter working hours and in gradually introducing a legal entitlement to a basic income. It is not difficult to see why. In the first place, the more working hours are shortened – and the more not only employers but also employees are given the right to arrange their working hours flexibly in accordance with actual requirements – the more time will become available for participation in cooperative networks outside the sphere of paid employment. Secondly, the better and more widely the right to an indispensable minimum of money needed for civilized living and for participation in a complex society where none is sufficient unto himself is secured, the more will people living in this society be prepared to give up gainful employment, with its chances of increased income, temporarily or even permanently, and to transfer their abilities and energies to types of activity that are not rewarded in money. We can thus envisage a 'package' of reform strategies, in which the element of cooperative, non-monetary exchange is just as important as either of the other two elements and in which each element plays the dual role of a strategic goal and a facilitating condition for principled acceptance and political implementation of the other two.

Theorists of the market and the money economy have always viewed as a morally and economically unsurpassable advantage of a free money economy the fact that it stimulates the powers of competition and initiative. Ought we not to take them at their word by suggesting that human initiative can be even more effectively stimulated if the monopoly still enjoyed by the money economy for the satisfaction of human wants is broken by creating the conditions for a 'second order competition' between monetary and non-monetary methods of satisfying human needs?

Notes

Chapter 2 Time, Money and Types of Household: The Example of the Federal Republic of Germany

1 This count does not include the 'unmarried couples living together', where at least one of the partners is in employment; statistics on these are very incomplete. Estimates of the numbers of 'unmarried persons living together' vary between c.500,000 (for 1980, cf. Schwarz 1982:198) and 1.24 million (for 1983, cf. BMJFG 1985:12). What is certain is that the number of such households has greatly increased, especially in the 18–35 age group, and that people with higher educational qualifications more frequently live together in the unmarried state.

2 The following remarks are also based largely on the following studies: Schweitzer and Pross 1976:384ff.; Scheuch 1977:38ff.; EMNID 1983, 1985; Keller 1984; Kössler 1984; Lakemann 1984; Berger-Schmitt 1986a; Krüsselberg et al. 1986: Büchtemann and Schupp 1986:36ff.

3 This could be due to differing standards of cleanliness and order, to the (necessarily) higher working efficiency of employed women, to housewives' efforts to prove how 'useful' they are to the family, or to identification with the role of housewife.

4 The total value of durable, high-value household consumer goods increased about *fourfold* between 1970 and 1984 in the Federal German Republic (cf. Schäfer 1985:115).

5 Because of the raised expectations concerning health, nutrition, home furnishings and equipment, child education, etc. brought about by the change in lifestyles, traditional sources of wisdom are becoming more and more irrelevant. This increases the importance of acquiring skills through the study of 'counselling' literature, attendance at advanced education courses, advice from consumer counselling organizatoins, etc.

6 'The value of a given amount of money [is] equal to the value of each individual object of which it is the equivalent plus the value of freedom of choice between an indefinite number of such objects' (Simmel 1930:208f.)

7 The Allensbach Social Survey Institute found in repeated surveys that since the 1950s more and more adults have been experiencing feelings of boredom on Sundays and holidays (in 1958 23 per cent of the population, in 1982/3 38 per cent). Among the occupied population this feeling was always most frequently present among manual workers and low level employees and officials, and the greatest increase has been in this category (cf. Noelle and Neumann 1965:389; Piel 1987:59).

8 As the Gospel parable says, 'to him that has shall be given . . . and from him that has not, even what he has shall be taken' (Matt. 25:29).

Chapter 4 'Useful Activities': An Overview

1 This interrelation also shows up in a survey of unpaid compulsory public work, which has at times been extensively used in Eastern Europe under the name of 'voluntary construction work' or 'economic mass initiatives' or in Third World countries (e.g. dwelling construction campaigns in agricultural settlements in Brazil). Activities of this kind only bring the desired results if the administrative compulsion is backed up by neighbourhood and/or political and moral supervision. Conversely government-organized voluntary schemes seem not to be very attractive if they are suspected of being only a 'cleverly packaged' form of compulsory work.

2 In this connection we can omit other activities that are regarded as not only illegal in form but also criminal in intent, such as theft or trade in drugs, although they are often cited as examples from the broad field of the 'shadow economy'.

Chapter 5 Historical Excursus

The authors thank Klaus Novy and the Internationaal Instituut voor Sociale Geschiedenis in Amsterdam for kindly allowing them to publish archive material.

1 For example Ellen Ross (1983) describes in detail how under the specific conditions of a very homogeneous London working-class district between 1870 and 1914 there existed long-term reciprocal relationships between female relatives, friends and neighbours which provided an astonishing amount of mutual help and independent provision.

2 These would include for example the plans of François Marie Charles Fourier (1772–1837) for forming 'Phalanstères', as well as thoughts within the orbit of the American technocracy movement revolving around Howard Scott in the 1930s on the introduction of 'energy money'. Fourier's aims for his self-sufficient communities, where members were to live and work in buildings rather like palaces and have their internal relationships strictly hierarchically organized down to the

details, were to give them the greatest possible satisfaction of their needs (cf. Warschauer 1909:97ff.; Lichtheim 1969:38ff.).

3 For the history of the doctrines cf. Lichtheim 1969:119ff. On the cooperative movement in Britain see Potter 1893; Simon 1925:153ff., 211ff.; Garnett 1972. On 'equitable labour exchanges' see Oliver 1958; Elsässer 1984:189ff.; Simon 1925:218ff.; Diehl: 1968:239ff.; Garnett 1972:139ff.; Potter 1893:41ff.

4 The German state socialist Carl Rodbertus-Jagetzow (1805–1875) gave exhaustive consideration to the question of a logical application of the principle of labour value on the basis of Owen's and Proudhon's experience (cf. Hofmann 1965:116ff.; Diehl 1968: II. 185ff., 307ff.).

5 The thought that owing to its property of durability money can be 'hoarded' arose long ago. John Locke (1966:paras 48–51) said in his analysis that with the introduction of money the two inherent barriers to the unlimited accumulation of goods in the natural economy of the condition of nature, namely the satiety limit of the human stomach and the perishability of commodities, were abolished and would have to be replaced by contractual agreements.

6 The most recent work of Dieter Suhr, pointing to a (self-organized) model for the introduction of 'money without added value', indicates that it is not altogether out of place to take up some of Gesell's ideas on money theory. Cf. Suhr 1988a, 1988b.

7 In the first half of 1932 just 400 of the 4,000 inhabitants of Wörgl were out of work, and most of these were no longer receiving unemployment support. The municipality was bankrupt and owed the savings bank in Innsbruck about 1.3 million schillings. Also the Raiffeisen bank in Wörgl had almost come to a standstill. The commune could not be expected to start up any investment projects or work-creating schemes in the foreseeable future.

8 The periodical *Monthly Labour Review* contained reports by the US Bureau of Labour Statistics giving detailed assessments see especially the series of articles Anon. 1933, Anon. 1934, Anon. 1935, Anon. 1939 and Anon. 1941. Grinstead and Wissler (1933) surveyed *inter alia* 60 organizations of the unemployed in the winter of 1932–33 to find out how their organizational structures functioned and how effective they were and how far they lent themselves to transposition. See also Weishaar and Parrish 1933; Lester 1933; Bernstein 1972:416ff.; Mattick 1969:97ff.; Piven and Cloward 1977:68ff.; Schindler 1932. Pauline A. Keehn has assembled a good bibliography on the subject of 'barter' (1982).

9 The term 'scrip' is used in the American literature to cover all kinds of media providing moneyless exchange of goods and services. The expression also covers credit notes based on units of time, standardized units of performance and/or drawing rights, point accounts with account books or extracts giving the current points status, settlement cards to be processed decentrally and 'constantly decreasing money' with revaluation stamps and other local auxiliary currencies.

Chapter 7 The 'Service Credits' System in the United States

Many people in the United States have made themselves available for interviews, given us relevant documents, provided useful information in replies to letters and enabled us to visit individual projects. Of these we would mention, with thanks for the assistance they have given: Edgar Cahn, Miami; Ann Cravitz, Miami; Carroll Estes, San Francisco; Diane Montagne, Princeton; Joanne Polowy, Jefferson City; Terrie Raphael, Brooklyn; Joel Rogers, Madisōn; Rosa Salazar, San Francisco; Patricia Vallejos, San Franciso; Bernard Veney, Washington. The authors also thank numerous men and women colleagues and Fellows of the Center for Advanced Study in the Behavioural Sciences, Stanford.

1 For example, on 23 February 1987 the *New York Times* carried a front page report on the system and the first results of the experimental projects. The tenor of this very detailed report was overwhelmingly favourable; emphasis was laid on the originality of the idea underlying the scheme, which could function as a novel way for social services to be provided in hitherto neglected areas of assistance to old and sick people, supplementing the professional system of care. One month later the paper carried a commentary featuring somewhat more cautiously the arguments for and against, yet concluding that it should be given a trial with ample state and private support: 'Give service credits a try', *New York Times*, March 1987. In January 1985 a similarly positive assessment had been published in the *Washington Post*, when the first legislative initiatives were under way in the federal states (Raspberry 1985).
2 This is based on a personal visit and detailed discussions with VIP's project managers in January 1988.
3 Indeed, as regards technical qualifications trainees are expressly warned against carrying out services that they might well perform for themselves, but which might give rise to questions of liability. As an example of the borderline not to be crossed: if an electric light is not working, the bulb could be changed; but if that does not cure the problem, do *nothing* more. The importance of this question of liability is another illustration of the special difficulties that arise when the programme is focused on old people.

Chapter 8 The Netherlands: A Case Study of the Exchange Economy

The authors wish to thank all who have contributed to the creation of the Netherlands case study, in particular George Berger (Amsterdam), René Boomkens (CREA, Amsterdam), Greet Hettinga (Stichting Buurteconomic

Amsterdam), Koos Koopal (Amsterdam), Michael Krätke (Political Science Institute of Amsterdam University), Ton van der Pennen (R.O.V. Research Institute, Leiden), Piet Renooy (Regioplan Research Institute, Amsterdam), Alice Ruijzenaars (SARA, Academic Computing Services Amsterdam), Ingeborg Seelemann and the project team of 'Over & Weer' in Amsterdam, Els Vonk (Landelijke Vereniging van Vrijwilligerscentrales, Utrecht), David Weston (Centre for Urban Design, Oxford Polytechnic) and Frank Wiezer (Dit voor Dat, Utrecht).

1 See Oude Engberink 1986; on current developments of the welfare state in the Netherlands see Engbersen and van der Veen 1987; ch. 2; on the connection between unemployment and informal activities as discussed in Holland see Mevissen and Renooy 1986 and Sandwijk and van Waveren 1987.

2 Since about 1983 social policy in the Netherlands has been modelled on this pattern, the revitalization of neighbourhood and friendly relationships coupled with rigorous economies in the system of state benefits. Most recently, however, this policy has been renamed; the government now refers to it as a 'responsible society' (*verantwoordelijke samenleving*). There is a critical assessment of this model and policy in Koot and Stegerhoek 1986.

3 In February 1988 we carried out a first comprehensive written survey among the initiators and organizers of 28 exchange networks in the Netherlands. We received replies, mostly very detailed, from 19 projects. We supplemented the findings from this survey by intensive study of the information material issued by the various projects (including Stichting Over & Weer 1987, 1988; Stichting Wisselwerk) and by a number of interviews and 'on-site visits'. We have taken our information on the projects that did not reply to our enquiry from documents from the "Archief Ruildienstprojeckten" of the Landeslijke Vereniging van Vrijwilligerscentrales. At the end of March we carried out another written survey, directed this time to participants in the large Over & Weer network in Amsterdam, which at the time had 195 registered members; we also approached some members of the Dit voor Dat network in Utrecht. Of some 200 questionnaires sent out we received back in the following month 67 from Amsterdam and six from Utrecht.

4 Such distortions would occur, for instance, if as the number of participants increased the scope of supply (offer) were only to increase in a *particular qualitative direction* (for instance handicrafts or odd jobs), while the requirements multiplying at the same time were for quite different services, say technical repairs or language learning, and hence could not be satisfied from the growing pool of potential suppliers.

5 As a percentage of the current structure of offer and demand the "turnover corridor" in Tables 1 and 2 is of about the same size, whereas only its degree of clearance (column 4) is somewhat higher in the larger network (74 per cent compared with 51 per cent).

Chapter 9 The Search for New Ways of Organizing Social Commitment in the Federal Republic of Germany

The authors thank the project team of the 'Ownwork House' in Munich (especially Kurt Horz, Elisabeth Redler and Jens Mittelsten Scheid), the persons they interviewed at the Bielefeld Workers' Welfare Institute and the Dortmund office of Caritas; also Johann Jessen and Walter Siebel (both of Oldenburg University) and Thomas Olk (Bremen University), who were helpful in discussions right from the beginning.

1 For example, there have existed for some time several pilot projects and experiments seeking to promote an expansion of gardening and handi-craft activities by *individual* households (allotments, handicraft activity sites covering blocks and neighbourhoods; these were appraised in Jessen and Siebel 1988). There is also in Munich an initiative ('Nachbarschaft Georgenschwaige') which originally aimed at organiz-ing a wide variety of self-help activities at neighbourhood level, but which now undertakes socially innovative ward projects using unem-ployed in government job creation schemes, without the idea of net-working help services on an exchange basis to any significant degree (see Pieper 1989; Will 1987). We have also seen reports on a project in Hanover called 'ELM', assisted by the European Community, which tried to build up an exchange cooperative of long-term unemployed and recipients of social assistance on the pattern of the American 'food co-ops'; so far, however, the project as confined to this target group has not had any success (see Finkeldey 1987; ELM-Projekt 1988). All such projects have this in common, that a non-monetary exchange of goods and services between households does not play a serious part in their thinking.

2 This section is based on an on-the-spot visit in July 1988. In addition, the concept papers (Horz and Mittelsten Scheid 1985; Horz 1986; AN Foundation 1985–7:37ff., 46f.) and the publicity material have been evaluated. A first evaluation report of the concomitant academic research is very informative (Redler 1988).

3 This very high sum is made up of personnel costs for 14 male and female staff members holding various positions and contracts, monthly rental payments of 7,300 DM (including heating) and the cost of the considerable public relations effort and of some large purchases to complete the equipping of the building.

Bibliography

Andorka, R. 1987: Time budgets and their uses. *Annual Review of Sociology*, 13, 149–64.

AN Foundation/ANstiftung 1985–7): *Jahresbericht 1985–87 der Forschungsgemeinschaft ANstiftung e.V..* Munich. Angele, J. 1988: Budgets ausgewählter privater Haushalte 1987. Ergebnisse der laufenden Wirtschaftsrechnungen. *Wirtschaft und Statistik*, 574–82.

Anon. 1933: 'Cooperative self-help activities among the unemployed'. *Monthly Labor Review*, 36: 34, 449–95; 36: 4, 717–70; 36: 5, 979–1038; 36: 6, 1229–40.

Anon. 1934: Production by self-help organizations of unemployed. *Monthly Labor Review*, 39: 1, 25–30.

Anon. 1935: Self-help among the unemployed in California. *Monthly Labor Review*, 41: 61, 504–9.

Anon. 1939: Self-help organizations in the United States, 1938. *Monthly Labor Review*, 49: 6, 1335–47.

Anon. 1941: Activities of the Washington (D.C.) self-help exchange. *Monthly Labor Review*, 53: 1, 35–49.

Anthony, D 1977: *The Ideology of Work*. London.

AWO/Arbeiterwohlfahrt Bundesverband e.V. 1988: *Humanitäres Handeln aus politischer Verantwortung. Grundsatzprogramm der AWO*, 2nd edn. Bonn.

Baartmans, K., Meijer, F. and Schaik, A. van 1987: *Zelfwerkzaamheid, woningonderhoud en bouwwerkgelegenheid*. Delft.

Bahrdt, H.-P. 1983: Arbeit als Inhalt des Lebens ('denn es fährt so schnell dahin'). In J. Matthes (ed.), *Krise der Arbeitsgesellschaft? Verhandlungen des 21. Deutschen Soziologentages in Bamberg*, Frankfurt/New York, 120–37.

Balbo, L. and Nowotny, H. (eds) 1986: *Time to Care in Tomorrow's Welfare Systems: The Nordic Experiments and the Italian Case*. Vienna.

Barrios, N. B. 1986: Evaluation of the Volunteer Service Credit Program. E-86-14, MS, Tallahassee, Florida, December.

Battelle Institut 1984: *New Information Technologies and Small-scale Job*

Creation: *The Alternative Economy and Job Creation in the USA, with Policy Recommendations applicable to the European Context*, by S. van Buiren. Luxemburg.

Bauer, R. and Diessenbacher, H. (eds) 1984: *Organisierte Nächstenliebe. Wohlfahrtsverbände und Selbsthilfe in der Krise des Sozialstaates*. Opladen.

Baumol, W. J. 1967: Macroeconomics of unbalanced growth: the anatomy of urban crisis. *American Economic Review*, 57: 415–26.

Beck, U. 1986: *Risikogesellschaft. Auf dem Weg in eine andere Moderne*, Frankfurt.

Bedau, K. -D. 1986: Vermögenseinkommen der privaten Haushalte in der Bundesrepublik Deutschland 1970 bis 1985. *DIW-Wochenbericht*, 53, 353–60.

——1987: Die Vermögenseinkommen der privaten Haushalte, *DIW-Wochenbericht*, 54, 525–31.

Benseler, F., Heinze, R.G. and Klönne, A. (eds) 1982: *Zukunft der Arbeit*. Hamburg.

Berger, J., Dohmeyer, V., Funder, M. and Voigt-Weber, L. (eds) 1985: *Alternativen zue Lohnarbeit? Selbstverwaltete Betriebe zwischen Anspruch und Wirklichkeit*. Bielefeld.

Berger, P. L. and Neuhaus, R. J. 1977: *To Empower People: The Role of Mediating Structures in Public Policy*. Washington D.C.

Berger-Schmitt, R. 1986a: Innerfamiliale Arbeitsteilung und ihre Determinanten. In W. Glatzer and R. Berger-Schmitt (eds), *Haushaltsproduktion und Netzwerkhilfe*, Frankfurt/New York, 105–40.

——1986b: Arbeitsteilung und subjektives Wohlbefinden von Ehepartnern. In W. Glatzer and R. Berger-Schmitt (eds), *Haushaltsproduktion und Netzwerkhilfe*, Frankfurt/New York, 141–74.

Bernstein, I. 1972: *The Lean Years: A History of the American Worker 1820–1933*. Boston.

Blosser-Reisen, L. 1988: Kostensenkung im Gesundheitswesen: Ein Beitrag der privaten Haushalte? *Sozialer Fortschritt*, 37, 159–66.

BMJFG/Bundesminister für Jugend, Familie und Gesundheit 1985: *Nichteheliche Lebensgemeinschaften in der Bundesrepublik Deutschland*, Stuttgart/Berlin/Cologne/Mainz. Vol. 170 of the BMJFG series.

——1986: *Vierter Familienbericht: Die Situation der älteren Menschen in der Familie*, BT publication 10/6145, 13 Oct 1986. Bonn.

Boll, F. and Olk T. (eds) 1987: *Selbsthilfe und Wohlfahrtsverbände*. Freiburg.

Böltken, F. 1987a: Ortsgebundenheit und Ortsverbundenheit. Empirische Befunde im Zeit- und Regionalvergleich. *Informationen zure Raumentwicklung*, no. 3, 147–56.

——1987b: Soziale Disparitäten und soziale Netzwerke im regionalen Vergleich. *Informationen zur Raumentwicklung*, nos 9/10, 543–9.

Bose, C. E., Bereano, P. L. and Malloy, M. 1984: Household technology and the social construction of housework. *Technology and Culture*, 25, 53–82.

Boulding, K. E. 1981: *A Preface to Grants Economics: The Economy of Love and Fear.* New York.

Braun, H. -U. 1985: Grundvermögen privater Haushalte Ende 1983. Ergebnisse der Einkommens- und Verbrauchsstichprobe. *Wirtschaft und Statistik,* 967–74.

Braun, R. and Röhrig, P. 1987: *Praxis der Selbsthilfeförderung. Das freiwillige soziale Engagement am Beispiel von vier Städten.* Frankfurt/New York.

Büchtemann, C. F. and Schupp, J. 1986: *Zur Sozio-Ökonomie der Teilzeitbeschäftigung in der Bundesrepublik Deutschland. Analysen aus der ersten Welle des 'Sozio-ökonomischen Panel,* discussion paper IIM/LMP 86–15. Wissenschaftszentrum, Berlin.

Burgdorff, S. (ed.) 1983: *Wirtschaft im Untergrund.* Reinbek.

Cahn, E.S. 1986: Service Credits: a new currency for the welfare state. Suntory Toyota International Centre for Economics and Related Disciplines, discussion paper 8, London. Summarized in Heinze and Offe 1990: 125–46.

——1987a: The time dollar. MS, Miami.

——1987b: The Florida Service Credit Project: implementation of the service credit concept. MS, North Miami.

Clausen, L. 1988: *Produktive Arbeit, destruktive Arbeit.* Berlin/New York.

Coughlin, T. A. and Meiners, M. R. 1987: Service Credit banking: issues in program development. MS, National Center for Health Services Research, Rockville, Md, November.

Dahrendorf, R 1983: Wenn der Arbeitsgesellschaft die Arbeit ausgeht. In J. Matthes (ed.), *Krise der Arbeitsgesellschaft? Verhandlungen des 21. Deutschen Soziologentages in Bamberg,* Frankfurt/New York, 25–37.

Dalton, G. 1982: Barter. *Journal of Economic Issues,* 16: 1, 181–90.

Data Report 1985 *Datenreport 1985. Zahlen und Fakten über die Bundesrepublik Deutschland,* Statistisches Bundesamt, Bonn. Vol. 226 in The Federal Office for Political Education Series.

Deimer, K., Jaufmann, D., Kistler, E. and Pfaff, M. 1983: Selbsthilfe in der Sozialpolitik – ein Lösungsansatz? *Aus Politik und Zeitgeschichte,* 33: 34, 14–29.

Denis, H. 1986: Proudhon und die Prinzipien der Tauschbank. *Zeitschrift für Volkswirtschaft, Sozialpolitik und Verwaltung,* 5: 2, 283–95.

Der Spiegel: Besonderer Reiz. No. 40, 149–50.

Diehl, K. 1968: *Pierre Joseph Proudhon: Seine Lehre und sein Leben,* 3 parts in 1 vol. Aalen. First published in Jena, 1888–96.

Diewald, M. 1986: Sozialkontakte und Hilfeleistungen in informellen Netzwerken. In W. Glatzer and R. Berger-Schmitt (eds), *Haushaltsproduktion und Netzwerkhilfe,* Frankfurt/New York, 51–84.

Ehling, M. and Schäfer, D. 1988: Internationale Erfahrungen mit Zeitbudgeterhebungen im Rahmen der amtlichen Statistik, *Wirtschaft und Statistik,* 451–61.

ELM-Projekt 1988: 2. Bericht für den Zeitraum 1987, ed. L. Finkeldey et al., MS, Hanover.

Elsässer, M. 1984: *Soziale Intentionen und Reformen des Robert Owen in der Frühzeit der Industrialisierung. Analyse seines Wirkens als Unternehmer, Sozialreformer, Genossenschaftler, Frühsozialist, Erzieher und Wissenschaftler.* Berlin.

EMNID 1983: Freizeitbedingungen und Freizeitentwicklungen – Kommentar. MS, Bielefeld.

——1985: Wer hat die meiste Freizeit? *EMNID-Informationen,* 37: 6/7, 24 and A44–A67.

Engbersen, G. and Veen, R. van der 1987: *Moderne armoede: overleven op het sociaal minimum. Een onderzoek on der 120 Rotterdamse huishoudens.* Leiden.

Euler, M 1985: Geldvermögen privater Haushalte Ende 1983. Ergebnis der Einkommens-und Verbrauchsstichprobe. *Wirtschaft und Statistik,* 408–18.

Evers, A 1988: Volunteering oder: Chancen mehren und Zwänge abbauen. Einige internationale Erfahrungen und Beispiele. In Fink 1988: 155–72.

Federal Statistical Office (German)/Statistisches Bundesamt 1955: *Statistische Berichte (Arb. -Nr. VIII/12/26): Die Wanderung im Bundesgebiet im Jahre 1955.* Wiesbaden.

——1970: *Volkszählung vom 27.5.1970, Heft 9: Bevölkerung und Kultur.* Wiesbaden.

——1985: *Fachserie 1, Reihe 3: Haushalte und Familien 1985.* Wiesbaden.

——1986: *Fachserie 1, Reihe 3: Haushalte und Familien 1986.* Wiesbaden.

Federal Study Group/Bundesarbeitsgemeinschaft der Freien Wohlfahrtspflege 1985: *Gesamtstatistik der Einrichtungen der freien Wohlfahrtsverbände.* Bonn.

Fink, U 1986: Subsidiarität – Lösung für sozialpolitische Probleme der Gegenwart. In R. G. Heinze 1986: 157–69.

——1987: Der neue Generationenvertrag. *Die Zeit,* no. 15, April.

—— (ed.) 1988: *Der neue Generationenvertrag. Die Zukunft der sozialen Dienste.* Munich/Zurich.

Finkeldey, L. 1987: Selbsthilfe im Armutsbereich – ein Irrweg? Überlegungen zu einem praktischen Beispiel: MS, Hanover.

Frankfurter Rundschau 1988: Computer hilft beim Tauschen. Barter-Datenbank führt Verkäufer und Abnehmer zusammen. 24 Oct.

Gaitskell, H. T. N. 1936: Four monetary heretics. In G. D. H. Cole (ed.), *What Everybody Wants to Know about Money: A Planned Outline of Monetary Problems* (section on Silvio Gesell). London, 385–401.

Garnett, R. G. 1972: *Co-operation and the Owenite Socialist Communites in Britain 1825–45.* Manchester.

Gernert, W., Heinze, R. G., Koch, F., Olk, T. and Thränhardt, D. (ed.) 1986: *Wohlfahrtsverbände zwischen Selbsthilfe und Sozialstaat.* Freiburg.

Gershuny, J. 1978: *After Industrial Society: The Emerging Self-service Economy.* London.

Gershuny, J. and Jones, 1987: The changing work/leisure balance in Britain, 1961–1984. In J. Horne, D. Jary and A. Tomlinson (eds), *Sport, Leisure and Social Relations,* London/New York, 9–50.

Gershuny, J., Miles, I., Jones, S., Mullings, C., Thomas, G. and Wyatt,

S. 1986: Time budgets: preliminary analyses of a national survey. *Quarterly Journal of Social Affairs*, 2: 1, 13–39.

Gesell, S 1922: *Die natürliche Wirtschaftsordnung durch Freiland und Freigeld*, 5th edn. Berlin. First Publ. 1906.

Glatzer, W 1984: Haushaltsproduktion. In W. Glatzer and W. Zapf (eds), *Lebensqualität in der Bundesrepublik. Objektive Lebensbedingungen und subjektives Wohlbefinden*, Frankfurt/New York, 366–88.

——1986: Haushaltsproduktion, wirtschaftliche Stagnation und sozialer Wandel. In W. Glatzer and R. Berger-Schmitt (eds), *Haushaltsproduktion und Netzwerkhilfe*, Frankfurt/New York, 9–50.

Gorz, A. 1982: *Farewell to the Working Class: An Essay on Post-industrial Socialism*. London.

——1989: *Critique of Economic Reason*. London.

Graham, F. D. 1933: Die Schaffung von Arbeitsgelegenheit. *Annalen der Gemeinwirtschaft*, 9, 384–97.

Gretschmann, K., Heinze, R. G., Hilbert, J., Schulz, E. and Voelzkow, H. 1989: *Neue Technologien und Soziale Sicherung. Antworten auf Herausforderungen des Wohlfahrtsstaates: Maschinensteuer – Mindestsicherung – Sozialgutscheine*. Opladen.

Grinstead, L. H. and Wissler, W. 1933: *Barter Scrip and Production Units as Self-Help Devices in Times of Depression*. Columbus, Ohio.

Grubiak, O. and Grubiak, J. 1960: *The Guernsey Experiment*, Glasgow.

Guggenberger, B. 1988: *Wenn uns die Arbeit ausgeht*. Munich/Vienna.

Habermas, J. 1981: *Theorie des kommunikativen Handelns*, 2 vols. Frankfurt. Trans. by Thomas McCarthy as *The Theory of Communicative Action*, 2 vols, Cambridge, 1984 and 1988.

Harman, J. D. (ed.) 1982: *Volunteerism in the Eighties: Fundamental Issues in Voluntary Action*. Washington.

Haugg, K. and Schweitzer, R. von 1987: Zeitbudgets von Familien – eine Literaturstudie mit haushaltstheoretischen Anmerkungen. *Zeitschrift für Bevölkerungswissenschaft*, 13, 215–41.

Hegner, F 1986a: Solidarity and hierarchy: institutional arrangements for the coordination of actions. In F. X. Kaufmann, G. Majone, V. Ostrom (eds), *Guidance, Control and Evaluation in the Public Sector*. Berlin/-New York, 407–29.

——1986b: Zukunftswege der Industriegesellschaft. Ausbau der 'Einbahnstraße' oder Umbau zur 'Zweibahnstraße'? In R. G. Heinze 1986: 303–38.

——1988: Die absehbare Arbeitsmarktentwicklung und das sozial-ökonomische Gewicht der Bedarfs-und Haushaltswirtschaft. In P. Gross and P. Friedrich (eds), *Positive Wirkungen der Schattenwirtschaft?* Baden-Baden, 51–86.

Heidenreich, H. -J. 1986: Mikrozensus und Erwerbstätigkeit im Juni 1985. *Wirtschaft und Statistik*, 974–85.

Heinze, J., Schedl, H. and Vogler-Ludwig, K 1986: *Wachstumsfelder am Rande der offiziellen Wirtschaft. Auswirkungen expandierender Produktions-und Beschäftigungsformen auf Producktivität und Strukturwandel*, Ifo studies in structural research. Vol. 7. Munich.

Heinze, R. G. (ed.) 1986: *Neue Subsidiarität: Leitidee für eine zukünftige Sozialpolitik?* Opladen.

Heinze, R. G. and Offe, C. (eds) 1990: *Formen der Eigenarbeit.* Opladen.

Heinze, R. G., Olk, T. and Hilbert, J. 1988: *Der neue Sozialstaat, Analyse und Reformperspektiven.* Freiburg.

Hinrichs, K. 1988: *Motive und Interessen im Arbeitszeitkonflikt. Eine Analyse der Entwicklung von Normalarbeitszeitstandards.* Frankfurt/New York.

Hirsch, F. 1980: *Die sozialen Grenzen des Wachstums. Eine ökonomische Analyse der Wachstumskrise.* Reinbek.

Hirschman, A. O. 1982: *Shifting Involvements: Private Interest and Public Action.* Princeton, N.J.

Hofmann, W. 1965: *Einkommenstheorie. Vom Merkantilismus bis zur Gegenwart,* Studies in social economy, vol. 2. Berlin.

Hornung, A. 1934: *Das Ergebnis des Wörgler Schwundgeldversuches. Ist Wörgl ein Freigeld-Experiment?* Innsbruck.

Horz, K. 1986: Haus der Eigenarbeit. Konzept einer sozial-kulturellen Einrichtung. MS, Munich.

Horz, K. and Mittelsten Scheid, J. 1985: 'Haus der Eigenarbeit.' Thesen zu einem sozialen Experiment in München, A paper read at the Evangelische Akademie conference in Loccum on 'consumption beyond the market' held on 15–17 November, MS.

Huurne, A. ter 1985: Meeste werklozen willen geen onbetaald werk. *Volkskrant,* 64: 18537, 8 Aug.

IfD/Institut für Demoskopie Allensbach (Allensbach Social Survey Institute) 1985: *Die Situation der Frau in Baden-Württemberg. Eine Repräsentativuntersuchung unter Frauen, ihren Partnern und Kindern über die Situation der Frau im Spannungsfeld von Beruf und Familie,* commissioned by the Baden-Württemburg Ministry of Labour, Health, Family and Social Order, Stuttgart.

IfF/Institut für Freizeitwirtschaft 1984: *Spezialstudie Do-it-yourself. Heimwerken und Heimwerkerbedarf in der Bundesrepublik bis 1990,* 2 vols. Munich.

IISG/International Instituut voor Sociale Geschiedenis: Archief Door Arbeid Welvaart. Amsterdam.

Jessen, J. and Siebel, W. 1988: Wohnen und informelle Arbeit. Konzepte zur Förderung. Final report on the project on 'Housing policy, leisure and the grey economy' commissioned by the Ministry of Urban Development, Housing and Transport of Land North Rhine-Westphalia. MS, Oldenburg.

Jessen, J., Siebel, W., Siebel-Rebell, C., Walther, U.-J. and Weyrather, I. 1985: Mythos informelle Ökonomie. *Leviathan,* 13, 398–419.

——1988: *Arbeit nach der Arbeit. Schattenwirtschaft, Wertewandel und Industriearbeit.* Opladen.

Joerges, B. 1983: Konsumarbeit – zur Soziologie und Ökologie des 'informellen Sektors'. In J. Matthes (ed.), *Krise der Arbeitsgesellschaft? Verhandlungen des 21. Deutschen Soziologentages in Bamberg.* Frankfurt/New York, 249–64.

Keane, J. 1988: *Democracy and Civil Society*. London.

Keehn, P. A. 1982: *The Barter Economy: A Partially Annotated Bibliography*. Chicago.

Keller, B. 1984: *Die Zeit als ökonomisches Gut. Eine theoretische und empirische Analyse des Konsumentenverhaltens*. Institute für Angewandte Wirtschaftsforschung, Tübingen.

Klauder, W., Schnur, P. and Thon, M. 1985: Arbeitsmarktperspektiven der 80er und 90er Jahre, Neue Modellrechnungen für Potential und Bedarf an Arbeitskräften, *Mitteilungen aus der Arbeitsmarkt- und Berufsforschung*, 18: 1, 41–62.

Knapen, M. and Heerdink, H. 1986: *Kan het een beetje meer zijn? Een oriënterende studie naar het zorgvermogen in de samenleving*. Nikjmegen.

Knulst, W. P. 1977: *Een week tijd. rapport van een onderzoek naar de tijdsbesteding van de Nederlandse bevolking in oktober 1975*, Study no. 10., Sociaal en Cultureel Planbureau, 's-Gravenhage.

Knulst, W. and Schoonderwoerd, L. 1983: *Waar blijft de tijd. Onderzoek naar de tijdsbesteding van Nederlanders*, Study no. 4. Sociaal en Cultureel Planbureau,'s-Gravenhage.

Kohler, H. and Reyher, L. 1988: *Arbeitszeit und Arbeitsvolumen in der Bundesrepublik Deutschland 1960–1986. Datenlage – Struktur – Entwicklungen*, Research Studies on the labour market and occupations, vol. 123. Nuremberg.

Koot, T. and Stegerhoek, N. 1986: *Zorgzame samenleving tussen recht en ruil*. The Hague.

Kössler, R. 1984: Arbeitszeitbudgets ausgewählter privater Haushalte. *Baden-Württemberg in Wort und Zahl*, 32: 114–19.

Kotler, P. 1984: *Marketing Management: Analysis, Planning, and Control*, 5th edn. Englewood Cliffs, N.J.

Kramer, U. and Lakemann, U. 1987: Entwicklungen der erwerbsgebundenen und erwerbsfreien Zeit in der Bundesrepublik Deutschland nach 1950. Unpublished draft of the final report on part I of the research project on 'Policy on leisure' commissioned by the Minister for Urban Development, Housing and Transport of Land North Rhine – Westphalia, MS, Bielefeld.

Krause, D. and Schäuble, G. 1986: *Einkommensquellen und Lebenschancen. Eine Untersuchung zur Einkommenssituation der Haushalte in der Bundesrepublik Deutschland*. Berlin.

Krüsselberg, H.-G., Auge, M. and Hilzenbecher, M. 1986: *Verhaltenshypothesen und Familienzeitbudgets – Die Ansatzpunkte der 'Neuen Haushaltsökonomik, für Familienpolitik*, vol. 182 in the publications of the Federal Minister for Youth, Family and Health. Stuttgart/Berlin/Cologne/Mainz.

Kück, M. 1986: Alternative Ökonomie in der Bundesrepublik. In M. Berg, M. Kück, and M. Makowski (eds), *Alternative Finanzierungskonzepte. Bestandsaufnahme, Konflikte, Modelle, Perspektiven*, Berlin, 10–20.

Lakemann, U. 1984: *Das Aktivitätenspektrum privater Haushalte in der Bundesrepublik Deutschland 1950 bis 1980: Zeitliche und inhaltliche*

Veränderungen von Erwerbstätigkeiten, unbezahlten Arbeiten und Freizeitaktivitäten. Eine vergleichende Auswertung empirischer Untersuchungen. discussion paper IIM/LMP 84–19. Wissenschaftszentrum, Berlin.

Landelijke Vereniging van Vrijwilligerscentrales (ed.) 1987: *Ruilen past iederen. Elkaar helpen in straat, buurt en stad.* Utrecht.

——: *Archief Ruildienstprojekten.* Utrecht.

Lederer, E. 1933: Arbeit für Erwerbslose. Ein Vorschlag. *Annalen der Gemeinwirtschaft*, 9, 280–3.

Lehr, U. 1988: So einsam sind sie nicht. *Psychologie Heute*, 15:7, 36–41.

Lester, R. A. 1933: A million men return to barter. *National Municipal Review*, 22: 3, 125–8.

Levitt, T. 1973: *The Third Sector.* New York.

Lichtheim, G. 1969: *Ursprünge des Sozialismus.* Gütersloh. Trans. as *A Short History of Socialism*, London, 1970.

Linder, S. B. 1971: *Das Linder-Axiom oder Warum wir keine Zeit mehr haben.* Gütersloh/Vienna.

Locke, J. 1966: *The Second Treatise on Government.* Oxford. First published in England, 1690.

Loon, T. van 1987: Vrijwilligerswerk: maatwerk!. In R. C. Kwant (ed.), *Dat doe je gewoon? Vrijwilligerswerk in sociaal, cultureel en economisch perspectief*, Amsterdam, 54–76.

Lüschen, G. 1988: Familial-verwandtschaftliche Netzwerke. In R. Nave-Herz (ed.), *Wandel und Kontinuität der Familie in der Bundesrepublick Deutschland*, Stuttgart, 145–72.

Lutz, B. 1984: *Der kurze Traum immerwährender Prosperität. Eine Neuinterpretation der industriell-kapitalistischen Entwicklung im Europa des 20. Jahrhunderts.* Frankfurt/New York.

Luxemburg, R. 1913: *Die Akkumulation des Kapitals.* Berlin. Trans. as *The Accumulation of Capital*, London/New Haven, 1951.

Marx, K. 1969: Das Elend der Philosophie. Antwort auf Proudhons 'Philosophie des Elends', in *MEW*, Bd. 4, Berlin (DDR), 62–182. First published in French in Paris, 1847; English translation, *The Poverty of Philosophy*, Moscow, 1975.

Mattick, P. 1969: *Arbeitslosigkeit und Arbeitslosenbewegung in den USA 1929–1935*, ed. F. Hermanin and C. Pozzoli, Frankfurt. Written in 1936.

Merz, J. and Wolff, K. 1988: Eigenarbeit, Nebenerwerb und Haupterwerb. Versorgungsstrategien privater Haushalte in der Bundesrepublik Deutschland. *Mitteilungen aus der Arbeitsmarkt- und Berufsforschung*, 21, 206–21.

Mevissen, J. W. M. and Renooy, P. H. 1986: *De informele economie gelokaliseerd. Een studie naar achtergronden en verschijningsvormen van de informele economie in Nederland.* The Hague.

Mooser, J. 1984: *Arbeiterleben in Deutschland, 1900–1970. Klassenlagen, Kultur und Politik.* Frankfurt.

Mückenberger, U. 1985: Die Krise des Normalarbeitsverhältnisses. Hat das

Arbeitsrecht noch Zukunft? *Zeitschrift für Sozialreform*, 31:7, 415–34 (part 1); 31:8, 457–75 (part 2).

Müller, S. and Rauschenbach, T. (eds) 1988: *Das soziale Ehrenamt. Nützliche Arbeit zum Nulltarif.* Weinheim/Munich.

Müller-Krumholz, K. 1987: Entwicklung des Realeinkommens begünstigte Spartätigkeit 1986. *DIW-Wochenbericht*, 54, 515–24.

Muralt, A. von 1934: Der Wörgler Versuch mit Schwundgeld. *Annalen der Gemeinwirtschaft*, 10, 295–311.

New York Times 1987: Give service credits a try. 12 March.

Niessen, H.-J. and Ollmann, R. 1987: *Schattenwirtschaft in der Bundesrepublik. Eine empirische Bestandsaufnahme der sozialen und räumlichen Verteilung schattenwirtschaftlicher Aktivitäten.* Opladen.

Noelle, E. and Neumann, E. R. (eds) 1965: *Jahrbuch der öffentlichen Meinung, 1958–1964.* Allensbach/Bonn.

Novy, K. 1978: *Strategien der Sozialisierung. Die Diskussion der Wirtschaftsreform in der Weimarer Republik.* Frankfurt/New York.

——1986: Aspekte einer Theorie der Arbeitsbeschaffung auf der Basis lokaler Selbsthilfe – Historisch Gewonnen. In H. E. Maier and H. Wollmann (eds), *Lokale Beschäftigungspolitik*, Basle/Boston/ Stuttgart, 360–87.

Offe, C. 1984: Arbeit als soziologische Schlüsselkategorie? In C. Offe, *'Arbeitsgesellschaft': Strukturprobleme und Zukunftsperspektiven*, Frankfurt/New York, 13–43.

Offe, C. and Heinze, R. G. 1986: Am Arbeitsmarkt vorbei. Überlegungen zur Neubestimmung 'haushaltlicher' Wohlfahrtsproduktion in ihrem Verhältnis zur Markt und Staat. *Leviathan*, 14, 471–95.

Oliver, W. H. 1958: The labour exchange phase of the co-operative movement. *Oxford Economic Papers*, 10, 355–67.

Olk, T. 1987: Das soziale Ehrenamt, *Sozialwissenschaftliche Literatur Rundschau*, 10: 14, 84–101.

Opielka, M. 1988: Garantiertes Grundeinkommen ist keine reformierte Sozialhilfe, *Frankfurter Rundschau*, no. 214, 14 Sept.

Ostner, I. and Willms, A. 1983: Strukturelle Veränderungen der Frauenarbeit in Haushalt und Beruf? In: J. Matthes (ed.) *Krise der Arbeitsgesellschaft? Verhandlungen des 21. Deutschen Soziologentages in Bamberg*, Frankfurt/New York, 206–27.

Ostrander, S. A. and Langton, S. (eds) 1987: *Shifting the Debate: Public/Private Sector Relations in the Modern Welfare State.* Rutgers.

Oude Engberink, G. 1986: *Minima zonder marge*, vol. 2, Gemeentelijke Sociale Dienst Rotterdam, Rotterdam.

Ours, J. C. van 1986: Huishoudelijke produktie als economische buffer? *Economisch Statistische Berichten*, 71, 424–30.

Owen, R. 1967: Report to the County of Lanark . . . , May 1, 1820 In *The Life of Robert Owen, Written by Himself*, supplementary appendix vol. IA, New York, 261–320. First published in London, 1888.

Pahl, R. E. 1984: *Divisions of Labour*, Oxford/New York.

——1988a: Some remarks on informal work, social polarization and the social structure. *International Journal of Urban and Regional Research*, 12, 247–67. Summarized in R. G. Heinze and Offe 1990.

——(ed.) 1988b: *On Work, Historical, Comparative and Theoretical Approaches*. Oxford.

Parsons, T. 1951: *The Social System*. New York.

Petersson, K. 1989: Nebenwährung als Sozialvertrag: Kanadische Erfahrungen mit dem 'Local Employment and Trading System' (LETS). In R. G. Heinze and Offe 1990: 147–58.

Piel, E. 1987: *Im Geflecht der kleinen Netze. Vom deutschen Rückzug ins Private*. Osnabrück.

Pieper, R. 1989: Selbstorganisation in der Nachbarschaft. Ein Modellprojekt zur Institutionalisierung von Eigenarbeit. In R. G. Heinze and Offe 1990: 225–43.

Piven, F. F. and Cloward, R. A. 1977: *Poor People's Movements: Why They Succeed, How They Fail*. New York.

Potter (Webb), B. 1893: *Die britische Genossenschaftsbewegung*. Leipzig.

Powell, W. W. (ed.) 1987: *The Nonprofit Sector: A Research Handbook*. New Haven/London.

Proebsting, H. and Fleischer, H. 1987: Bevölkerungsentwicklung 1986. *Wirtschaft und Statistik*, 610–17.

Prognos AG (publisher) 1986: *Entwicklung der freien Wohlfahrtsverbände bis zum Jahr 2000*. Basle.

Proudhon, P. J. 1973: *Ausgewählte Schriften in drei Bänden*, ed. A. Ruge and A. Darimon. Aalen. First published in Leipzig, 1850–1.

Rammert, W. 1987a: Der nicht zu vernachlässigende Anteil des Alltagslebens selbst an seiner Technisierung. In B. Lutz (ed.), *Technik und sozialer Wandel. Verhandlungen des 23. Deutschen Soziologentages in Hamburg*. Frankfurt/New York, 320–5.

——1987b: Mechanisierung und Modernisierung des privaten Haushalts: Grenzen ökonomischer Rationalisierung und Tendenzen sozialer Innovation. *Österreichische Zeitschrift für Soziologie*, 12: 4, 6–20.

Raspberry, W. 1985: Earning more than money. *Washington Post*, 12 June.

Rauschenbach, T., Müller, S. and Otto, U. 1988: Vom öffentlichen und privaten Nutzen des sozialen Ehrenamtes. In Müller and Rauschenbach 1988: 223–42.

Redler, E. 1988: *Eigenarbeit fördern. Die Entstehungsgeschichte des Hauses der Eigenarbeit in München*. ANstiftung papers 1/1988, Projekt 'Eigenarbeit', Munich.

Rehn, G. 1977: Towards a society of free choice. In J. J. Wiatr and R. Rose (eds), *Comparing Public Policies*, Warsaw, 121–57.

Rerrich, M. S. 1983: Veränderte Elternschaft. Entwicklungen in der familialen Arbeit mit Kindern seit 1950. *Soziale Welt*, 34, 420–49.

Ronge, V. 1988: Theorie und Empirie des 'Dritten Sektors'. *Jahrbuch zur Staats- und Verwaltungswissenschaft*, 2, 113–48.

Ross, E. 1983: Survival networks: women's neighbourhood sharing in London before World War One. *History Workshop*, 15, 4–27.

Rotstein, A. 1985: The second economy and the social welfare system. Final report to the Policy Analysis Division, Department of Health and Welfare. MS, Toronto.

Sachsse, C. 1986: Verrechtlichung und Sozialisation: Über Grenzen des Wohlfahrtsstaates. *Leviathan*, 14:4, 528–45.

Sandel, M. J. 1988: Democrats and community: a public philosophy for American liberalism. *New Republic*, 22 Feb.

Sandwijk, P. and Waveren, B. van 1987: *Sleutelen aan de buurt: een onderzoek naar de relatie tussen buurt, informele ekonomie en stadsvernieuwing*. Rotterdam.

Schäfer, D. 1985: Wert des Gebrauchsvermögens der privaten Haushalte. *Wirtschaft und Statistik*, 110–18.

——1988: Haushaltsproduktion in gesamtwirtschaftlicher Betrachtung. *Wirtschaft und Statistik*, 309–18.

Scharpf, F. W. 1985: *Strukturen der post-industriellen Gesellschaft oder: Verschwindet die Massenarbeitslosigkeit in der Dienstleistungs- und Informations-Ökonomie*, discussion paper IIM/LMP 84–23. Wissenschaftszentrum, Berlin.

Scheuch, E. K. 1977: Soziologie der Freizeit. In R. König (ed.), *Handbuch der empirischen Sozialforschung*, vol. 11 on 'Leisure and consumption', 2nd edn, Stuttgart, 1–192.

Schindler, P. G. 1932: Bartering of services among the unemployed in Los Angeles. *Monthly Labor Review*, 35:3, 501–2.

Schöpp-Schilling, H.-B. 1988: Und der Frau wieder das Ehrenamt? In Fink 1988: 99–115.

Schüler, K. 1987: Demographischer Bezugsrahmen zur Einkommensverteilung nach Haushaltstypen in den Volkswirtschaftlichen Gesamtrechnungen. *Wirtschaft und Statistik*, 361–70.

Schwarz, K. 1980: Zur Einkommenslage junger Familien in der Bundesrepublik Deutschland. *Zeitschrift für Bevölkerungswissenschaft*, 6, 317–34.

——1982: Bericht 1982 über die demographische Lage in der Bundesrepublik Deutschland. *Zeitschrift für Bevölkerungswissenschaft*, 8, 121–3.

Schweitzer, R. von and Pross, H. 1976: *Die Familienhaushalte im wirtschaftlichen und sozialen Wandel*. Göttingen.

Simmel, G. 1930: *Philosophie des Geldes*, 5th edn. Munich/Leipzig. Trans. as *The Philosophy of Money*, London, 1978.

Simon, H. 1925: *Robert Owen. Sein Leben und seine Bedeutung für die Gegenwart*, 2nd edn. Jena.

Smith, A. 1977: *The Wealth of Nations* (1776). Harmondsworth.

Statistical Yearbook 1988: *Statistisches Taschenbuch 1987. Arbeits- und Sozialstatistik*, Bundesminister für Arbeit und Sozialordnung, Bonn.

Stichting Over & Weer 1987: *Jaarverslagen 1986*. Amsterdam.

——1988: *Jaarverslagen 1987*. Amsterdam.

Stichting Wisselwerk: *Jaarverslagen 1984, 1985, 1986*. Alkmaar.

Suhr, D. 1988a: *Gleiche Freiheit. Allgemeine Grundlagen und Reziprozitätsdefizite in der Geldwirtschaft*. Augsburg.

——1988b: *Der Kapitalismus als monetäres Syndrom. Aufklärung eines Widerspruchs in der Marxschen Politischen Ökonomie*. Frankfurt/New York.

Teltsch, K. 1987: Program allows elderly to barter for services. *New York Times*, 23 Feb.

Thiede, R. 1986: Die Situation von Privathaushalten mit pflegebedürftigen Haushaltsmitgliedern, *Nachrichtendienst der Deutschen Vereins für öffentliche und private Fürsorge*, 66, 123–30.

Thiele-Wittig, M. 1987:. . . der Haushalt ist fast immer betroffen – 'Neue Hausarbeit' als Folge des Wandels der Lebensbedingungen, *Hauswirtschaft und Wissenschaft*, 35, 119–27.

US Senate 1987: Hearings of the Subcommittee on Aging, Committee on Labor and Human Resources. 12 Nov., including testimony of the American Red Cross by M. P. Smith. MS, Washington D.C.

VDR/Verband Deutscher Rentenversicherungsträger (publishers) 1975: *Der Rentenzugang und der Rentenwegfall im Jahre 1974*, Statistik der deutschen gesetzlichen Rentenversicherung, vol. 44, Frankfurt.

——(ed.) 1987: *Rentenzugang des Jahres 1986 in der deutschen gesetzlichen Rentenversicherung einschließlich Rentenwegfall/Rentenumwandlung*, VDR-Statistik, Bd. 75, Frankfurt.

Vlek, R. 1986: Een verkenning van modern thuiswerk, In D. Läpple, T. van der Pennen and R. Vlek, *De woning als 'werkplek'. Nieuwe en oude vormen van arbeid in en rond het huis*, Utrecht, 135–95.

Warschauer, O. 1909: *Zur Entwicklungsgeschichte des Sozialismus*. Berlin.

Weber, M. 1924: Der Sozialismus, In *Gesammelte Aufsätze zur Soziologie und Sozialpolitik*, Tübingen, 492–518. First publ. 1918.

Weishaar, W. and Parish, W. W. 1933: *Men without Money: The Challenge of Barter and Scrip*. New York.

Will, C. 1987: 'Nachbarschaft Georgenschwaige' – Self-Reliance in der Praxis. *WohnBund Journal*, 11, 45–51.

Zander, W. 1934: Eisenbahngeld und Arbeitslosigkeit. *Annalen der Gemeinwirtschaft*, 10, 111–35.

Zandstra, J. M. 1987: The paradoxical field of informal service. In J. W. M. Mevissen and J. Heijink (eds), *Workshop Informal Economy, Research and Policy: Compilation of Discussion papers*, paper no. 6, 0244H 1–11. Nijmegen.

Zapf, W., Breuer, S. and Hampel, J. 1987a: Technikfolgen für Haushaltsorganisation und Familienbeziehungen. In B. Lutz (ed.), *Technik und sozialer Wandel. Verhandlungen des 23. Deutschen Soziologentages in Hamburg 1986*, Frankfurt/New York, 220–32.

Zapf, W., Breuer, S., Hampel, J., Krause, P., Mohr, H.-M. and Wiegand, E. 1987b: *Individualisierung und Sicherheit. Untersuchungen zur Lebensqualität in der Bundesrepublik Deutschland*. Munich.

Index